MESSAGES OF LOVE

The Mother of the Savior Speaks to the World from Naju, Korea

The Blessed Mother's Messages to Julia Kim
Translated by Sang M. Lee

Published by
MARY'S TOUCH BY MAIL
1996

In conformity with the decrees by Pope Urbanus VIII, the Publisher recognizes and accepts that the final authority regarding the apparitions in Naju, Korea rests with the Holy See of Rome, to whose judgment we willingly submit.

The decree of the Congregation for Propagation of the Faith A.A.S. 58, 1186 (approved by Pope Paul VI on October 14, 1966) states that the Imprimatur is no longer required on publications that deal with new revelations, apparitions, prophesies or miracles, provided that they contain nothing contrary to faith and morals.

Published by:

Mary's Touch By Mail
P.O. Box 1668
Gresham, OR 97030 U.S.A.

Contents

A Prayer By Julia

+ In the name of the Father, of the Son and of the Holy Spirit. Amen.

God loved us so much that He sent His Only Son, Jesus Christ, to the world to save us.

But the devil's violence is increasing and his control over humans is becoming stronger every day. That is why the Blessed Mother came to this world to hold our hands, suffering pains for us.

But, because her children do not understand her well, she called me, a poor and unworthy sinner, to use as an instrument by rescuing me just before I was about to cease functioning.

So, Lord, open our spiritual eyes and ears and soften our hearts that have hardened like a rock so that we may recognize the loving voice of the Blessed Mother who is imploring us with tears and tears of blood. Help us become more humble and lowlier persons and walk the way of a little person's love, holding the Blessed Mother's hands, following her will and giving her thanks.

May the Lord be glorified and praised and may we lead a life of unending thanksgiving. Amen.

Foreword

The Blessed Mother participates in human history as the Mother of Jesus and the Helper to the Savior. As the new Eve, she has been deeply involved in the salvation of the human race, sharing in the Passion of Jesus Christ, Who came into this world to remit the sins of mankind.

Since the Resurrection and Ascension of Jesus, the Church has grown and developed under the guidance of the Holy Spirit and with the help of the Blessed Mother. This will continue until the end of the world.

Through centuries, the Blessed Mother has appeared at different places and given us the messages of Jesus—for example, in Guadalupe, Paris, Lourdes, Fatima, Banneux, and so on. In recent years, she has been weeping at several locations in the world. Especially, in Naju, Korea, she has been shedding tears and tears of blood.

In Naju, she shed tears for the first time on June 30, 1985, using a small plaster statue 55 cm *(about 22 inches)* tall. This statue had been given to Julia by Rufino Park, former catechist at a mission station, as a gift to Julia when he was miraculously cured from bronchitis after three days of prayer with her.

Some of the first witnesses of the Blessed Mother's tears made the following remarks.

A Pagan: I'd better start going to the Catholic Church. I don't think I can continue my sinful life any longer.

A Protestant: I made a wrong choice. I am going to convert to Catholicism.

A *Non-Practicing* Catholic: Oh, my goodness! She is weeping because of me. Mother! Please don't cry. I will start going to church again and living according to the Lord's Will.

A *Practicing* Catholic: Forgive me, for I have been a lukewarm Catholic. Give me a fervent faith and help me to work for the Blessed Mother. You are letting me smell the fragrance of roses. Thank you, Mother.

Julia: Mother! Now I can be happy, even if I have to die. For some time, many people had doubts about your tears, but, now, many are repenting and returning. Thank you. (There were about 2,000 people attending the prayer service today.) —From Julia's diary, July 17, 1985.

Until January 14, 1992, the Blessed Mother has shed tears and/or tears of blood for a total of 700 days. In my case, I had heard about the weeping statue of the Blessed Mother, but had not been very interested. I visited the Chapel in Naju twice, but didn't experience anything special. But, when I came to the Chapel for the third time on May 23, 1991, I had an urge to pray as follows, *"Mother! My faith is weak. Please give me a sign."* Then, I approached the statue and saw the Blessed Mother's eyes starting to sparkle with tears. I rubbed my eyes to make sure that I was not dreaming. But they were really tears. I began crying loudly and begged for her forgiveness. Julia held my hands and prayed for me. Since then, I have visited the Chapel frequently and have had spiritual experiences.

Why is the Blessed Mother weeping? You will find the answer, when you read her messages. She says the messages are more important than the tears. The following is a summary of the major messages.

● Pray the rosary fervently for world peace and the conversion of sinners.

● Pray and do penance for the babies who are being aborted and for their parents.

- Pray constantly for priests.

- Families are suffering. Love one another and strive for the sanctification of families.

- There are too many who receive Holy Communion sacrilegiously. Teach them the importance of the Holy Eucharist and Confession. Make frequent visits to the Blessed Sacrament and console me.

- Observe the First Saturdays for the consecration to the Immaculate Heart and the Holy Hours every Thursday for the consecration to the Sacred Heart of Jesus in reparation for the sins of the world.

- Make a habit of praying all the time. Live a consecrated life with sacrifices, reparation, self-denial, poverty and self-renunciation.

- Hold my hands. I am the string connecting Heaven and earth. Come aboard Mary's Ark of Salvation and sail to Heaven.

- Build the Basilica of Mary's Ark of Salvation so that all may be saved.

- The souls who accept my words will be changed and reborn by my messages.

The Blessed Mother has clearly emphasized that her messages are not just for Korea but for the whole world. She promises that we will be saved, if we put her messages into practice.

Julia, who receives the Blessed Mother's messages, is also experiencing terrible pains. These include the pains of giving birth to the babies being aborted, crucifixion, arrows penetrating the heart, leg-screw tortures, and pouring sewage water and human excrements into the mouth. Sometimes when she experiences the pains of the Crucifixion, the five wounds of Jesus appear on her. Frequently, I have witnessed her praying for people in pains and receiving the same pains in their place. It is said that sufferings are a mystery. To Julia, they are love.

I sincerely hope that the Blessed Mother's messages will be approved by the Church soon, as she wishes, and that they are made known all over the world so that all will be able to avoid condemnation and falling into hell. In the name of the Blessed Mother, I would like to sincerely thank Sang M. Lee, who translated the Blessed Mother's precious messages into English and Sister Mary Noreen, S.C., who did the proofreading.

January 14, 1992

Rev. Hong Bin Aloysius Chang
Kwangju, South Korea

Introduction by Rev. Raymond Spies
—Julia's Spiritual Director
(Translated from French)

THE VIRGIN WEEPS. . . . This reality touches the loving souls. . . .

How many are responding to the sorrowful and anguished calls by Jesus and Mary? Only a small minority. . . a handful indeed.

The most sad aspect of this situation is that Love is not loved; Love is not desired; and Love is being rejected.

Many people say and think that they love God, Mary and neighbors, but, in reality, they remain themselves, their own egos. . . .

People do not change themselves—remaining at the human level only and without truly becoming spiritualized through the Love of the Triune God and of Mary, living in Them and with Them, reflecting on Them and becoming mirrors of Their Love, Humility and Meekness.

The Apostle John and Mary Magdalene obtained, through their prayers and efforts, this sublime grace of the Divine Love. For that, they had to be spiritually strong in soul, heart and spirit so that they could stand at the foot of the Cross, close to the crucified Jesus, and close to Mary, suffering with Them.

Our life and response to the loving thirst of Jesus and Mary should become like those of John and Mary Magdalene. Jesus and Mary are the noble Beggars thirsty for our souls— each and every one of us. They implore us without ceasing to give Them the most precious (widow's) mite that They desire, which is to help Them save the souls who are perishing and are on the road to hell.

This is what Their messages are reminding us of. Like the

Apostle John and Mary Magdalene, let us also stand close to the Cross every day, looking at Jesus and Mary, Who continue suffering and weeping so much for each sinful soul. . . .

Let us belong to the small minority, the handful who respond filially, lovingly, faithfully, generously, and heroically to the pressing calls by Jesus and Mary.

It is this handful who, sacrificing and praying without ceasing, will help Jesus and Mary to pull from the quagmire of sins the innumerable souls who are lying there, having lost all hope.

Would't it be the greatest sign of love for us to have pity on such souls and become little redeemers for them?

*   *   *

I have been asked to write an article for the English translation of the messages given by the weeping Virgin in Naju, Korea. I am very happy to do so.

For years, I have been thinking about the English translation. As I speak French, I have had to be content with the translation of the messages into French. I sincerely thank the translator and Mary's Touch By Mail, which is publishing the translation. I pray that the gentle Virgin Mary will bless them.

Several times, the Virgin has asked that the messages become known all over the world. She confirmed this by saying: *From this small land (Korea), a land made fertile with the blood of so many martyrs, the light will shine over the whole world through my little, poor souls.* (November 4, 1991)

Then, how have the messages been spread until this date?

To better understand the status of dissemination of the messages, it may be useful to say a few words about my background.

I am a Belgian born in Lorraine, France. I arrived in Japan as a Salesian missionary in 1951. I was 28 years old. In 1958, I asked the *Edition Don Bosco* (Salesian) to publish a book on the Virgin of the Poor in Banneux, Belgium. They agreed, and a book in Japanese was published. Later, this book was translated into Korean.

My first publication in Korea was a translation into Korean of the wonderful book by Jean Guilton (a famous writer in France) on the Virgin Mary. Pope Paul VI once said that it was the most beautiful book on the Virgin he had ever read.

In April 1986, I received a book which mentioned a statue of the Virgin of Fatima shedding tears in Canada. This statue belonged to a man called Brother Joseph François. I summarized some of the contents of this book and published it in Korean in September 1986. There have been two editions. A total of 15,000 copies have been distributed over a period of several months.

On December 7, 1986, Sunday, I was offering a long prayer to the Holy Virgin asking her to give the Christians of Korea, who love her so much, a special sign of her Love, as she did in Akita, Japan. I stopped praying at 7 p.m. for a break. At 7:30, the telephone rang. The call was from Father Matthias Park, a Korean priest in Busan, aged about 75 years. He said: *I have read your book on the Virgin who weeps in Canada. Thank you very much. . . . Do you know that, in Korea also, a statue of the Virgin has been shedding tears since June 1985?* I answered: *No.* He continued: *I ask you to contact Julia, who receives messages from the Virgin. . . .* I promised him to do so. On December 8, the Feast of Immaculate Conception, I first telephoned the Pastor of Naju and, then, Julia.

On January 13, 1987, I met Julia. Until then, there had been no priest spreading the messages or guiding and supporting Julia's efforts. She asked me for help. First, I prayed to consult with the Virgin. The next day, I accepted Julia's request.

In June 1987, the messages (in Korean) were published for the first time. Several articles were added to explain the meaning and motives of the tears.

Additional editions followed. One edition reached 30,000 copies; another 50,000 copies; and still another 80,000! . . . Subsequent editions came out without interruption. To this date, the total including some leaflets and magazines has exceeded half a million copies.

Who is taking care of the expenses? The Virgin herself. . . through the fervent Christians, especially those who gather in the mountain church not far from Anyang* to attend the Mass offered for the Virgin every first Saturday, which started quite some years ago. I have never had to make any special request. Help comes spontaneously. *(*Anyang is a small city located about 10 miles south from downtown Seoul. Father Spies runs the Father Damien Center in Anyang where many poor and sick*

sick people are being taken care of.)

What about the spreading of the messages in other languages?

I translated the messages into French. Copies of the translation were sent to my friends and the benefactors of our work for the poorest at the Father Damien Center. Some have undertaken the work of spreading the messages. Father Rene Laurentin, who was invited by me and saw the Virgin's tears on December 8, 1987, has been spreading the messages in the *Chretiens* Magazine. Mr. Andre Castella has done the same in his magazine: *Stella Marie*, published in French and in German. Mr. Fernand Corteville, who is president of the *Association des Enfants de Notre Dame de La Salette*, has used his bulletin called *L'Impartial*. There are many more. The following are results so far in translating the messages into different languages.

Translation into French: Printing has proceeded without interruption and copies have been sent to people abroad. One edition came out in France and Switzerland in 1990. A new edition has been completed and has been scheduled to be published in January 1992. Another edition in French appeared in Canada in November 1991—five thousand copies of which have been distributed. Distribution has been free thanks to the help by the Korean Christians.

Translation into Flemish (Dutch): There have already been two editions with 8,000 copies in total. A complete, integrated edition will be published this summer.

Translation into Spanish: One edition was published at the beginning of this year including all the messages received so far, some commentaries and explanations. Another text in Spanish is going to be published in Madrid this year.

Translation into Italian: The third edition complete with messages, commentaries and explanations will appear this summer.

Translation into German: I have been informed that it will be published very soon by the Editions du Parvis in Switzerland, which published the French edition twice.

Translation into Japanese: Translation has been completed. It will also include commentaries and explanations.

Translation into Arabic: An Egyptian priest expressed his desire to translate the messages for the Christians in his country.

Translation into Vietnamese: The Vietnamese edition has been published in San Jose, California, the U.S.A.

I sincerely hope that the messages will be translated into Chinese, Russian and other languages.

* * *

The Tears of the Virgin

From June 30, 1985 to January 14, 1992, the Virgin shed tears for exactly 700 days. Julia was amazed at seeing that tears stopped flowing after precisely 700 days. She informed me of her surprise by telephone.

Her surprise awakened my spirit. I opened my Dictionary of Biblical Theology. I found the commentaries on the subject of "Numbers." *The figure "7" signifies a very important number. "Cain shall be avenged 7 times." (Genesis 4:15) "The just man falls 7 times per day." (Proverbs 24:16) "Peter would forgive 7 times." (Matthew 18:21) "Jesus chased 7 demons out of Mary Magdalene." (Luke 8:2)* But this number has a superlative. *"Lamech will be avenged 77 times." (Genesis 4:24) "Peter had to forgive 70 times 7 times." (Matthew 18:22)*. . . Furthermore, there is a triple repetition of a gesture or word as a mark of a strong emphasis and insistence—the superlative of the superlative, *"Holy, holy, holy is the Lord of hosts!" (Isaiah 6:3)*.

In our case, regarding the tears, we have this triple repetition, but multiplied twice by ten:

$$\underline{7} \times 10 = \underline{70} \text{ and } 70 \times 10 = \underline{700}$$

The conclusion: the Virgin never stops weeping, because there are and will always be her children every day who, having fallen prey to sins, are falling into hell or trudging on the road that will lead them to eternal perdition.

A mother like Mary can only suffer horribly and her sufferings will be as long as the sufferings of her Son Jesus for every person until the end of time. Our gentle and loving Mother sheds tears at each moment for everyone. Our prayers and sacrifices can diminish the frightful intensity of her sufferings.

*   *   *

From the messages, we learn about our Heavenly Mother's maternal desire, anguish and sorrow she experiences when she sees her children rejecting Love, her words, and the cross, preferring the poisoned nourishment that gives them a life trapped in the three passions, three sensualities and three concupiscences that offer them to Satan to be chained and thrown forever into the kingdom of eternal hatred, hell: (1) pride, (2) impurity, and (3) cupidity *(the thirst for money in many forms)*.

The Virgin's messages constitute a truly beautiful treatise on spirituality, which is so practical and shows us the life of a spiritual childhood after St. Theresa of Lisieux. The Virgin shows and teaches us the way and the means of becoming meek, humble and little and of becoming victims of penitence, reparation, expiation and the cross together with Jesus.

At the end of the messages given on September 17, 1991, the Virgin summarized her thoughts and desires so clearly: *The souls who are elevated high on the Cross and offer themselves gracefully as victims to the Lord are truly the souls who glorify the Lord and are the little souls closest to me.*

Occasionally in the messages, there were words said by Jesus and the Virgin but were not comprehended by Julia. Julia asked others to explain them. One such word, that was difficult and is not commonly used anymore, was spoken on two occasions: once by Jesus at the beginning of His message on May 16, 1991 about the Holy Eucharist and another time by the Virgin during her second message on August 27, 1991. This word was *"Chock-Bum,"* which is a word made of two Chinese characters and contains all the details the Prophet Isaiah (Chapter 53) enumerated to describe the sorrows and contempt that the Messiah was going to experience during His Passion.

*   *   *

Let us accept the messages with love and have within us the hearts of the Virgin Mary, the Apostle John, and Mary Magdalene, while standing close to the Cross at Golgotha. Let us also help the Virgin, the Heavenly Beggar, who is imploring us to help her save those of her children who are going away from their Heavenly Father, from Jesus, the Redeemer, and from Mary, their Mother and Co-Redemptrix, immersed in the quagmire of sins.

Let us become like the Apostle John and Mary Magdalene who are burning with the fire of love. Love is so simple and meek, but is not easily found.

Let us offer the following prayers often:

Oh, Holy Trinity—Our Good Father of Heavens, His Most Beloved Son and the Spirit of Love! The gentle Hearts of Jesus and Mary! Fill me up, fill us up with Your Love so that, by living in Your Love, we may give it to all our brethren without ceasing.

Make us reflections and mirrors of Your Love, Your Gentleness, Your Mercifulness, and Your Patience—in our thoughts, our affections, our words, our actions, our expressions, our gazes, our gestures and our behavior every day.

Let us offer the sacrifice most agreeable to the Lord: always forgiving our enemies, those who do not love us and those who hurt us.

April 6, 1992

Rev. Raymond Spies
Anyang, South Korea

The Blessed Mother began weeping through her statue in Naju on June 30, 1985, and began giving messages to Julia Kim on July 18, 1985, for the conversion of sinners.

THE MESSAGES

July 18, 1985

While I (Julia) was praying, the Blessed Mother let me participate in her pains of the chest. After about thirty minutes of intense suffering, she began speaking through her statue with a sorrowful, anxious, and indescribably beautiful voice.

THE BLESSED MOTHER:

I am sad. Many people still have doubts even after they see my bloody sweat and tears and say that these may be just plain drops of water. They do not believe. I ask you to spread the truth.

Do you know how the Heart of my Son Jesus is being torn apart? His Heart is being torn apart continuously, as human sins multiply and disorder spreads. Make reparations.

Spread the fragrance of roses all over the world for the prevention of wars and for the conversion of sinners. This is truly a weapon.

My Heart is broken because of the unlimited birth control. Prevent abortions and pray for those who carry out abortions.

Spread the fire of love that is flaming up in my Heart. The fire of love. . .

I want you to be happy. A husband and a wife are joined together so that they may lead a happy life. But my Son becomes broken-hearted when they hate each other and do not forgive each other. You must love one another. Who are your closest neighbors? How can you say that you love me and love the Lord when you cannot even love those in your family? Sanctify your family through love and harmony. This is what my Son Jesus thirsts for.

Achieve unity among those who do my work. In doing so, become sacrificial victims. Those who are working for me and for Jesus lack unity among themselves. As the Father, the Son and the Holy Spirit are One, you must become one, too. Be a good example to others by uniting in humility.

August 11, 1985

During my prayer, a strong wind was blowing noisily, almost extinguishing the candlelight in front of the statue. I heard the Blessed Mother's voice, which was the same as on July 18.

THE BLESSED MOTHER:

Praise the Lord.

Do not weep for my tears, but look at and console my Son Jesus who wears a crown of thorns and sheds blood and sweat.

Pray for priests without ceasing. They are now like a light before wind. They are being subjected to temptations. The windows of rectories are left open. Through the open windows, three devils *(of pride, materialism and lust)* are peeking in. Close the windows of rectories.

Become sacrificial offerings for priests. I am helping them, too. So, support them to the end, because they are my most precious and beloved sons.

September 15, 1986
—Feast of Our Lady of Sorrows

As I was beginning to participate in the Blessed Mother's excruciating pains of the chest, she implored with a voice filled with sorrows.

THE BLESSED MOTHER:

The path that leads to my Son Jesus is a narrow and difficult one of the cross. The human race can be saved by this path, but most do not come near it.

Combine your forces. Pray without ceasing for the souls that are not turning away from the road that leads to their perdition.

October 19, 1986
—First tears of blood

Today, the Blessed Mother shed copious amounts of dense tears of blood. Fr. John Park, the Pastor of Naju, also came with other parishioners and witnessed the tears of blood. Her statue turned into the beautiful, merciful, living Blessed Mother. But she looked so sad, as she was crying and imploring us.

THE BLESSED MOTHER:

As the Father, the Son and the Holy Spirit are One, you must all become one, too, and console me.

October 20, 1986
—Ordinary tears

Three Sisters from the Naju Parish, three other Sisters from the City of Kwangju and five lay people came. While I was praying with them, I fell down because of pains. I participated in the pains that the Blessed Mother was suffering. The Blessed Mother's loving voice came from her statue.

THE BLESSED MOTHER:

This world is decaying with sins. Even with the Sacred Blood of my Son Jesus, it is difficult to appease the just anger of God the Father. Let me borrow your body and your mouth.

I am shivering with cold. Who can comfort me? Who can console my Heart that is shaking with cold? Now, you are not praying to me, but I am imploring you. Pray for priests, my sons. They continue to be tempted. To protect them, you need to give clothing, food and water to those people whose souls are naked, hungry and thirsty. Through these souls, the devils are becoming stronger and more violent. To prevent them, you must offer prayers combined with sacrifices and self-denial, and also offer up poverty and penance gracefully.

Come back to my Immaculate Heart. . . . I called you today for a special purpose. Renounce your ego and abandon selfishness. I will be your shield. Even the arrows of fire thrown by the devils will not harm you. Pray much without worrying. I want you to stand on my side and become courageous guides in saving this world permeated with evil.

October 21, 1986

While I was offering an evening prayer, the warm voice of the Blessed Mother came from her statue.

THE BLESSED MOTHER:

My daughter, my beloved daughter! Listen to my words well. I have implored with tears at many places in the world. It has been very difficult to find souls who are consecrated to converting sinners by participating in sufferings with me for the sake of my Son Jesus and me.

The Blessed Mother weeps through her statue in Naju.
(July 23, 1985)

But you have promised martyrdom. Therefore, I ask you to find such souls for me. I want you *(plural)* to offer your pains combined with more prayers, sacrifices, penance, poverty and self-denial.

Julia: *. . . Mother, your words be done unto me.*

THE BLESSED MOTHER:

Thank you. The sins in the world are so numerous that God the Father's just anger has reached an extremely high level.

(Shedding tears) My daughter! I will call the religious. Through them, I will blow my spirit into those of my children who do not know me and let the light shine from them like a river. But how can they understand my words, if they keep their hearts closed?

My daughter! Help me. Quench my burning thirst.

October 22, 1986

While I was praying, I began feeling a heavy pressure on my shoulders and was losing energy in my whole body. I fell down, as an extreme pain was starting.

THE BLESSED MOTHER:

Listen to the sounds of nails being driven on me. I am being crucified together with my Son.

Julia: *. . . How can we soothe the painful wounds of Jesus and how can we pull out all the nails from His hands and feet?*

The Blessed Mother showed me the scene of her being crucified and asked me to experience it with her. It was an indescribably miser-able scene. She was being crucified, every time we sinned and every time we judged others. Her body became full of wounds and it was hard even to breathe. Who will cry for us and who will put into practice what Our Lady is asking of us?

Julia: *Mother, please tell me. Your servant is listening. I am not afraid of pains. I want to comfort you by suffering more.*

I received the pains of crucifixion and of being hit by arrows and swords. The Blessed Mother spoke again.

THE BLESSED MOTHER:

Who will pull out these nails, arrows and swords? The nails are bigger, go deeper and are harder to pull out when they are caused by my close children.

Now, my children! Receive pliers from me and hand over the hammers that you have been holding in your hands until now. Pull out all the nails with the pliers. Also, keep these weapons well. The devils' job is to take the pliers away from you and give back the hammers. They constantly keep an eye on you, so be alert and on your guard. The shields and weapons that you can use against them are prayers and the arrows of love. Before love, all the devils will capitulate.

October 23, 1986

While I was praying the rosary, light was shining from the Blessed Mother's statue like the sunlight and her merciful voice came from the statue.

THE BLESSED MOTHER:

Go to the Pastor. As I told you before, I need a helper. I called him to be an apostle and a vanguard of my Immaculate Heart and I want you to work with him.

It is time to consecrate yourselves to me. Why do you hesitate again and again? I am asking you for this together

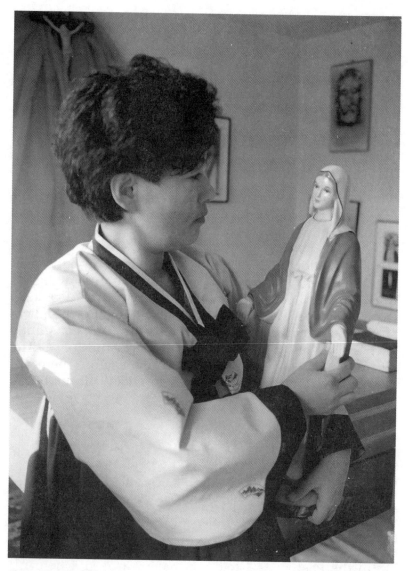

Julia Kim holding the Blessed Mother's weeping statue. This statue was a gift to Julia from Rufino Park, who had been cured of bronchitis through Julia's prayers.

with my Son Jesus because of the pains in Our Hearts caused by many who do not live a consecrated life.

Also consecrate the Blue Army. Offer more rosaries and sacrifices for world peace and human salvation.

Sacrifices are truly the beautiful fruits of mortification, penance, poverty and self-denial. Always work as a very little person with obedience. Then, I will be with you always.

October 24, 1986

I was ironing clothes. Because I was in a hurry, I was using the iron at the highest temperature setting. In the middle of ironing, the Blessed Mother called me and I hurriedly went to the other room where the statue was. Her statue turned into the living Blessed Mother speaking with a warm, soft voice.

THE BLESSED MOTHER:

My beloved daughter! Do not feel so sad. Am I not with you? Do you think the path that the Saints and martyrs walked was an easy one? It was a narrow and dangerous path of the cross. Now, hold my hands and those of your brothers and sisters. Let's go together to the flower garden of paradise, where the martyrs and Saints are.

Suddenly, I fell down and entered an ecstasy. I saw Father Andrew Dae-Gun Kim *(the first Korean priest, martyred in 1846 and canonized in 1984)* and many other martyred Saints. They were walking on a narrow, thorny path, exhausted with fatigue, and bleeding. Their destination was Heaven, where the Blessed Mother was waiting for them with laurel crowns. Jesus was welcoming them with open arms. Jesus was wearing a white cloak and a red mantle. God the Father was sitting in a high throne nodding His head. He had a long, white beard and was wearing white clothes. He was welcoming the Saints with a most merciful appearance. The Blessed Mother was welcoming them and was wearing a shiny laurel crown on her head. Father Andrew Kim also welcomed them and many angels were dancing gracefully. While I was watching all this in amazement, the Blessed Mother held my shaking hands and spoke.

The Blessed Mother's face became so miserable with tears and blood, as she weeps for her children in the world who are mired in sins and refuse to repent. (October 25, 1986)

THE BLESSED MOTHER:

You promised that you would accept sufferings. Why are you shaking? What are you afraid of? Now, stand up and, with courage, entrust your heart to my Immaculate Heart.

Because I love you, my Son Jesus and I called you, when your body was about to cease functioning, to deliver you from many sins. You did not take the initiative to entrust yourself to me, but I called you so that you could entrust yourself to me—as an apostle of my Immaculate Heart. This is only the beginning. There will be many sufferings. But do not be discouraged. Entrust everything—without exception—to my Immaculate Heart. Entrust even all your sins to me.

Together with those brothers and sisters whom I united with you spiritually, pray, do penance and sacrifices and approach me walking the way of a little person with humility. My spirit is flowing in you and in them. So, work together. Also tell my beloved priests that the way of the martyrs is a narrow and difficult one and is like a sailboat in the middle of a violent storm. But tell them that I will sustain them and be with them always.

I got out of the ecstasy and saw my helpers using a tape recorder. Suddenly, I remembered the iron and rushed to the room where it was. But the iron was only mildly warm and none of the clothes were burnt. In a moment, however, the iron became very hot again and all of us were amazed and praised the Lord. When we turned on the tape recorder, we could hear my voice but not the Blessed Mother's. I thought how wonderful it would have been, if her voice had been recorded, too.

October 29, 1986

The Blessed Mother's statue looked so miserable with lots of blood and tears on her face. I had never seen her looking so miserable. I was crying loudly, feeling much pain in my heart. Others present also cried aloud.

"Mother, who made your face like this? I cannot look at your face. Mother, please forgive us. We have not seen your face looking so miserable. Mother, tell us. Tell us what we can do." I kept crying.

At that moment, the Blessed Mother spoke with an anxious voice through her statue.

THE BLESSED MOTHER:

Practice obedience. Obey all—your superiors as well as those who are of a lower status than you. As I obeyed all, you should do the same. I feel so anxious, but will give you energy. So, do not cry but stand up courageously. What can we do, if people refuse to accept our love? Even God cannot force them. Do not expect too much too soon. Be patient and wait for the good time.

After the Blessed Mother finished speaking, the Pastor came with another priest and asked me to wipe the tears of blood from the Blessed Mother's statue. I felt so sad, but wiped the tears of blood from the statue beginning from the face down to the feet, contemplating the Blessed Mother's words that we should practice obedience.

October 31, 1986

I felt much pain in my left hand. It looked as if it were going to begin bleeding. At about 10 p.m., my feet began to harden. It was becoming late, but I did not want to leave the Blessed Mother. At about 2 a.m., pains intensified, and I fell down. I heard the Blessed Mother speaking.

THE BLESSED MOTHER:

Emphasize to everyone the importance of the Holy Eucharist. By the Holy Eucharist, the Lord will be in you. He will live in you and stay there always, if you open your heart and receive Him with a clean heart. How can the Lord enter you, if you do not have a clean heart or keep the door closed? Look at those receiving Holy Communion. . . .

I saw many people receiving Communion. There only were a few who were receiving the Lord sincerely. The Blessed Mother was at the Lord's side. She was crying because of so many sacrilegious Communions. She wants us to make frequent Confessions so that even one more soul may be saved.

November 5, 1986

I saw the Blessed Mother nailed to the Cross suffering excruciating pains. I took part in her pains. They were so hard to endure. As she was speaking from the Cross, I was repeating her exact words without realizing it. Some of my helpers wrote down what they were hearing.

THE BLESSED MOTHER:

Is there anyone who can lower me from the Cross? Moment after moment, there are more people who crucify me. I am suffering on the Cross together with my Son Jesus.

Help me. I cannot appease God the Father's anger without your help.

Can you participate in my sufferings? . . .

Because of birth control and abortions, I feel extreme pains in my womb. Little lives are roaming about in limbo after having been deprived of their human dignity and treated only as a lump of bloody flesh—which was a consequence of the human cruelty, desecration and failure to recognize the dignity of human life. Pray and soothe their wounds and offer atonements for the sins commited at night.

Do you see the blood flowing out of my throat? God the Father's just anger is overflowing. Because I love you all, I am holding on to you all even to the extent of vomiting blood. . . in order to save even one more soul that is failing.

I will dwell in you, if you renounce yourselves and come to me. Unite with one another in love. If you do, Satan will retreat. Become apostles of my Immaculate Heart. Console me by doing so.

Father Raymond Spies, a Salesian missionary priest from Belgium, became Julia's spiritual director in January 1987.

February 13, 1987

Today I received the pains of crucifixion together with the Blessed Mother. Our Mother laments over the world covered with darkness. She is begging for our help, because the just anger of God the Father is overflowing.

Mother, we are already yours. Use us as you wish.

THE BLESSED MOTHER:

Renounce yourself.

Do not worry. I know what is in your mind. Entrust everything to me and rely on me.

My daughter who is most pleasing to my Heart! I feel sorrow when you suffer. When you feel pain, I do, too; when you go through agonies, I agonize, too; and when you are sad, I am sad, too. But the pains, sorrows and agonies in this world will turn into happiness in the next world, because the happiness of this world is not the happiness of the next world. That is why you must endure the hardships well. Then, you will enjoy happiness in the next world with me.

Therefore, my sons and daughters, become persons smashed and trampled by all the people of this world and offer even these matters as penance. Then, you will come to me as humble persons, as little persons. . . .

Receive the light from my Immaculate Heart. Thus, become apostles of my Immaculate Heart who shine the light upon all the sick souls.

Achieve unity by loving one another. I want you to trust each other, be respectful and faithful to each other, and fulfill your duties.

My beloved children! I trust you and will abide in you.

February 25, 1987

While I was praying and contemplating for the conversion of sinners, the area around the Blessed Mother's statue became bright and foggy. There were angels flying over me. They looked so pretty with short, curly hair. The color of their wings was grey. The statue turned into the living Blessed Mother. As she was lifting her arms, two streams of red light began radiating from her hands and spreading like sunlight. She spoke, while shining the light.

THE BLESSED MOTHER:

My beloved daughter! When you come to me by walking on the path of a little and poor person, which is a narrow and

difficult path, a painful and lonesome path, and a dangerous, thorny path, I will hold your hands. So, come to me.
You will receive heavenly consolations. Come to me by becoming a lowlier and lowlier person. I am preparing a laurel crown for you.

Now, my daughter! Look at me. Receive the light of my
burning Immaculate Heart and shine it upon all the people
living in darkness. I will be with you.

Julia: *I am so powerless and unqualified. . . . But I am a
servant of the Lord; let it be done to me as you wish.*

THE BLESSED MOTHER:

Yes, that's it. Who can say he (or she) is qualified? What is
needed is a determination to live according to the Lord's
Will and to make an effort to repent with tears before the
Lord when mistakes are made.

March 13, 1987

While I was in deep meditation with my eyes closed in front of the
Blessed Mother's statue, it became bright. I opened my eyes and
saw the Blessed Mother's statue changed and shining. I felt as if I
were floating in the air and felt a close union with the Blessed Mother.

THE BLESSED MOTHER:

Oh, my daughter! Look around you. This world is being
covered with darkness, as sins multiply. There cannot be
peace in the world, because many families are getting sick.
The couples combined together to live a happy life are becoming isolated individuals, as they are unable to forgive
and love each other and are becoming jealous, resentful
and hateful of each other. My daughter, see how serious
family troubles are.

She showed me the scenes of many families, as in a movie.

Only a few were trying to live according to the Lord's Will. The sick families looked so terrible and miserable. Conflicts between mothers-in-law and daughters-in-law, between husbands and wives, among brothers and sisters, and between parents and children. . . Their eyes were burning with hatred and permeated with poison. They were hating each other, because their thinking was self-centered. As the adults were fighting and hurting each other, their children were being trampled on. The wounds gave rise to more wounds.

What a tragedy that they had to go on living like this! Insisting on equal rights between men and women. . . being unforgiving to each other. . . The devils were clapping their hands and giggling in an ugly manner for the divisions and hatred they had promoted. Even those who believed in God were falling into temptations frequently because of their weakness. This was offending the Lord and giving Him such sorrows.

Julia: *Mother! . . . What can I do?*

THE BLESSED MOTHER:

Help me open my eyes. My eyes are bloodshot because of the shocks from all sorts of insults. Wipe away my tears that flow every day.

Julia: *Teach me what to do.*

THE BLESSED MOTHER:

Tell people about your family. The life you have lived has not been yours. I have guided it since a long time ago. It was not an easy matter to select one family. I will give you the strength to overcome difficulties, as I called you and chose your family in this age when many families are sick and, as a result, the world is deprived of peace and is being covered with a thickening darkness.

Live a consecrated life filled with constant prayers, sacrifices, penance and love.

Julia: *How can I do it?*

THE BLESSED MOTHER:

Do not think that you have been living a chosen life because of your perseverance. . . . I have planned and prepared your life and you have consented to living accordingly. So, do as you promised. Good-bye. An-nyoung! ("An-
nyoung" is a short form of the the Korean equivalent to "Good-bye."
It is normally used between friends and by anyone to a younger
person in a friendly way.)

Julia: *Mother! Please tell me more.*

I kept asking, but she did not speak any more.

April 18, 1987

The Blessed Mother spoke while I was undergoing pains in ecstasy.

THE BLESSED MOTHER:

My beloved daughter! Pray for priests ceaselessly. Your severe pains to the extent of shedding blood and sweat will
help priests. When priests work to help those people who
fell into errors because of their ingratitude, how can they
be liberated from their sins, unless your sacrifices and reparations accompany (the priests' work)?

Now, stay awake and pray for priests without ceasing. It is
urgent. Also pray for peace in this country and for the end
of anarchic birth control.

April 21, 1987

After I suffered the pains of crucifixion for two hours, the Blessed
Mother spoke through her statue.

THE BLESSED MOTHER:

I want you all to participate in my work of Salvation, united with priests. Keep the Bishop informed through your spiritual director so that many of my children may participate in my Kingdom. Do you know how intensely my Immaculate Heart is burning to save even one more soul that is contaminated with sins and is weak? I want to save souls from the miserable vice that makes them live as blind people, even though they have eyes, and makes them live as deaf people, even though they have ears. I want to help them renounce themselves and amend their lives.

When they do renounce themselves and return to me, I will become their strength. I will give energy to the weak souls and help them free themselves from sins.

April 23, 1987
—The Blessed Mother sheds tears of blood for the third time.

The Blessed Mother began shedding tears at about noon and tears of blood at 5:30 p.m. Her tears of blood were reaching her feet. Her statue turned into the living Blessed Mother.

THE BLESSED MOTHER:

Daughter! Today I shed tears of love burning in my Immaculate Heart for my most beloved priests to wash their wounds and console their hearts. I want you to become their comforters, too.

Priests!! My most beloved priests are now walking on the path of loneliness and a painful cross. They are climbing Mt. Calvary tired and suffering. They are walking on an alienated path of the cross, suffering many pains in their wounds. Help them. For the conversion of sinners who are deeply mired in evil habits and to follow the Will of my Son Jesus, priests are carrying the burden of teaching the way of love to the numerous souls who despise and ignore them countless times and the burden of offering sacrifices and reparations for those souls. I want you to pray with me for them so that they may not be infected by the world but be

The Blessed Mother wept tears and tears of blood for priests and asked us to constanly pray for them. (April 23, 1987)

faithful to their vocation. They are my sons who deserve respect and love by all.

Julia: *Mother, what should I do?*

THE BLESSED MOTHER:

Listen well and tell people. From now on, all of you must treat priests and religious like your parents who gave birth to you. You must also become their comforters. That is because this age is very evil and filled with errors and, because of this, the devils are so active and are employing all the available means to destroy priests. They know that they gain more by ruining one priest than destroying one thousand or ten thousand lay people.

Now, look. Those who left the priesthood had been good priests. That is why I am praying, shedding tears that they do not walk on the road to hell but repent. I want you to pray for them, too.

Now, look! Many priests are suffering because of criticisms by those who have family-life vocations. How can you, who have been called to family life, judge priests and religious, while not being able to be faithful to your own vocations? Why are you trying to remove the speck from others' eyes while missing the plank in your own?

My most beloved priests. . . I implore you today to wash the wounds of my priests whom I love so much that I can put them in my eyes without feeling any pain. (This is an idiomatic expression in Korea used by adults about a child whom they love very much.)

Julia: *Mother, tell me.*

THE BLESSED MOTHER:

Be awake and pray. It is my Son's wish to save many souls through them *(priests).* . . . The religious *(the nuns)!* Pray for my beloved daughters. They have many knots in their hearts. They have a human nature just like yourselves and, therefore, can make mistakes. Whenever they do, offer them up with prayers.

May 12, 1987
—Ordinary tears

The Blessed Mother shed tears from midnight to 8 a.m. I saw her eyes filled with tears.

Julia: *Mother, why are you weeping?*

Momentarily, I fell down and saw many souls. Some of them were walking with a cane; some did not have any legs; some were without shoulders or arms; some did not have eyes or ears; some had disfigured noses or mouths. They were going somewhere, pushing each other, fighting with each other in noisy and mean ways and falling again and again. I was astonished and screamed. I thought they were the souls in Purgatory.

THE BLESSED MOTHER:

. . .Look! Many souls are going toward hell because of abortions. I have to implore with tears like this in order to save those numerous souls. I intend to save them through you— through your sacrifices and reparations. How can I be unaware of the pains you endure? Now, would you participate in the pains of the little babies who have been abandoned by their ignorant and cruel parents?

Julia: *Yes, Mother. I can do anything, if you stay with me.*

At that moment, my posture became that of an unborn baby—with arms and legs crouched. My face became red like blood. I suffered for four and a half hours. When these pains ended, pains of delivery began. My face became swollen like a pumpkin and I could not move myself. I suffered all day. The spiritual pains were harder to endure than the physical pains.

May 17, 1987

While I was in a deep meditation after praying fifteen decades of the rosary, the Blessed Mother implored with an anxious voice.

THE BLESSED MOTHER:

I ask the Pope, Cardinals, Bishops and all priests.

You must carry the cross and pray together at Gethsemane in order to save this world contaminated with errors. Share the pains that my Son's Sacred Heart and my Immaculate Heart suffer.

Always be awake and pray at Gethsemane to avoid falling into sins of impurity.

Love alone will lead you to Jesus.

Oh, my sons! Live with me so that I may not be disappointed. Offer up small sacrifices, because my Heart is filled with sorrows for those who commit sins.

Do not seek your own satisfaction, but love me in a simple way.

Satan's violence is increasing day after day with a terrible force. He is becoming more active to make even fervent souls reject me. Help me. I will give you the light from my Immaculate Heart so that all of you may be saved. Become apostles of my Immaculate Heart by receiving the light from my burning Heart.

June 13, 1987
—A vision at 3 a.m.

I entered an ecstasy while thinking about many brothers and sisters who were in pains. The Blessed Mother came to me with a merciful and graceful appearance and spoke to me quietly—almost whispering anxiously and lovingly.

THE BLESSED MOTHER:

My children who have faith and try to live according to the Lord's Will are going to suffer more pains. Offer up all your pains. Offer more sacrifices. If you offer sacrifices and penance out of true love, you will be helping much in saving many souls. Let everyone know this.

June 14, 1987

It was late at night. I was praying and whipping myself, fervently imploring the Blessed Mother. The weeping Blessed Mother embraced me warmly like a close friend and like an elder sister. She spoke with a merciful and soft voice.

THE BLESSED MOTHER:

Do not brag about anything. Instead, have humility and love. Do not own luxuries. Daughter, let's live like a pilgrim and a traveler—until you reach the bosom of your Heavenly Mother. Always be poor and little. Serve all in everything all the time. Daughter! While following the footsteps of the Saints for the sake of Jesus, do not concern yourself too much with criticisms. Even when you suffer pains from others, give them peace. Through sacrifices and penance, do the things that can benefit them.

Every day, lower yourself further, thinking about Jesus on Mt. Calvary. Through poverty, humility, obedience and purity, keep going down from the high place to the low place following this Mother who wants you to walk the way of perfection. Shouldn't we become more humble like Jesus, Who chose to be humble? Change your life further—throwing away every attachment. Change your value system. Live a life of conversion. Convert every moment and converse with Jesus. Conversion does not just mean repenting sins.

It means trying to live the life that God wants you to live. Abandon the worldly life and live a life based on the Gospels. Live like a lily. As the higher-grade protein gives rise to a more foul odor, the shiny things of the world entail a greater darkness. Let's die again and imitate Christ.

June 15, 1987

The Blessed Mother did not shed tears today, but spoke with a crying voice.

THE BLESSED MOTHER:

Yes, you make very frequent Confessions. The devils do not lead people to commit mortal sins at first. They make people commit venial sins and, then, when many venial sins have accumulated, mortal sins. Therefore, try to receive Jesus with a clean soul by making frequent Confessions, even when you only have venial sins.

Jesus established the Sacrament of the Holy Eucharist to nurture us with His Body and Blood, to unite with us, and to resurrect our bodies after death. We must praise this amazing Sacrament, but many souls are becoming unclean by failing to make frequent Confessions.

As you would put on freshly washed clothes before meeting a high-ranking person, prepare to receive Our Lord with a clean soul by making frequent Confessions. However hard one may try to keep the soul clean, it cannot remain spotless indefinitely.
. . .
So, through the Sacrament of Confession, open your eyes and ears and, thereby, open your hearts widely to receive Jesus.

The Blessed Mother wept because of sacrilegious Communions.

June 27, 1987

I felt so sorry because of many people who were walking on the sinful way by judging the Blessed Mother. Also because of the anxiety about my work, I was trembling and praying for the Blessed Mother's help.

THE BLESSED MOTHER:

Do not tremble. Have faith in the power of my Motherhood and wake up the sleeping souls. I will welcome all the repenting souls.

Your love must be fervent. It can burn in shining flames only through unending sacrifices.

Make a constant effort to blind Satan. On Thursdays, offer reparations to the Blessed Sacrament. Pray without ceasing to constrain the evils that offend the Lord and to compensate for the sacrileges committed against the Holy Eucharist.

June 29, 1987

As I was praying in preparation for the second anniversary of the Blessed Mother's first weeping tears, a golden light and a blue light came from the altar in the Chapel. I fell and received the pains of crucifixion and of the Sacred Heart and the Immaculate Heart. The Blessed Mother appeared at that moment. She was wearing a sparkling crown and was carrying the Baby Jesus. The Baby Jesus was wearing white clothes with golden hems and was holding a blue globe with a small cross on it.

When my pains were over, Jesus and the Blessed Mother blessed me and others. The Blessed Mother's voice was overflowing with love. It was the most loving voice I have ever heard.

THE BLESSED MOTHER:

Daughter! Many of my children testifying for me are living

without self-renunciation and, therefore, are unable to spread love as they should.

Julia: *Mother! Tell me. I am unworthy, but will spread your love.*

THE BLESSED MOTHER:

Even at this moment, it is necessary to make more sacrifices and do penance because of the sins being committed by many of my children. For this reason, you need to suffer more. By doing this, you are participating in my sufferings.

When you accept my words, my messages will renew and change your souls. In this age filled with errors, even my beloved children are being deeply permeated with errors. Because of this, I wish to spread my voice through you. I wish to save the people in the world from darkness by shining the light from my burning Immaculate Heart upon them. Therefore, become a sacrificial victim.

Julia: *Teach me, Mother!*

THE BLESSED MOTHER:

I am carrying the burden of reparation for you; so carry the burden for others. There are too many souls who fall into hell and bruise my Heart. When you offer penance and prayers to compensate for the sins and ingratitude of so many souls, they will be saved.

I love you despite your weaknesses. I want all of your love to be directed toward me. I want the lay people to obey the Pope, Cardinals, bishops and all the priests. They are my most beloved sons and have received the power to forgive the sins of countless people who have become contaminated with sins. For this reason, even my Son Jesus comes down from Heaven to earth in obedience to them.

June 30, 1987

—Second anniversary of the Blessed Mother's first weeping

THE BLESSED MOTHER:

Oh, my sons and daughters! Come back to me, to my bosom. . . .

I wish to be your refuge in this dangerous world. I will burn you with the flames in my Immaculate Heart. Oh, my beloved children! I will fight on your side, when you renounce yourselves and return to me. I will help you with my power that crushes the serpent.

July 15, 1987

I was praying in front of the weeping statue of the Blessed Mother. I was crying loudly because of my unworthiness.

Julia: *Mother, what can I do? I am so indiscreet and foolish, only hurting your Heart. I am a most sinful one, a most ignorant one. Why did you choose me, such a sinful person?*

THE BLESSED MOTHER:

My daughter! I did not come to call the just. Because the sinners are walking on the road to hell, I wanted you to work with me to save even one more soul. For this purpose, I delivered you from death while you were in pains and my Son Jesus saved you when you were about to cease functioning.

Julia: *Mother! I am very sorry. It is difficult to move my body.*

THE BLESSED MOTHER:

When you suffer bodily pains, offer them up for those with

dying souls. You know that I am now suffering many of the same pains that I suffered on Mt. Calvary for my Son. If you offer sacrifices and penances for those who do not know this, your small sacrifices will quench my immense thirst.

Julia: *Mother! I will try. But again and again I only give you my shortcomings. What can I do?*

THE BLESSED MOTHER:

Do not worry too much about awkward mistakes in your daily life. Do not get upset or try to defend yourself, but have trust in me. This will make you more humble. I will rescue sinners as much as you request with your sacrifices and penances. When you suffer in even small matters and begin feeling as I do, I feel comforted. Good-bye! Annyoung!

August 11, 1987

Because so many people were coming to see the Blessed Mother's statue, those who were living in the same apartment complex were protesting, even with public demonstrations. So, I was trying to find a new place and a new house for the Blessed Mother's statue. Feeling tired, I was praying before the statue. The Blessed Mother's voice came from the statue.

THE BLESSED MOTHER:

Give alms to this Heavenly Beggar, who is waiting for you, calling you and longing for you.

October 19, 1987
—Ordinary tears; First anniversary of the Blessed Mother's first shedding tears of blood

I received messages in ecstasy.

Father Hee-Dong John Park, former Pastor of Naju, celebrated Mass today commemorating the anniversary. About eighty people attended.

The Blessed Mother began shedding tears at 4:25 p.m., lasting until 8:25 p.m. While I was participating in her pains, she spoke to Father Park through me.

THE BLESSED MOTHER:

Father Park, I called you, because I love you. You must testify for me together with Father Lee *(Pastor of Naju at the time of this message)*. Nobody fully understands my sufferings. I have difficulty breathing because of the sinners. You must help me. Many priests are avoiding me.

Father Park: *How may I help you?*

THE BLESSED MOTHER:

Many sheep are walking toward hell. I have implored at many places in the world with apparitions and with tears, but my messages have not been spreading well.

Father Park, my beloved priest! You did not come here by accident, but by my call. I chose you. I am in pains and need your help. I chose Father Spies, too. The messages must spread fast. They must spread all over the world. Tell the Bishop. Tears are important, but the contents of the messages are more important. You must spread my messages fast.

Those who say they are testifying on behalf of my Son Jesus are giving me such pains. . . You must get involved. Father Park, hold the hands of Father Lee and Father Spies and help me. Report to the Bishop. To the Bishop!

Father Park, I chose you. I will always be with you. Do not feel lonesome, as I am always with you. So, with me, tell people about the Passion of my Son Jesus. You must climb Mt. Calvary carrying the cross of love—with Jesus. In order to help many people with prayers, sacrifices and reparations, you must pray and work with Father Lee and Father Spies. You must get involved together. I am preparing a laurel crown for you. You must be awake and pray together with my Son Jesus in Gethsemane and spread the messages all over the world.

I chose Father Lee, Father Spies and Father Park. You must work holding hands with Father Lee and Father Spies. Father Park, I chose you. Do not forget this. Julia is only an instrument. You must hold her hands. Don't let go of her. Many priests are turning their eyes from me. Father Park, please help me.

In order to save many souls, we must carry the cross of love together and offer reparations with prayers and sacrifices and, thereby, appease the just anger of God the Father.

The flames in the Sacred Heart of Jesus and of my Immaculate Heart are burning every moment. They are burning intensely. The Hearts are becoming torn apart.

I love all priests. Every day, I shed tears to wash their wounds. The tears of priests should not be tears from pains but tears united with mine.

December 11, 1987

A light similar to sunlight was shining from the weeping statue. The statue turned into the living Blessed Mother and began speaking. Her voice was serious but also friendly and warm.

THE BLESSED MOTHER:

. . .

My beloved priests. I brought them here. I brought him *(Father René Laurentin)* here from a distant land. I chose the date of his coming and also changed the flight schedule so that he could testify.

(Father Raymond Spies had asked Father Laurentin to visit Korea from December 7, 1987 so that he could arrive in Naju on December

Holy Rosary Church in Naju

Julia's house next to the Chapel

8, the Feast of the Immaculate Conception. Kimpo International Airport is near Seoul, and Naju is about 200 miles south of Seoul; but Father Laurentin had a busy speech and travel schedule and could arrive in Seoul on December 8 at the earliest. Suddenly and unexpectedly, however, many flight schedules in Asia changed and Father Laurentin was able to arrive in Seoul on December 7 and in Naju the next day.)

He will inform the Pope. He is a very little, simple, graceful and beloved son of mine.

. . .

It is urgent that people put the messages into practice. But prayers are lacking. If the approval can be obtained soon, many children walking toward hell will change their course. It will also become a shortcut to world peace. That way, the prayers of Korea's blessed children will be answered faster.

Many children gather under my mantle, but they disperse easily. So, help me.

. . .

Priests who come to me, who is weeping, will receive abundant light and burning love from me. Good-bye!

January 1, 1988
—Feast of Mary, the Mother of God

The Blessed Mother's statue shed blood from her eyes and nose from about 10:15 a.m. She appeared to me in my ecstasy. She spoke filled with sorrows and shedding tears of blood. I was weeping in pains.

THE BLESSED MOTHER:

In this age when the whole world is in need of unity, this nation *(Korea)* is being divided and unable to love one another. It is painful enough to be divided between the South and the North. Why do you distrust, hate and resent each other and confront and fight with each other? You are all brethren, one nation and children of one God.

Julia: *What should we do?*

THE BLESSED MOTHER:

Pray that you may be united. Offer reparations and prayers. Also ask all priests to offer fervent rosary prayers for unity, to remember the voice of the Lord on the Cross all the time, to avoid getting angry and to make reparations for the sins of those who do wrong unknowingly. They will convert at a proper time.

God the Father was going to punish (this country) severely for the intense strifes, but the small sacrifices and penances offered by the little ones together with me helped to avoid this. More penance is needed, however.

Today I will gather all of you under my mantle. Since you know my pains, I want you to spread the messages to all so that my beloved children may receive the light from my Immaculate Heart and that my tears and blood may not flow in vain.

As I told you before, the rosary defeats the devils. Tell all the faithful to offer five more decades of rosary prayers. If they pray more for the unity of this country, it will be saved from a calamity.

Julia: *My Mother Mary! My beloved Mother who is suffering because of the division of my country and because of the lack of harmony within my country! I pray that all you wish will be realized so that it may become a glory to the Lord and a cause of our unending gratitude.*

January 10, 1988
—Feast of the Baptism of Jesus

Because of severe fatigue and pain, I went to bed early but could not fall asleep. As my mind was full of thoughts about the Blessed Mother, I got up and went to the Chapel at 11:15 p.m. and began praying the rosary. I only prayed one decade by 12:40 a.m., as I was crying with the Blessed Mother.

I entered an ecstasy at that moment and saw the Blessed Mother wearing a crown on her head and holding the Baby Jesus, Who was not wearing any clothes. She handed over the Baby Jesus to me and said that we should become like children. After the Baby Jesus touched me softly several times, the Blessed Mother received Him back and said that it would be difficult for us to enter Heaven unless we become like children.

The Blessed Mother, shedding tears, was extremely beautiful. She was smiling and was filled with love. Instead of the veil, she was wearing a laurel crown decorated with twelve shining stars.

THE BLESSED MOTHER:

Daughter! Forget about your weaknesses and remember my love. As my love will sustain you in your weaknesses, empty your heart. Only then will I be able to work in you. Give me even your present sufferings. There are always some temptations to overcome in this world.

Daughter! You know that the children who love me will be tested a lot. Yes, you are going through the pains of labor. I hope there will be more children who can suffer such pains, but most of them hurt me while suffering.

You understand that there can be birth because of the pains of labor that you suffer now, don't you? Help save many souls by patiently suffering these pains and remember the rewards that I am preparing for you. You should know that everything will be purified through love, as gold becomes purified in the furnace.

My little soul! However many good works you may have accumulated, they will collapse one after another if you neglect little things and speak ill of others. Be slow in opening your mouth and control your tongue wisely. When you feel like criticizing others, cover them with love. This will be a good work, too. Be holy in your words and deeds.

Daughter! You feel very anxious now. I am anxious, too. It hurts my Heart so much, when I see my intensely beloved children—who should climb up into my love and seek the treasures of Heaven—harming their own souls by trying to become higher than others, by being jealous and resentful of others, and by having doubts about my mercy.

My daughter, practice humility. This will give me a special, precious joy. Never try to become higher than others. Your penance, kindness, sacrifices, and reparations become fragrant oil for my wounds.

My daughter! Have a special love for my children with whom you work. The devils of pride, envy and resentment have an eye on them, because they try to become higher. You must practice love through sacrifices. Didn't I tell you that all the devils will be defeated when you practice love? Unite. Unite by loving one another.

There is something I want to show you. You know well that I wish to tell everyone through you.

There was a high mountain with fourteen stairs to the top. There also were trees by the stairs, bearing fruits whenever we did good works. But, when we judged others or committed other sins, the fruits of good works fell down to the ground. It was difficult to climb up the stairs, as I saw some people falling down from halfway to the top, others not going straight up but going in a circuitous way, and so on. Above the fourteen stairs was Heaven. There were God the Father, Jesus, the Blessed Mother and St. Joseph. All the Saints and angels were welcoming us with loud, joyful cheers.

They were looking at every deed of ours—without exception. The largest fruits came from repentance and conversion. When we suffer pains and offer them for other people, the light shines on them and the fruit of good works is borne for us. Those who die after climbing even one step will go to Purgatory. If one reaches the fourteenth step, it is almost Heaven. The fifteenth step is Heaven. I was trembling, because so many people were falling off the stairs. The Blessed Mother spoke.

THE BLESSED MOTHER:

Did you see, daughter! It is easy to start climbing the stairs, but it is so difficult to complete all fourteen stairs *(the fourteen stations to Golgotha Hill)*. Therefore, tell everyone to be careful not to fall off the stairs and turn all the accumulated good works into nothing. Good-bye! An-nyoung!

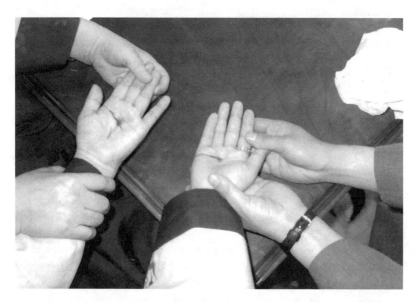

Several times, Julia received the Stigmata (the Five Wounds of Christ) while suffering the pains of the Crucifixion. The above photograph was taken in Naju on January 29, 1988.

January 30, 1988
—9:45 – 11:45 a.m.

I was suffering, because people were criticizing and judging each other and, therefore, were unable to achieve unity. As I began suffering the pains of the burning Immaculate Heart, the Blessed Mother appeared, weeping, suffering and looking sorrowful.

In the small room upstairs, I was throwing up and suffering without a moment's rest. The Blessed Mother loves us so much that she speaks to us even to the extent of throwing up blood in order to save even one more soul. But people do not understand her or follow her. She tries to embrace all, but they refuse. Because of this, she feels much pain in her arms.

The Blessed Mother is thirsty, because unity is so hard to achieve; people make promises easily but do not keep them; and there are many priests but they do not fill her dear children's spiritual needs.

The Blessed Mother speaks *(to Julia's helpers)*.

THE BLESSED MOTHER:

Father Spies is also suffering pains. But don't worry. Many priests will be persecuted, but I am going to help them.

My pains are intense, because so many of my children are not accepting my messages. Pray much so that the messages may spread fast. You did not come here on your own, but by my call. Do not leave me. Until I call you, you must work with Julia and help her. I will prepare your rewards. So, trust and follow me. When the sufferings are great, rewards will be great, too.

Different responsibilities are assigned to all of you, as you are different members of the same body and have different functions. Do not refuse the cross given to you. I will purify you by placing you in the furnace of my love and melting your impurities. Children, achieve unity.

Many members of the body must form a unity and love each other. But they are not accepting the Love of God. How can God help?

So, you are called to be the apostles of my Immaculate Heart and, therefore, you must accept me well and share each other's burdens.

Do not weep or worry for my pains, but make the Passion of Jesus known all over the world. Some priests and religious do not carry out their obligations properly and fall into sins of impurity. For this reason, Jesus is being hit by more arrows and is bleeding on His Head with more crowns of thorns. But there are no children to wipe away His Blood.

Therefore, the Immaculate Heart must be made known quickly. My Heart is being torn apart and my throat is burning with thirst, but there aren't many children who are helping. Unite your efforts.

My Son Jesus and I are trembling with cold, but who is giving us clothes? I feel thirsty, but who is quenching my thirst? My womb is being torn apart because of abortions, but how many have you prevented?

Priests, priests, my beloved priests are falling into sins of impurity.

. . .

I am suffering so much pain. Pray and sacrifice incessantly for priests. Pray for them with sacrifices and penances so that the devils may not tempt them. I also feel sorrows because of the Divine Office offered out of habit by religious.

If you truly love me and love your neighbors, then, you are loving Jesus and will be appeasing the just anger of God the Father. When my messages are spread to the world and put into practice, the just anger of God the Father will be softened and the terrible punishment will be turned away.

My dear children! I called you with love. I will protect you until the end of the world and until you come here where I am. So, hold on to my arm tightly and follow me. I will guide you, when you do penance, sacrifices and reparations and when you joyfully consecrate all the poor souls. I will fight on your side when you fight the war in the world. I will help you.

Because I called you to be apostles of my Immaculate Heart, the devils will become more active and tempt you. Hold my hand tightly so that you may not fall into temptations.

Your goal should not be just to prevent wars. This country is going toward a division because of hatred, jealousy and resentment. So, your sacrifices are necessary. You must work together holding each other's hands.

People are carrying out abortions even at this moment, causing intense pain in my womb. Pray the rosary more fervently.

You are brothers and sisters united by love. So, do not fight because of jealousy and selfishness. Instead, love one another and work in unity.

My dear daughters! My beloved souls! Whenever you sin, my Heart becomes torn apart and bleeds and bleeds in vain. Now you must pray for the conversion of sinners and pray the rosary more fervently for peace in this country and in the world. As I said before, if you offer more rosary prayers, this country will avoid a calamity. I want all the faithful to do it. . . .

If all of you unite, this country will triumph. I love this Korea. I have loved Korea so much. Now I am here. If you unite, you can overcome any temptation. Hold each other's hands for unity. As I hold your hands, you must hold all others' hands. I will embrace you all.

If you do not unite, more blood will flow from my eyes and I will suffer more. Give alms to me. Give alms to this Heavenly Beggar.

You will live in my Immaculate Heart. So, rejoice and keep your hearts on heavenly matters, desire heavenly things, renounce self-love and walk the way of self-renunciation and of a little person's love. Come back to my bosom and become a comfort to me.

January 30, 1988
—10:30-11:30 p.m.

While I was crying a lot because of many kinds of severe pains, the Blessed Mother appeared and called me. Her appearance was as usual, but she looked taller than before and also very sad and full of pains. She spoke very intimately and lovingly.

THE BLESSED MOTHER:

My beloved daughter, who has to experience much pain! I did not shed tears in vain. I called you, a weak and poor child, to lead the whole human race to the road of redemption. So, what can I do about your suffering? What can I do, if you feel sad? So, do not be troubled too much. Since a long time ago, I have been tempering you with pains from the fires of justice. You even said that God was harsh. I can understand.

So much pain has been given to you. Your heart is pierced with a sword, stops functioning and becomes cold on the cross, which is a terrifying instrument of torture. Frightful pains that come from twisting your arms and legs (with heavy wooden sticks) and crushing your heart. Your heart becomes paralyzed because of the countless arrows. Your body is full of wounds from scourgings and becomes unmovable. Your throat becomes so dry that you cannot even swallow saliva. Your head is bleeding under the pressure from the crown of thorns.

But I tell you again that, through such terrible pains that you suffer, the spiritually blind will see, those chained to the world will be set free and many souls imprisoned in darkness will return to the Immaculate Heart.

Do not worry about those who are against us. Those who have ears will hear, those who have eyes will see, and those who practice my messages are accepting me and, therefore, will experience a renewal of their souls. They will surely see the triumph of my Immaculate Heart.

So, my daughter, rejoice in your sufferings. Offer me all your pains—even the smallest ones. The burden of atonement is heavy, but I will be with you as you climb Mt. Calvary with Jesus in love. An-nyoung!

February 4, 1988
—A visitation by Father Raymond Spies

Father Spies came to see the Archbishop of Kwangju and also witnessed the weeping of the Blessed Mother's statue in Naju.

He arrived at about 10 a.m. with Sister Dina and saw the tears on the statue. He began celebrating Mass at 11 a.m.

Overnight, the statue had moved forward a few steps, looking toward the side window. Father Spies was thinking about this as he was getting ready for the Mass. He thought that, only if the Blessed Mother wanted, she could go back to her original place and look toward the altar. That way, she could participate in the Mass better.

"Should I move her back to her original place or should I put her on the altar so that she can see the people better? Is she going to walk back to her place by herself? . . ."

With these thoughts in his mind, he did not make any decision. When the Mass started, the Blessed Mother gave an answer through me. (I was attending Mass sitting on the floor because of pains.)

THE BLESSED MOTHER:

Julia! Tell Father Spies. I can go back to my original place by myself, but I prefer to be placed there by the priest. I do not just mean the original place for the statue, but my original place as the Mother of the Church. I should be respected by all, but, instead, I am despised, abandoned, neglected, handled carelessly, and avoided. I feel much sadness in my Heart. Help me quickly.

When Father Spies heard the message, he asked me to help move the statue back to the original place. I stepped forward to help despite the pain. When I stretched my hands to assist the priest, however, I almost screamed, because my two hands were punctured and bleeding.

THE BLESSED MOTHER:

Daughter! You must help me in the rear by offering pains.

Julia: *Yes, Mother. I will follow your will.*

I fell down and entered a state of ecstasy at the moment the priest was giving a blessing at the end of Mass. The Blessed Mother showed me many children who were walking toward hell, because they did not have love.

THE BLESSED MOTHER:

Daughter, look. I have chosen numerous souls with love, but they are giving much pain to my Son Jesus by considering themselves lofty and deserting my messages, which amounts to a betrayal. Jesus continues suffering on the Cross, because they scourge Him cruelly and despise and insult Him.

My daughter! My Son Jesus paid a dear price to save the poor, sinful souls—the souls who are walking toward ruin because of their hypocrisy, ingratitude and indifference. Do not have any doubt in following my wish that you offer your sufferings gracefully to lead many souls to the path of salvation. Also, believe that when you suffer much, you accumulate much joy in Heaven.

As my messages are founded on love, mercy will overflow into any soul who repents and practices the messages.

Daughter! I am being comforted by Father Spies, who is a simple and little soul. I rejoice, because he offers his fidelity and love fervently.

My little daughter! My daughter who has to suffer pains! Will you participate in the Lord's Passion so that many souls may return to the Lord?

Julia: *Yes, Mother.*

THE BLESSED MOTHER:

Receive this pain for the sake of the Pope, Cardinals, Bishops, and priests; also for the conversion of sinners.

I received intense pains of the Cross, the crown of thorns and the heart. Whenever people sinned, spears, arrows and sharp swords pierced the heart. After about twenty-five minutes, Father Spies felt so much compassion on me that he blessed me, ending the pains.

June 5, 1988
—Feast of the Holy Eucharist (Corpus Christi)

I had been in bed for several days because of the intense pains—not even able to go to the bathroom. Several people had to help me. But it was a great feast day and I did not want to stay in bed. Because of the pains, I prayed more fervently that the Lord wash the dirt away from my soul and help me work more effectively as His instrument. While praying, I went to church, supported by others, and attended Mass. In the church, I was not able to keep myself sitting up and had to be supported by Mark, Philip and Martha. It was a pain that would have been unbearable without love for Jesus. I cried and offered up the pains.

The Blessed Mother was extremely beautiful. She was about 165 cm (5' 5") tall and was holding a rosary in her right hand. She was wearing a white dress with a white mantle stretching from head to feet. The hems of her mantle were sparkling gold. Her burning Immaculate Heart was red and looked like it was moving. About seven swords pierced her Heart. Under her feet were three roses—white, red and yellow. Jesus was bleeding and a bright light was radiating from His whole Body like the sun. Above the Crucifix, there was a white dove radiating a bright light.

Julia: *Jesus! Many of Your children aspire to see You, but are unable to do so, because they don't know how. Please start a fire of love in them. I will offer my sufferings, though inadequate, for them. Help us. Even in this, not my will but Yours be done.*

I received Holy Communion, and, when I was coming back to my seat supported by Philip and Mark, I felt my mouth being filled with the Body and Blood of Jesus. I smelled blood, too. Then, I felt as if I were floating in the air and fell down to the floor. At that time, I heard the strong voice of Jesus from the tabernacle.

JESUS:

Look at Me!

I was very surprised when I looked in the direction of the voice. Jesus was there bleeding so miserably. The Blood was not falling to the ground, but into the beautiful chalice and paten on the altar to be brought to us by the priests. The Blessed Mother, our Mediatrix, was standing by Jesus.

She always looks beautiful, and, today, looked particularly anxious and very shiny. She suffers pain, because Jesus is bleeding for His Love for us. But she rejoices, because, by bleeding, He comes to us, sinners, and, by our receiving Him, we become renewed and united with Him. For this reason, the Blessed Mother wants and prays that each and every one of us renounce the ego and receive the Holy Eucharist with a clean heart. Jesus speaks.

JESUS:

I am still bleeding on the Cross to save the whole human race and My Blood will not flow in vain. I am the Transfuser Who washes away your dirty sins. My precious Blood is a special medicine that will open the eyes of the sick souls and wake up the sleeping souls—through priests. I am so troubled that people receive Me out of habit and with indifference.

I wish to pour down all My Love upon all the souls on this earth. Help them participate in the heavenly banquet *(the Blessed Sacrament)*.

My Mother Mary has often encouraged frequent Confessions. But many children make the Confession without a sincere repentance or even try to receive Me without going to Confession *(when it is necessary)*. A Confession out of habit or without true repentance is an insult to Me and will not enable one to see Me. Therefore, let Me work within you by confessing your sins with sincere repentance.

I also want to tell you that I desire to pour down all My Love upon all the children in this world, but too many of them cannot meet Me because they do not go to Confession.

Those children who have true repentance and a desire to meet Me in reconciliation but are unable to go to Confession can still receive Me by promising to make a good Confession. But, if that promise is not kept, it will constitute an even greater sacrilege. When the promise is kept, I will set a fire of a greater love in them than in the case of a Confession out of habit.

It is My Love that prompted Me to come down to this world and call the sinners rather than the just. I want everyone, without a single exception, to belong to Me, and I am relying on My Mother Mary for that. Therefore, by following her, you will be following Me.

Come now, all the children of the world! Today, as always, I become a sacrificial offering and am waiting for you. Let's gather at the heavenly table and share Love. When you open your heart widely and return to Me, I will not question your past, but will bestow the cup of blessing on you instead.

My little soul! I ask you again. Pray for the Pope, My Vicar, all the Cardinals, Bishops and priests. Offer sacrifices and reparations without ceasing so that they may carry out their duties loyally. I want them to follow Me with self-renunciation and poverty. I entrusted all the work to them, and so, all the liturgical celebrations they offer are what I offer. Without penance, how can they follow Me? I want you to offer more sufferings and reparations so that they may carry out their duties faithfully. Little, hidden sacrifices are what comfort My Heart and help precious graces flow into all the people.

I send My Love continuously to My High Priest, the Pope, Cardinals, Bishops and priests. My Mother will help them so that My Love may flow abundantly into all the souls. Have total confidence in My Mother.

Jesus gave a blessing and I made a Sign of the Cross. As I came out of the ecstasy, the Pastor was also giving the blessing at the end of the Mass. I found my body restored to a normal healthy condition. Those who saw this were delighted and amazed.

Julia: *Truly good Jesus! You have such a great love for sinners. I am a sinner who deserves death, but You shed Blood for me. I cannot even find words to express my gratitude.*

Jesus! When Your precious Love is transfused to the whole world, it will turn into a paradise. But how sorry it is that so many of Your children do not understand this precious Love, make their own judgment and walk toward hell. You feel so lonely because of this.

Jesus! I am Yours, though unworthy. Make me Your dwelling place and be comforted.

July 24, 1988
—9:30 p.m.–12:30 a.m.

At about 9 p.m., I suddenly lost energy in my whole body and fell down. I went upstairs to my room supported by others, where I was struggling with excruciating pains. A while later, I entered an ecstasy and saw Heaven, Purgatory and hell.

It was a world of difference. Such a tremendous difference! The saved children were sharing peace, joy and love in the flower garden, but the condemned ones were burning in the intense flames with resentment and hatred.

Heaven—Our True Home

Countless angels were playing a beautiful and majestic symphony welcoming the souls who were entering Heaven. Also, numerous Saints were welcoming them with loud cheers. Jesus was waiting for them with open arms, and the Blessed Mother was stretching out her hands to hold them. God the Father smiled, expressing a welcome with His eyes. St. Joseph was also welcoming them.

It was a place without any jealousy or resentment. All were sharing love with one another. It was filled with love, peace and joy. It was a place of heavenly banquet where one does not become hungry even without eating.

The Blessed Mother prepared crowns of flowers and put them on people, who were then dancing holding each other's hands. In the flower garden, Jesus and the Blessed Mother together held up her mantle, and all were entering the inside of the mantle. All were humble to each other and were keeping order to avoid inconveniencing others. Their faces were full of smiles and were beautiful.

Purgatory

It is a place where one must walk into the terrible flames of fire. There, one does the unfinished penance of this world and becomes purified.

It is a place far away where those who die in grace but have unfinished reparations must walk the way of atonement. When they are completely purified, they are lifted into Heaven by the angels with the help of the Blessed Mother. The process can be expedited, if we in this world pray for them. We can also help them by making sacrifices and doing penance for them.

It will be too late to regret not having done penance in this world. So, while still alive in this world, one must offer love constantly through sacrifices for others.

Hell

When the angels tie the hands of the condemned souls and drop them, the devils snatch them violently. Then, they fall into the flames of fire. It is a place of eternal perdition. It is useless, however hard one may regret and struggle. It is a sea of fire filled with hatred. Who will hold their hands? Nobody.

People struggle like a person drowning and trying to grab even a straw, but only run around in the fire, tear each other down, and try to take food away from others, but all the food burns in the fire, and nobody can eat anything. So, they are growling with eyes that are sticking out. They become horrible devils.

It was a terrible scene one could not even look at.

THE BLESSED MOTHER:

Daughter, did you see that?

The string that connects Heaven and earth together is I, your Mother. My Heart suffers so much pain, because errors abound everywhere in the world and penetrate even my chosen children to an outrageous degree.

That is why I intend to spread my voice to the children of the world through you. I want to let them recognize the light that comes continuously from my Son Jesus and understand my love. I want to exhort them to come out of the darkness into which they are now falling.

My little daughter, who rejoices in suffering pains for my Son Jesus and me! My Heart is hurt so much, because numerous children who have been called to Heaven are walking toward Purgatory and hell.

Even some of my priests, whom I love so much that I can put them in my eyes without feeling any pain, are going toward Purgatory and hell. I want to save them through you, the poorest one. When you endure and offer sufferings well, you are treating my wounds with fragrant oil.

Julia: *But Mother, I am so incapable. Many times, I do not satisfy your Heart, and, many times, I find it difficult to renounce myself completely for you.*

Help me. Oh, my Mother! Our shield and our comforter! I entrust myself, such a weak and unworthy one, to you com-

pletely so that your will may be fulfilled.

THE BLESSED MOTHER:

Even at this very moment, numerous souls are walking toward hell. I wish to save them through your sacrifices and sufferings. Will you take part in the pains?

Julia: *Yes, my Mother! How joyful it is to suffer with you for the conversion of many souls!*

Before I knew you, I had been so unhappy and miserable. But now I thank God and you for allowing me to take part in the sufferings despite my unworthiness.

THE BLESSED MOTHER:

Now, my dear daughter! My beloved daughter who asks for more sufferings! Now you are suffering pains. But daughter! I suffer even greater pains than you do.

Julia: *Mother! Let me have all those pains. Do you, our most gracious Mother, have to suffer these great pains?*

THE BLESSED MOTHER:

Through the pains that you and I suffer, the children mired in errors will be saved and the dirty souls will be cleansed by the precious Blood of my Son Jesus and saved by amazing miracles.

Julia: *Mother, I offer myself to you truly and completely.*

THE BLESSED MOTHER:

Daughter! My daughter who has to suffer! Even though your sacrifices and penances are heavy in this world, I will hold your hands. So, do not worry. I will stand by you.

Julia: *Mother! I am so unworthy. How can I desire great things? If many souls can go to the Lord by my suffering the* *pains of hell, I will be glad to do so. I wish to offer my pains with love and joy according to your will, to save even one more soul.*

THE BLESSED MOTHER:

Yes, my daughter! That is why I love you so much. Such a heart will flow into the world and make the spiritually blind see and the sick souls recover. But, if they refuse to respond to my calls, I will not be able to do anything after their death. Because, at that time, the justice of my Son Jesus will have to be realized. The evil ones will be ashamed and regret, but it will be too late.

Terrible Pains of Hell

I was crying and screaming in extreme despair that cannot even be imagined with a human mind.

The Blessed Mother is suffering and calling us incessantly to prevent us from going to the cursed abyss where the condemned souls separated from God are punished in many different ways under the just judgment by Jesus—bitterly lamenting, screaming, regretting, and struggling in vain. We must say *"Yes"* to the endless and endless calls by Our Mother.

July 27, 1988

From 11:30 p.m. to 2 a.m., I received the pains of delivery. My womb began hurting intensely and my eyes were also hurting so much, as if pricked with thorns, that I could not open the eyes.

The Blessed Mother was curing the wounds of the babies who had never been born but aborted. The pains of delivery were in reparation for the sins of the mothers who killed their babies before birth. Through my pains, Mother Mary was giving them the spring water of grace for their repentance.

If we try hard and entrust everything to Mother, we will surely be comforted. The pains in my eyes were because of the pains the Blessed Mother suffers in her eyes when she sees numerous sins of the humans. I could not see the Blessed Mother, but heard her voice.

THE BLESSED MOTHER:

Daughter! I feel anxious when I see you suffer so much. But I feel comforted by your willingness to sacrifice even your life for many souls, as they will repent thanks to your sufferings.

Julia: *Mother! I am only a truly unworthy sinner. This sinner belongs to you completely. Let your will be done.*

THE BLESSED MOTHER:

Thank you, my daughter! You think you are unworthy, but, as all of you are precious to me, you are also an indispensable instrument for me.

Julia: *Mother! I am only an unworthy instrument. I will not spare anything for my Lord, even if it means a complete laceration and destruction of my body. Help me walk toward you, Mother, as a useful instrument.*

THE BLESSED MOTHER:

Don't your eyes hurt very much now?

Julia: *Yes, Mother, they do.*

THE BLESSED MOTHER:

I cannot look at those numerous sins committed with eyes. You and I are doing penance for these sins. You are also suffering the pains for the aborted babies and for the conversion of those poor souls who carry out abortions. These pains will not be in vain.

Julia: *Mother, thank you. Make fuller use of me, your instrument.*

These sufferings ended, but I could not fall asleep because of the remaining pains. I was able to endure them, because the Lord was with me. I still could not open my eyes.

July 29, 1988

I suffered the pains of delivery and the pains of unborn babies who were struggling and screaming to avoid being killed.

It was Friday, a day of rest, but, in the morning, there were thirteen visitors who had leprosy. Despite the pains, I went out supported by others and shook and kissed their hands. I prayed for them fervently.

As I was struggling with pains alone in the room, Mark and Martha came to say good-bye to me before starting their journey home after many days of work. It was 3:40 p.m. My abdomen was becoming larger and the pains of delivery and of unborn babies began. I entered an ecstasy and heard the Blessed Mother speaking.

THE BLESSED MOTHER:

My beloved daughter! Can you take more pain?

Julia: *Yes, Mother! I will take any pain, only if it can help them be saved.*

THE BLESSED MOTHER:

Thank you, my daughter! Today five thousand souls will convert and be offered to the Lord thanks to your sufferings. We must let many people know that we are suffering for them. Many souls will also receive the grace of conversion by learning about the images of aborted children.

People are walking on the road toward hell, because they commit cruel murders and yet do not know they are murderers. These little lives are deprived of their human dignity and receive terrible punishments that their parents deserve. Aren't these punishments too cruel for them?

I am overcome with sorrow, because these innocent lives, precious lives given by God, are cruelly trampled, brutally kneaded, crushed, torn, and killed by ignorant and indifferent parents.

Therefore, I want to show you these little babies begging for their lives and, thereby, convert many sinners and bring them back to me. Tell everyone that a little baby is not a bloody lump, but has a life flowing in it from the moment of conception in the mother's womb.

Julia: *Yes, Mother! Let all the things you wish be done.*

Pains started, as my posture became that of an unborn baby—with two arms crossed, two hands holding knees, and crouched legs.

"No! No! No!"—there were loud screams because of the pains caused by the steel sticks used to kill the babies. It was hard to describe the babies' screams.

"Mommy! Mommy! Mommy!" These little lives were trying to avoid the steel sticks calling their mothers countless times.

It was no better than hell.

With the posture of a baby, I was jumping and rolling around in the room and writhing in pains. Mark and Martha could not handle me and, so, called several other people to come and help. They all became exhausted.

An unborn child who wants to live implores its mother.

Baby: *No, Mommy! No, Mommy! No, Mommy! I want to live, Mommy! Let me live! Mommy, let me live! Mommy! Mommy! Mommy!!!* . . .

Repeating these screams countless times, the baby was running around for life. Actually, I had not eaten that day and was completely exhausted. If it were not for a supernatural mystery, I could not have jumped around so forcefully for three hours. I suffered the pains of being killed after struggles four times. . . .

Those who were present in the room wept so much that they could not even pray.

Julia: *Praise and glory be to the Lord. . . !*

September 14, 1988

While I was seeking the Lord in the middle of pains, I heard the Lord's voice.

JESUS:

Children! Look. The devil will try to shake your faith and trust (in Me). You should not think that such things will not happen. Enter My Sacred Heart and deepen your understanding of My Heart and My Love. Do not lose trust even briefly so that the devil may not sneak into your hearts. When you are lacking in trust, you not only hurt My Heart, but also sadden God the Father.

Be sure that the only way you need to walk is the way of love, a little person's way of love. Until you reach the Heavenly Kingdom by walking this way, trusting Me completely, live only for love and preserve a loving heart through sufferings, even if your sufferings may be constant. Even when you make mistakes by misusing your free will, I still love you. You know well that I will not leave you.

November 6, 1988
—Sunday

How I miss Akita! I still feel sorry that we did not spend even one night or have enough time for prayer in Akita, whereas, in Tokyo, we spent two nights. But I feel joyful by remembering that Bishop Ito, Sister Sasagawa and other Japanese Sisters were happy and amazed by the photographs of the Blessed Mother's statue in Naju weeping blood for priests *(taken on April 23, 1987)* and that we all shared the same love of the Blessed Mother.

At 11 a.m., we attended Mass in the Franciscan Hall in Tokyo. The Mass was celebrated by Cardinal Stephen Kim, the (Japanese) Pastor, and also Father Ki Sun Oh, Father Keum Koo Chang and Father Byung Il Kim, who came to Japan together with me.

It was a special joy to see our Cardinal in Japan. Back in May 1987,

I attended the Mass offered by Cardinal Stephen Kim in Manila, the Philippines, celebrating the unveiling of the statue of Father Andrew Kim. Now we were in Japan offering Mass together again!

At the time of the consecration, there was a sound of wind from above, and the front area behind the Cardinal became foggy. Soon there was the Blessed Mother—extremely beautiful, wearing a white dress and a white mantle. She looked exactly the same as in Naju. She was standing a little higher than the Cardinal, holding a rosary in her right hand and praying. It seemed that she was standing on clouds. As she was stretching out her arms, bright light was radiating from her hands like the sunlight and shone upon the Cardinal, the priests and the faithful present there.

Then, her appearance became that of the wooden statue of Akita. Her beautiful and gentle voice was the same as in Naju.

THE BLESSED MOTHER:

Look at me. Isn't my present appearance that of the wooden statue in Akita?

My symbolic images look a little different from each other, but I am the same Mother in Heaven who has been appearing and imploring with tears at many places in the world.

Listen well. It is I who called you here. It is not by accident that a Mass is being celebrated here by the Cardinal and Father Oh from Korea. I want to bind you all together into one—the Cardinal, priests, the lay people. . .and Japan and Korea—with a string of love. I ask you, because more prayers are needed for unity.

This age is becoming too evil. Because people should entrust everything to my Immaculate Heart but are not doing so, they fall into temptations by the devils. Thus, they make preposterous errors insisting that evil is good.

Greater sacrifices and self-renunciation are necessary, because the majority of the shepherds are falling into errors, as they are not leading a life according to the Gospels.

Even within countries, people are fighting in division rather than uniting and are trampling peace by hating instead of loving each other. Thus, the fire in my Immaculate Heart is flaming up intensely, because people are not practicing my messages, become fanatic slaves of the world, close their hearts to the precious opportunities to share love and are wasting everything because of their selfishness.

This is a time when nations are confronting each other, causing evil to spread in all directions and making the dangers more imminent. I ask for more prayers with trust and love so that nations may unite with each other, individuals may join together and, thus, the Kingdom of the Sacred Heart may be established.

December 8, 1988
—Feast of the Immaculate Conception

It was a great feast of the Blessed Mother and the first anniversary of moving the Blessed Mother's weeping statue from the apartment to the Chapel. So, we decided to hold an overnight prayer meeting after the Pastor and Father Spies gave permission.

I had been planning to offer preparatory prayers in the Chapel with Rufino, the Chapel administrator, and to start a visitation of the Holy Eucharist from 10:30 p.m. But there were several phone calls and I was also congratulating Father Spies on the big feast. The time was already 10:17 p.m. and I hurried to the Chapel. In the Chapel, I made the Sign of the Cross with holy water and began singing, *"Jesus is crucified on the Cross. . . ."* As I was singing and approaching the statue, I noticed that tears of blood were streaming down on the statue.

At this moment, Rufino was lighting the candles in front of the statue and Immanuel, who was visiting Naju from Onyang *(another city in Korea)*, was watching a video *(on Naju)* in the back room. Rufino and I looked closely at the statue and saw the bloody tears already reaching the feet. They were tears mixed with some blood.

Rufino, Immanuel and I were singing and praying in front of the statue and, at about 10:30 p.m., I entered an ecstasy.

The Blessed Mother was holding a rosary and was weeping as usual. She looked so beautiful and kind. Her tears continued to flow reaching her feet. They were tears of mercy and love. She came to this world as the Helper to Jesus in washing and healing the sinners. She spoke with a beautiful and kind voice.

THE BLESSED MOTHER:

I will call the Pastor. So far, the devils have been using all the available means to prevent cooperation with the Pastor and to cause divisions. For this reason, you must be awake and pray harder—for the Pastor and Father Spies. I will shine the light of my Immaculate Heart on all of you so that you may work together for unity.

I called them *(the Pastor and Father Spies)* to work together, holding my hands, and to walk the way of martyrdom. Now they will walk that way. Maintain a closer cooperation with Father Spies. This work is not what Julia, who is unworthy and weak, is doing. Julia is only a channel. The work is being done by me.

Oh, my beloved children! Too many of you are walking toward hell. Ask the Bishop to restore my position in the Church. Then, my messages will spread to the world and people will amend their lives, will be liberated from the road leading to hell, will convert and start walking on the way toward Heaven, and, thereby, will soften the just anger of God the Father.

Julia: *Mother! Even now, aren't there many of your children converting and amending their lives by accepting your call?*

THE BLESSED MOTHER:

But an enormous number of my children are walking toward hell. I am asking you again, because I am so anxious. Do you want to see, daughter?

Julia: *Yes, Mother. Please show me.*

THE BLESSED MOTHER:

Yes, my lovely daughter! My dear daughter who has to suffer pains! Now, look! Look at the children who are going toward hell by judging and criticizing others.

I screamed, when I saw the sight.

Julia: *Oh, no! Oh, no! Mother! Jesus!*

I could not look, because it was so ugly. Every time people judged and criticized each other, worms *(maggots)* crawled out of their mouths. Then, the worms fell on the ground and joined the devils. These worms were crawling onto other unwatchful people and making them sin, too.

On the other hand, when people spoke well of others with love, beautiful melodies flowed out of their mouths and melted the worms with the fire of love.

So many children were governed and controlled by the devils, because they were hating each other and not forgiving each other. The worms could not be killed, however many times they were trampled upon, but were just melting away, when people practiced love and charity through sacrifices and won the spiritual battle. But there were too few people, among so many, who were willing to practice love through suffering.

THE BLESSED MOTHER:

Daughter, did you see that? That is why the just anger of God the Father has reached an extremely high level and punishment is near at hand.

I screamed loudly.

Julia: *Please forgive the numerous sinners. If they can convert by my suffering the pains of hell, I will offer all of myself for them. I have deserved hell since long ago. . . .*

I have been able to give a little love, because you called me, who was so poor and miserable. Moreover, you have allowed me to see the Lord and Mother. Participating in the sufferings has been my proper duty.

I pray that the Lord's Will be done through this shameful sinner with certainty. I cannot help being happy, even if I go to hell. So, please do not punish them.

I implored so loudly that others who were present heard me scream, "No!"

THE BLESSED MOTHER:

Yes, thank you. Pray with that kind of deep sacrifice and self-denial. When you offer sufferings gracefully and without despair in spite of all kinds of criticism and slander, the Lord will save many sinners from the miseries of sin and will be with you.

The sufferings, so many sufferings. . . these are what you will receive in the course of your life as you asked for.

My little soul, who anguishes even over small mistakes and makes new resolutions! I find joy in you. Through mistakes, you overcome pride and you can reach the highest degree of perfection through humility.

Have a stronger confidence in me. Follow me with greater courage. An-nyoung!

I got out of the ecstasy at midnight. I could not move my body and was carried on a stretcher to the Chapel office, where I stayed with the Blessed Mother. But, as many people were gathering around me instead of praying, I felt sorry and asked to be carried to the upper room. Seven people had to help. The Blessed Mother was weeping in great sorrows.

Julia: *Mother of the Lord! Thank you. I cannot stop thanking you always, because the more sufferings I experience,*

*the more sinners will convert. I do not want to spare any-
thing, if my unworthy sufferings can be used in realizing
the Lord's Will.*

*May the Lord be glorified through my little sufferings and let
this unworthy and lowly sinner offer unending gratitude.*

*Oh, my Mother Mary! I want to become your daughter who
gives you only joy. Help me!*

January 8, 1989
—Ecstasy from 9:10 a.m.

I was still in bed, without having slept at all during the night because of pains, when my mother told me by intercom that the Blessed
Mother's statue was shedding tears of blood. First, I reported this to
the Pastor by phone, but I could not reach Father Spies. When I
went to the Chapel, there were several people praying. They told me
what had happened.

When they arrived at the Chapel at about 7:30 a.m., there were no
tears on the statue. But, when they looked again after some prayers,
she was shedding tears of blood. It was about 7:40 a.m. The tears of
blood continued flowing until 8:30 a.m. When I got to the Chapel, it
was 8:50 a.m. I saw that the blood was already dry, but there were
threads of clear tears still flowing.

We started praying the rosary together, but, after one decade, I lost
energy and fell down, even though I tried to hold on to the altar. I
entered an ecstasy.

I was so surprised at the scene I saw. There was a big riot among so
many people screaming and trying to kill each other. Then, the beautiful Lady of the Stars, the Blessed Mother, appeared with a bright
light.

She was wearing a laurel crown with twelve sparkling stars. Her
dress was the same as before, but her face was filled with sorrows.
She was shedding tears, as she spoke to me while I was praying the
rosary.

THE BLESSED MOTHER:

Daughter, look. Those numerous children are mired in sins and are provoking the just anger of God the Father. More prayers are needed. Greater sacrifices and atonement are necessary. There are too few consecrated children. Superficial prayers, visitations out of habit, service without heart, lukewarm Legio Marie activities, and so on. . . all these must be revitalized.

You must meet your neighbors as you would meet Jesus—with true love and a praying heart. Tell everyone. I give my love to all my children. But my Heart is hurting so much, because too many of them reject and insult my love. My ears are hurting very much because of the evil words that are so hard to listen to.

At this time, my ears also began hurting intensely because of so many people's criticisms, accusations, judgments, insults, flattery, sacrileges, pride, resentment, anger, slanders, and extremely loud screams.

THE BLESSED MOTHER:

I should be respected as the Queen of Heaven, but I am suffering constantly because of the children on earth.

Daughter! Do not feel sad. All your sufferings make you participate in the Passion of Jesus and, together with mine, are being offered for the conversion of sinners.

I do not want to remove this fierce battle that afflicts you, because this battle involves prayers, sacrifices and penance and your fierce battle will turn them into graces and blessings for many souls. It is an intense fight planned by God to sanctify souls.

Do you know about the Deluge in the time of Noah and the Tower of Babel? Who can say that the sins now are less than in those times?

The city of Naju

The Chapel in Naju

You must not ignore the wrath of God. But the Lord does not wish that you avoid sins for fear of punishments. What He wants is love.

I pray and suffer pains constantly for the children who have fallen into evil habits and corruption so that fire may not fall upon the earth from the sky.

But, if they refuse to accept my messages and continue accommodating to the world instead of the heavenly matters, it will be too late to regret.

I implore you, because punishment can come from human beings themselves *(meaning a Third World War)*. Hell is a place of terrifying and irreversible punishments, a pit of death and ruin, and a place of inextinguishable fire and maggots that will not die.

Let's pray that these souls may not be condemned and all may be saved. An-nyoung!

The Blessed Mother was tilting her head a little to the left as she was saying *"An-nyoung!"* She was also waving her right hand gently. I have never seen a more beautiful appearance. I felt as if I were being soaked into her.

January 15, 1989
—From 6 a.m.

It was the Blessed Mother who woke me from a deep sleep.

THE BLESSED MOTHER:

Wake up and let's pray. Julia, get up and let's pray for priests.

I woke up and saw the Blessed Mother above my dresser where she had shed tears of blood before. She continued with a beautiful voice.

THE BLESSED MOTHER:

Oh, my beloved daughter! My little soul who follows me happily even while suffering. Often you groan and get depressed under the pressure of pains, fall down with the heavy cross, and struggle to get up but cannot. Instead of getting help, a heavy rock is placed upon the cross. How painful you must be feeling! I am comforted in your heart, which anguishes even over small mistakes.

Daughter! Everyone has shortcomings and imperfections. But when you try to overcome them and, if you fail again, promptly repent, ask for the Lord's forgiveness and, renew the sincere resolution to amend your life, my Son Jesus and I will rejoice and help.

Daughter! Who cares about me as you do? The loyal and little souls do. Pray with them.

The children who are called to the state of God's grace will experience many sufferings and temptations. But those who live according to my messages will be rewarded with a victory crown of flowers in the next world.

Offer sacrifices and reparations without ceasing for the Pope, Cardinals, Bishops and priests. They, too, must accept my messages, but many don't. In order to prevent the chastisement, my beloved priests must accept the messages quickly. I wouldn't spare anything for the Pope, Cardinals, Bishops and all the priests. . . .

My priests whom I love so much that I can put them in my eyes without feeling any pain. . . . I am praying and offering sufferings in their place today as always.

As you approach God more fervently in order to bear fruit, devils will intensify their attacks on you and become more active to prevent you from bearing fruit.

My Son Jesus comes to you through priests to give you His Blood. So, pray much that priests, who should be holy, may not fall into temptations. Pray that they may become holier and may worthily carry out their duty of giving His Blood to people so that they may not have anything to be ashamed of as the givers of the Blood of Jesus in His place. Pray that the Church, families and society may become united as one, as the Father, the Son and the Holy Spirit are One.

My beloved priests will work heroically for God and people, if they respond to this sacred mission by receiving the grace of suffering through our little sacrifices and reparations. The whole world is rushing toward its ruin and devils are employing all the available means to destroy it. But there will be certain victory, if unity is achieved.

I wish to rescue the world by the victory of my mercy and love. Therefore, if you pray with me, with confidence in me, holding my hands, my Immaculate Heart will triumph. It will surely triumph.

Daughter! I will see you again. Good-bye! An-nyoung!

January 29, 1989
—*2:40 p.m. to 3:55 p.m.*

Exhausted from the pains in the morning, I could not get up by myself and was carried to another room in a convent. There I received pains of the crown of thorns, crucifixion, piercing with the spear, the burning Sacred Heart, seven arrows penetrating the heart, and the martyrdom of Father Andrew Kim.

Jesus was crucified on the Cross and the extremely beautiful Blessed Mother was standing beside Him, wearing a white dress and a blue mantle, holding a rosary in her hand and weeping sorrowfully. In the surroundings, there was a large crowd making noises of fighting and screaming. Jesus was shedding blood and sweat, as He continued to be hit by the arrows thrown by sinners.

JESUS:

Is there anyone who can lower Me from the Cross?

He cried out to the crowd, but only a few came near Him. They were not able to lower Him. Whenever people sinned, the crown of thorns pressed deeper on His head, causing more pains. The Blessed Mother became broken-hearted watching all this. She was saying, *"No! No!"* It was an unbearably sorrowful scene.

Pains lasted for about an hour and there was the gentle and warm voice of the Blessed Mother.

THE BLESSED MOTHER:

My daughter who has to suffer pains. My Son Jesus and I are comforted, because the souls hardened like a rock are melting by your sufferings and reparations.

The devils' violence is becoming more severe everyday. They are mobilizing all kinds of methods to ruin even the fervent souls. Today you saw clearly in what manner Satan makes contact with humans.

You must know that my dear Saints also were subjected to severe temptations.

Julia! Today you won a victory in my Immaculate Heart. Satan wants to overthrow my Church and destroy life in the souls. But, when you fight against him holding a shield of love, his true character will be revealed.

Julia: *Yes, Mother. Please continue to help us.*

THE BLESSED MOTHER:

Look. This world is decaying with errors. My Son Jesus is being crucified unceasingly because of the proud and cow-ardly pessimists and the self-righteous egoists who are habitually involved in corrupt activities and hypocritical lies. I implore you again, because the punishment can come through a Third World War.

Daughter! Can you receive more pains?

Julia: *Yes, Mother! I will take any pains.*

I asked for more pains with two arms raised.

THE BLESSED MOTHER:

Look at them.

She pointed at a large crowd. There were loud noises of wars and skirmishes.

THE BLESSED MOTHER:

Because love has been destroyed, there is no unity among people. As a result, the outcries of human beings in the midst of their sins are turning into noises of wars, which, in turn, are reaching Heaven and provoking God's anger.

Through the pains of the crown of thorns and the crucifixion which you have suffered and also the pains of Father Andrew Kim's martyrdom that you are about to suffer now, the Pope, Cardinals, Bishops, priests and religious will form a unity and climb Mt. Calvary carrying the cross of love together with my Son Jesus.

You must pray together constantly for world peace and the conversion of sinners.

Then, I received the pains of Father Kim's martyrdom. Father Kim lifted his head and exposed his neck courageously. He did the same for the second time, despite the extreme pains and bleeding, for the glory of God. *(The executioners did not use full force with the sword to make the pains greater and longer.)* He did the same for the third time. He hardly was able to move his neck for the fourth time. His head fell at the eighth time. After these pains, Jesus shined light on all and I was relieved of the pains.

Julia: *Receive the light of Jesus!*

I opened my eyes while crying out. There were Father Spies, Father

Chung, another priest, sisters and lay people watching me. I felt shy. I sweat so much that my clothes were very wet.

February 23, 1989

I was not able to fall asleep because of the thoughts about the cunning violence of the devil. I suffered because of all kinds of attacks by the devil coming through people, but entrusted everything to God with a deep love and prayed to Him with a trusting heart.

I was trying to sleep. It was a while later. I was not sure if I was sleeping or not. Suddenly I heard a voice.

Voice: *Julia! Lately you have been suffering too much. Take a break now. Even Jesus rested between prayers.*

I was wondering if it was the Blessed Mother and if she was going to give me some rest, as she knew well about all my sufferings so far. But it was a little strange that she would give me a break during this Lenten season of fasting and penance. I was also remembering the Blessed Mother having asked that I offer gracefully all the numerous pains given to me—even those terrible ones that twist arms and legs and grind the heart.

Voice of Satan: *You have accumulated lots of treasures in Heaven so far by sacrificing yourself for sinners. These treasures are yours. Now, God will be very pleased, even if you rest comfortably and lead a life without pains. Let others take care of the work in the Chapel. You don't have to spread the messages any longer. I will take care of everything.*

Julia: *What should I do then?*

Voice of Satan: *Now my will is about to be realized. You can return to your family. If you focus on taking good care of your family, I will give you all the happiness, wealth and fame. So, listen to me. You don't have to worry about your husband's success in the world or your children's future. Do you understand?*

Julia: *No, I don't.*

It was hard to understand what I was hearing. Happiness, wealth and fame?

Voice of Satan: *Now I will let you live a comfortable life. Don't you like it?*

I kept feeling suspicious.

Julia: *Who are you? Show me yourself.*

Voice of Satan: *I am Mother Mary whom you love. Listen to my words carefully. Now you must sever yourself from Father Spies. You are a Korean. Why do you work with a foreigner? Now obey me only. I will direct you myself.*

Julia: *It was my Mother Mary who led me to hold hands with Father Spies. My life belongs to God. God will lead me. I have never wanted happiness, wealth and fame. I only wish that the Lord's Will be done on this earth.*

Voice of Satan: *You, a stubborn one! If you don't value your life, I will take it today. I cannot stand you taking away souls from me. If I only get rid of you, I will feel relief. I am also going to incapacitate the priests.*

From that moment on, I had to suffer without even being able to say a word. I thought I was dying—unable to resist under a heavy pressure.

After a while, I opened my eyes without full consciousness. There was the Blessed Mother, not speaking, but looking at me compassionately. Her appearance was that of the weeping Blessed Mother of Naju. Her expression was one of a mother watching her children in pains and wishing to suffer in their place.

I was trying to say, *"Mother!"* and start talking to her, but could not speak. I struggled and kept calling her, but could not make any sound come out of my mouth. Finally, I called, *"Mother!"* loudly and woke up. It was 5 a.m. My small desk was left turned over. I felt that

Mother had something to tell me and, so, washed myself and went to the Chapel.

When I opened the door of the Chapel, there was a strong fragrance of roses and lilies. As I was walking in, the Blessed Mother was walking toward me. When I stopped, she stopped also. She was within reaching distance from me.

THE BLESSED MOTHER:

Daughter! Thank you.

Julia: *Mother, why do you love this sinner so much, who is so ignorant and incapable?*

THE BLESSED MOTHER:

I give my messages of love to the simple and little ones. Little ones give admiration, honor and glory to the Lord and do not take away anything from me. Certain things that can be shortcomings to the big souls are not short-comings to the little ones. You are a little soul. You have many shortcomings, but these shortcomings can turn into good through sacrifices and reparations and can keep you humble.

Offer up everything, as I love within you, turning every-thing you do into a prayer of love. As you do not refuse anything to me, I will not refuse anything to you.

Julia: *Mother! I am an unqualified person unable to do anything. I am only a poor and unworthy sinner who should remain hidden.*

THE BLESSED MOTHER:

Yes. I called you, because you are poor and unworthy. I wish to spread my messages of love through you who wants to work hidden.

Julia: *Mother! That is difficult because of my unworthi-ness.*

THE BLESSED MOTHER:

Do not fear. When you feel uneasy, the devils will intensify their attacks and work harder to achieve their victory. They are becoming more active, employing all kinds of methods to defeat you, as many souls get to see the light thanks to the grace of conversion through your sacrifices and sufferings.

Look. Aren't they persecuting you through many people under the guise of good? I do not give up any single soul. Nobody can take away even one soul from me, but, because God gave humans free will, they run away, betray and deny the Lord and follow Satan, blinded by their stubbornness. There are too many children who lack trust in me and hurt my Immaculate Heart. Daughter! I implore you.

Julia: *Mother! Please tell me. I will not spare even my life for the sake of the realization of the Lord's Will. Let your will be done.*

THE BLESSED MOTHER:

Yes. Thank you. People know well that the Lord did not create them to become one team with the devils and, yet, they do become one and provoke God's anger. They should be sharing joy with each other in eternal love, instead. Therefore, my messages of love must spread fast for their amendment of their lives.

For this purpose, the approval is necessary. Talk to the Bishop again. My beloved Bishop, my dearest priest. He has devoted his whole life to the Lord and has always taken good care of the children as their parent in the Lord's place—despite many wounds, pains and sufferings. I am comforted by his many sacrifices and reparations. I will let him shine with the light of the Lord's glory. Offer Masses in the Chapel so that the arrows of fire thrown by the devils may be stopped.

My Son Jesus is shedding blood and sweat. Too many souls are joining their forces with the devils. Therefore, prepare a tabernacle in the Chapel so that we can pray with my Son Jesus. Then, there will certainly be a victory. Help me. Invite my Son Jesus in, Who will shine brightly in this dark world.

Julia: *Mother! What should I do?*

THE BLESSED MOTHER:

Consult with the Bishop, my son, together with the Pastor and Father Spies. Help me save many souls.

Julia: *What kind of method should we use?*

She did not answer. I asked again and again, but she was silent and weeping. It was 7 a.m.

July 5, 1989
—Feast of St. Andrew Kim, Priest and Martyr

FOR ALL PRIESTS

I had been in pains for five days. The pains were so severe that I could not open my eyes or stretch my back. I felt so bitter in my mouth, as if I had drunk bile. I also had an intense headache and felt so cold that I had to cover myself with a thick cotton blanket, normally used in winter, and turned on an electric heating pad. I was thinking, offering pains for the sanctification of priests, conversion of sinners, and world peace.

Our Blessed Mother must be suffering so much pain, because many children are being controlled by the devils because of their division and confrontation and are walking in darkness. My pains seemed to become lighter and more bearable with these thoughts.

At that moment, Rufino, the Chapel administrator, came and informed me that the Blessed Mother's statue was shedding tears of blood. It was 3:15 p.m. I wanted to go to the Chapel, but could not move myself at all. At 3:50 p.m., the Pastor came and conversed with me with great difficulty for one hour. Then, he blessed me and I was able to sit up. I was sweating and able to stretch my back. The bitter taste in my mouth was also gone and I felt refreshed and was able to walk. So, I went to the Chapel with the Pastor and saw the statue weeping. It was about 6:30 p.m.

After the Pastor left, I began praying the rosary and entered an ecstasy. I saw Father Andrew Kim blessing all the children in the world.

In spite of this, many children continue to be controlled by the devils. The devils influence people's minds, making them criticize each other with jealousy and resentment; making them justify their actions by speaking ill of and cheating others and by pride, hatred and selfishness; and making them confront each other with anger and indignation. They also make people live in disorder through lust and obscenity and make them accommodate to evil through hatred and the inability to forgive each other.

I saw the vicious rampage of the devils leading people to evil under the guise of good.

The Blessed Mother had told me about this many times in the past, but today she showed me the viciousness of the devil. The devil had a black shape, but was controlling people while hiding himself. In contrast, Father Andrew Kim was praying the rosary with us while chasing away the devils with palm tree leaves together with many other martyred Saints.

As Father Kim was blessing and embracing all of us, I got out of the ecstasy. The time was about 7:50 p.m. I felt that the Blessed Mother would be giving me messages in the upper room and had myself carried by someone there. After I prayed for a while, the Blessed Mother appeared in front of the dresser. She was wearing a queen's crown and a blue mantle. She was very beautiful, but looked sad.

Her appearance was as usual. It was somewhat foggy between the lower edge of her dress and her feet. I could see some roses near her feet—not very clearly, though, because of the fog. Her crown and whole body were so bright that I could not look at her closely. The crown looked similar to the one given to her by Father Matthias Park. The Blessed Mother was so bright that I could not look at her directly and listened to her while bowing my head and kneeling on the floor.

The message was for all the priests.

THE BLESSED MOTHER:

Oh, my beloved priests, my sons! Today, I bestow streams of mercy on you out of my Immaculate Love. Your High Priest, my Son Jesus, also bestows the cup of blessing on you today.

Thank you for fighting in the world of darkness where many souls have lost faith and are revolting against God and blaspheming Him because of their selfishness.

My dear sons! I know well that you are experiencing many pains, fatigue, loneliness, sadness, and, sometimes, blasphemies and insults in following my Son Jesus.

But that is unavoidable. Think of all the scourgings that my Son received. He was the Son of God, but, because He was Jesus with a human nature, He suffered pains when He was ridiculed and crucified. Then, for the salvation of the human race, He asked His Father to forgive those who were hurting Him. He did not drink the bitter chalice, because He wanted to, did He? He said, *"Father, if You will, remove this chalice from Me; but not My Will, but Yours be done."*

Oh, my beloved priests! My sweet priests whom I can put in my eyes without feeling any pain. Give me all your pains and sufferings.

Come to me and spread my messages of love courageously so that people may be freed from the Red Dragon and that the Kingdom of the Lord may come. In union with the Pope and all the bishops, let the victory of the Resurrection reach the whole world. In this age, the devil is becoming more active to control humans by means of human powers. My numerous poor children are following the Red Dragon and walking toward the deep darkness, hell, in their extreme pride. They are working in many different cunning ways to confuse people about the messages that I give.

Oh, my poor children. My priests, hold the hands of so many of my children who are recklessly walking into darkness.

There are some priests who have broken away from me and do not follow the Will of Jesus. But, through my priests and on this soil made fertile by the blood of so many martyrs, many souls are growing under the light from my Son and me. On the other hand, the Red Dragon is becoming more violent. So, tell people to be awake and pray.

Oh, my dear priests! I want even the most corrupt souls to receive the light from me. Therefore, be loyal to Jesus so that they may convert. Also, do not let my tears and blood flow in vain. I want my beloved priests to become sacrificial victims for the conversion of sinners.

Now, the devils are influencing people in the guise of all kinds of good. Oh, my sons! Shouldn't you discern (what the devils are doing) and defeat the devils? That is what is called for in my messages. Pray the rosary fervently. Offer sacrifices and reparations and consecrate yourselves totally to the Sacred Heart of Jesus. Trust more and follow me with confidence. Let all my children offer five more decades of the rosary for world peace, as prayers of love and unity.

Oh, my beloved priests! My precious ones who perform the amazing miracle of the Sacrament! Do not turn your eyes away from my messages, but have complete trust in my Immaculate Heart and entrust everything to my guidance. Rely totally on my Immaculate Heart through unending sacrifices and penances in order to crush the devils who are trying to afflict you by all kinds of cunning methods.

My Immaculate Heart will surely triumph. You will certainly see the victory, if you accept my words.

I will help you with my power that crushes the head of the

serpent and I will be with you. But, if you do not accept my words, many people will not be able to avoid the chastisement from God.

Now, come back to me and work together with me. Oh, the little priests of my Jesus! Sacred ministers of Jesus! Hold my hands. I ask each of you, who are my most precious and beloved little Jesus. Please put into practice the messages I give through Julia, who is so little and poor.

After these words, the Blessed Mother and the light disappeared. Actually, I was going to ask the Blessed Mother to tell the priests directly, as I was so incapable. But she left before I had a chance to say this. I felt sorry that I could not say anything. I only murmured, *"Lord, Thy Will alone be done."*

August 26, 1989

The Blessed Mother shed tears of blood. I was praying the rosary with Father Raymond Spies, who came for a three-day prayer; three Sisters, who came with Father Spies; other pilgrims; and my family. I entered an ecstasy during the Fourth Decade of the Sorrowful Mysteries. It was 11:38 a.m. I could not see the Blessed Mother, but heard her warm, soft and eager voice.

THE BLESSED MOTHER:

Daughter! Now is the time for a huge battle between me and my enemy. Our enemy is the army of the Red Dragon, who looks like a terrible animal. All the devils are out to conquer this earth from hell. They are challenging to corrupt many souls of this world by making them reject God, commit sins with all kinds of selfishness and defile everything. Thereby, they are trying to form an army.

Daughter! See how they allure people into the traps of hell.

The Blessed Mother had hardly finished her words when the black animal figures of the devils began appearing with their carts. The carts were well decorated but were black. The devils looked some-

The Blessed Mother: "A huge battle has begun already. Since it is a spiritual war, arm yourselves with me by entrusting everything to my Immaculate Heart. Also, practice my messages of love. Then, you will be able to escape from the terrible chastisement approaching the human race and the Church." (August 26, 1989)

what like eagles. They were snatching many souls and loading them into the carts. Around the carts were the black devils and many souls attracted to the carts. In order to make the souls join them, the devils were chattering in an inscrutable manner. Many souls were giggling and having fun with the devils without knowing that it was the road to hell and without running away from or rejecting it. Soon these souls, too, were turning black. I was so sad.

As I was trying to pray for these poor souls and rescue them, the devils, looking like eagles, began hitting me violently with their wings and scratched and pecked on my head with their claws and teeth. Despite the attacks, I did not retreat. As I was no match for them with physical force, I took out my rosary and struck them with it and this made them run away. They were pulling away the carts filled with the poor souls. I chased after them and began pulling out the souls one by one, with the rosary in one hand. When I hit the devils with the rosary again, they hurriedly overturned the carts and ran away. The people thrown on the ground were getting up, repenting their sins with tears and praising God.

At that moment, I began hearing the Blessed Mother again.

THE BLESSED MOTHER:

Daughter! Did you see that? A huge battle has begun like this already. Since it is a spiritual war, arm yourselves with me by entrusting everything to my Immaculate Heart. Also practice the messages of my love. Then, you will be able to escape from the terrible chastisement approaching the human race and the Church.

When I got out of the ecstasy, it was 1:38 p.m. I suffered pains during the two-hour ecstasy, but the remaining pains made me unable to move myself for a total of five hours.

Oh, Lord! Glory and praise to You.

August 29, 1989

The Blessed Mother was weeping from early morning. I went to the Chapel to be with her at about 10:30 p.m. I fell asleep while praying, contemplating and suffering pains. At 3 a.m., I woke up at the sound of someone being there. I felt that the inside of the Chapel was bright, but when I looked in the direction of the statue, there was no statue. Instead, there was the live Blessed Mother carrying the Baby Jesus and shedding tears. The Baby Jesus was not wearing any clothes and His eyes were also sparkling with tears.

She did not have the crown on her head, but was wearing a white mantle. Her appearance was as usual, but she was sitting in a chair looking tired and pale in her face and was surrounded by bright light. Momentarily, I knelt and prostrated myself. As I was trying to say something, the Blessed Mother began speaking with a beautiful voice.

THE BLESSED MOTHER:

Daughter! Look. In order to save the children who are wandering in a worsening darkness, I continue pouring down the light from my Immaculate Heart upon them. But even my closest children are not renouncing themselves and are hurting my Heart intensely!

Daughter! The vicious devils are even penetrating the inside of the Church causing division, confusion and darkness. How serious the harms to the sheep will be! Therefore, daughter, pray, make sacrifices and do penance with a greater love in this time of darkness.

In order to avoid the approaching calamities, the children who have been called must climb Mt. Calvary with a deep, silent love—without sighs or lamentations, even if they are ruthlessly despised and are insulted under the heavy burden of pains. Thus, they are being crucified together with my Son Jesus for the conversion of sinners.

Daughter! Can you receive pains for the suffering priests and for the conversion of sinners?

Julia: *Yes, Mother.*

I immediately fell down and suffered the pains of crucifixion. When I got out of the pains, the Blessed Mother spoke to me again with a very kind voice filled with love.

THE BLESSED MOTHER:

Daughter! Do not lose courage. The love, sacrifices and penance being offered by the little souls who are following me may even include the terrible pains of Calvary. But it is the Will of my Son Jesus and me that the little souls be called to help purify the world. Therefore, follow my sorrowful and wounded will with great love. Good bye! Annyoung!

The Blessed Mother disappeared with her light. I had so many things to tell her, but she left.

Julia: *Oh, Mother of love and mercy! Let your will be realized through the light of the wounded Sacred Heart of Jesus and the pierced Immaculate Heart of Mary. Also let us offer an unending gratitude. Amen.*

I prayed loudly. It was 4 a.m.

October 14, 1989

While I was in bed in the upper room because of intense pains, Father Raymond Spies and Father Louis Bosmans from Canada came and spoke to me.

"Julia, the Blessed Mother is shedding more tears today than ever. We will help you. Let's go and see the Blessed Mother." Then, they blessed me. After the blessing, we went to the Chapel and saw that the Blessed Mother had shed tears of blood copiously, making the cloth under the statue very wet.

I was crying and started praying the rosary with the priests. When we reached the Fifth Decade of the Sorrowful Mysteries and said, *"Let us meditate on the Crucifixion of Jesus,"* I fell down and entered an ecstasy. It was 1:10 p.m.

I heard the extremely beautiful, soft and, yet, anxious voice of the Blessed Mother.

THE BLESSED MOTHER:

Daughter! Can you receive pains for the Holy Father?

Julia: *Yes, Mother.*

I tried to speak, but could not make any sound. The Blessed Mother understood.

THE BLESSED MOTHER:

Daughter! Thank you. The International Eucharistic Congress *(held in Seoul and presided over by Pope John Paul II)* ended safely, thanks to your sacrifices, reparations and sufferings. But the cunning devils continue their attempts to hurt the Pope and are organizing assassination squads. Offer more sacrifices and sufferings for his safety.

As she ended speaking, I began receiving pains. They were pains of crucifixion, the heart being penetrated by an arrow and the chest flaming up after being hit by the arrows of fire that sinners dipped in oil and threw. I also received the pains that I had not even imagined—those suffered by the Korean martyrs—the pains of leg screws and of pouring rancid sewer water and human excrement into my mouth. It was so painful and hard to endure.

I was happy despite the pains, as I saw the devils collapse and run away whenever I suffered the pains of martyrdom. Again, I heard the anxious voice of the Blessed Mother.

THE BLESSED MOTHER:

Daughter! Leave everything to me and do not be anxious to know the end results. Pray and offer sacrifices and reparations constantly for the Pope, Cardinals, Bishops and priests. Those who are being controlled by the devils are trying hard to strike down the Holy Father and lead the Church to destruction. But all the devils will lose power, when my tears and blood are combined with your sacrifices and reparations.

But, today, even my children in the Church are experiencing confusion because of the false prophets. Priests, who

The Blessed Mother: "You will be saved, if you do not ignore my tears and tears of blood, accept my words well and live a life based on the Gospels." (October 14, 1989)

represent my Son, Jesus Christ, must be discreet and do their best to lead a life based on the teachings in the Gospels and within the orders of the Church.

You must understand well what kind of sacrifice my Son Jesus made for you and through what kind of pains your salvation has been won.

Display the power of love. My Heart is hurting so much because of the deafness and blindness of the children who do not love. Because they do not repent and, therefore, sink deeper into sins, my Heart is burning and burning so much that it bleeds. The blood gets mixed with tears and flows out of my eyes. Even so, they do not accept my words and, because of this, the anger of God is flaming up very vehemently.

Daughter! Look at the condition of many children in this

The Blessed Mother: *"Display the power of love. My Heart is hurting so much because of the deafness and blindness of the children who do not love."* (October 14, 1989; photo taken on October 15, 1989)

world. Because people complain even about small pains like headaches, bruises and scratches, the devils are laying traps of thorns, venom and atrocities. The human feet should be used for rushing to adore God, but are, instead, being used for running toward evil things. Their mouths should be used for praising and admiring the Son of God, but are being used for blaspheming and judging God. As a result, the whole world is being covered with darkness and is provoking the anger of God. The punishment is imminent.

You will be saved, if you do not ignore my tears and tears of blood, accept my words well and live a life based on the Gospels. But, if you do not, major calamities from the sky, on the ground, and in the seas will continue to happen. The world will experience all kinds of disasters. There will be moments of incredible distress in the near future. Therefore, do not think these are accidental happenings. Be awake and pray.

Children! I beg you. Like the Israelites who crossed the Red Sea and entered the fertile land of Canaan after the slavery in Egypt, you must also leave evil, practice my messages, and, thereby, walk toward Heaven. If not, you will not be able to escape the crisis of the Third World War. It will be too late to regret.

You must not forget that, as God called Moses to Mt. Sinai to save the Israelites, I am calling you without ceasing, imploring with tears in order to save you.

What might have happened, if Noah did not say "Yes" and obey, when Yahweh told him to build a ship to save him? Keep in your heart my words spoken with tears of blood. How can you be so blind and deaf? My Heart is flaming up intensely, my children, because families, the Church and society are becoming corrupt and the politicians are unable to achieve unity. Quickly renounce yourselves and come to me.

The Blessed Mother was sobbing and weeping, almost like lamenting.

Julia: *Mother! Mother!! Please tell the Bishop and priests what needs to be done. I am so incapable and unqualified.*

THE BLESSED MOTHER:

Do not worry. God loved the lowliness of His handmaid and worked in the heart that felt its weakness. Because many souls are being saved through your sufferings, the devils are afflicting you. Offer up your sufferings well.

Julia: *Mother! It is too hard because of my unworthiness. Help me.*

THE BLESSED MOTHER:

If I did not help you, the world would have become seas of fire already. But I will never leave you. Therefore, open your ears when you hear precious words and close your ears when you hear slanders. Even when you walk in darkness, follow me with confidence. Your sighs will turn into joys, if you accept my messages well and practice them.

When she finished these words, Jesus appeared with a bright light, wearing a white cloak and a red mantle. He blessed us and disappeared. The ecstasy ended at 4:10 p.m.

November 26, 1989
—Feast of Christ the King

The Blessed Mother had been shedding tears and tears of blood since October 13, 1989. At around 9:40 p.m. today, the Feast of Christ the King, she wept so much.

My pains began soon after 11 p.m. I prayed fervently that I could endure them. First, I had pains in my chest and felt as if it were going to burst, followed by pains of the crown of thorns and nailing of the hands and feet. My helpers carried me from the Chapel to my room. I wanted to receive pains alone and asked them to return home. But, as I was struggling with intense pains, they stayed and had a hard time holding me.

Because of so much pain in my chest, blood was coming up to my throat. While I was struggling with pains, one of the toe nails on my left foot came off. At that moment, the Blessed Mother began speaking.

THE BLESSED MOTHER:

Daughter! My chest is hurting so much because of many children who live in sins. My chest is burning so much that blood is coming up to my throat. Many souls will convert, because you offer your sufferings well. Sacrifices are necessary, because my burning Immaculate Heart does not want sinners to die, but to amend their lives. Events that no one can even imagine are waiting for you. But my Immaculate Heart is comforted by the prayers of the obedient children, the pains and hidden agonies of the innocent children, and the tears and earnest pleas of yourself, who has become a living sacrifice.

Deeply sorrowful lamentations, silent prayers, and crying out to Heaven because of betrayals, ingratitude and enormously heavy pressures; the pains of death experienced by my Divine Son for the salvation of the whole human race. . . Your participation in these pains will bring about the conversion of many sinners. Therefore, do not be troubled, but carry the cross further. My daughter!

My dear daughter who finds joy in receiving pains. Think of my urgent calls to the world and become like me.

How can the worldly people understand that the agonies befallen on you are coming from the Lord's Love? You must tell people that holy virtues cannot be attained without going through the cross. Also tell them that only through numerous sacrifices will the messages of my love spread to the entire world and guide all the people and can peace of mind be achieved.

The Blessed Mother: "Only through numerous sacrifices will the messages of my love spread to the whole world and guide all the people and can peace be achieved." (November 26, 1989)

Nothing can be achieved without sacrifices. The road to Heaven is difficult. But know that there are joyful relaxing places there.

I also experienced the same kind of weaknesses that you have and my human nature went through terrifying pains. That is why I love and nurture you, who is so poor.

My daughter! I could make you perfect, but I want you to walk the way of a humble and little person and to confess to God always as an unworthy sinner. Be more faithful to your duties of love.

All of you must know well that the refuge in my bosom is always ready for the souls who have been lost, but are turning themselves to me.

Since I chose you for the conversion of many souls, do not worry, and walk the little person's way of love—more humbly and straightforward.

The gate to Heaven is small and, therefore, little children enter it. For this reason, little souls must unite with each other more solidly and follow me in order to save the world.

The numerous souls who have brought about an imbalance in the universe because of their excessive pride will convert and world peace will be achieved through my fervent calls and tears and through the prayers, sacrifices and reparations by the little souls.

Thus, the walls of East Germany collapsed, the pagans will repent, the atheists will return, the Communist countries will convert, the barbed wires between South and North Korea will be cut, the devils will collapse, and a terrestrial paradise will be established on this earth. But if you do not accept my words and reject the Lord, the world will become seas of fire and perish through the Third World War.

The God of Love can also be a God of wrath. Pray harder and offer sufferings.

The sounds of this world become inaudible to me during my suffering. But I can hear the voice of the Blessed Mother despite the pains. The pains were too severe and my throat was too dry. It was hard to say anything, but I finished the prayers with a song, *"Lord, glory and praise to you. . ."* and the Glory Be.

How could I spare my life, if these pains give even the smallest comfort to Jesus and the Blessed Mother? Glory be to the Lord and let this unworthy sinner give unending thanks to Thee. Amen.

November 27, 1989

From yesterday evening until 1:30 a.m., I suffered many kinds of pains. I got up at 7:30 a.m. and was called by the Blessed Mother to the Chapel. At about 8:30 a.m., the statue began moving. I shouted, *"The Blessed Mother is moving!"* to those who had been praying before the statue. The statue became the live and beautiful Blessed Mother surrounded by a bright light.

She spoke with an extremely beautiful and kind voice. Not daring to look at her, I prostrated myself on the floor.

THE BLESSED MOTHER:

Daughter! Thank you.

Your suffering is like tearing off a piece of live flesh from the humanity. I am comforted, because you have offered your life for the glory of the Lord and have been willing to suffer all the pains for the conversion of sinners.

Daughter! See the Bishop. He knows how much I love him. But how could he fully understand my Heart that so anxiously longs for him? My beloved Bishop! Tell my son, the Bishop, of whom I am proud and who loves me. With his whole life devoted to the Lord and for the purpose of following the Lord's Will, he has been climbing Mt. Calvary and praying and making sacrificial offerings at Gethsemane together with my Son Jesus for the conversion of sinners.

But, because I felt incapable of doing it, I said to the Blessed Mother.

Julia: *Mother! I am so incapable of doing this work.*

I was feeling so anxious and weeping loudly, because I thought how much easier it would be if the Blessed Mother told the Bishop directly.

THE BLESSED MOTHER:

Do not worry too much. My Son Jesus uses an unworthy person like you and pulls you out of nothingness for His glory. Your humility in thinking that you are ignorant and unqualified is what I want. Entrust yourself completely to that grace.

Julia: *Mother! I am sorry. I only hurt your Heart all the time. I will do anything for the glory of the Lord. Please tell me.*

THE BLESSED MOTHER:

My Son Jesus chose the Bishop. My most beloved child, my sweet son, whom I can put in my eyes without feeling any pain. I have been with him and held his hands always, wherever he has been.

There have been so many crises for him until now. In all those difficult times, I have been his shield and his interpreter guarding his life. Thus, I want to receive the approval through him whom I love lavishly so that my messages of love may spread to the world. Since the world is still far from the truth and conversion, my voice can spread more forcefully to the world, sinners can repent, the chained people can be freed and peace can prevail, only if the Church approves my voice.

You must not turn your eyes away from your Mother for the sake of face-saving or public eyes. My tears will never flow in vain. I will perform amazing miracles of love through the Mass. Let there be Masses celebrated in this Chapel. The sanctification of priests will be accomplished through the Masses offered with me.

My dear and poor children. . .

Follow my will wholeheartedly to save many souls who are going toward hell without even knowing that they are going there.

Many children are revolting against God with enormous pride, breaking their vows, and even contradicting and ridiculing His Teachings. Therefore, I ask that my messages be spread fast.

When my messages are accepted by the Church and put into practice, the just anger of God the Father will be softened, order and truth will be restored, and the devils, who instigate confusion and cause turmoil, will be defeated.

But, if the world rejects my words and refuses to repent, the fire of God's justice will fall upon the world.

I am asking for help from the Bishop whom I chose with love in order to wash away the stains of sinners with my tears that flow endlessly like a river, even when they are not visible. When my Son Jesus came to the children of the world because of His Love, even to the extent of becoming their Food, He came through the priests, as He wanted to obey them. In the same manner, I want to spread my increasingly anxious voice to the world through the Bishop. Please follow my wish.

Daughter! You must unite with my son, the Bishop, and with your spiritual director. Obey them, entrust all to them and follow their guidance. They will surely receive the laurel crown from me. If they accept my words well, my Immaculate Heart will flame up with love and the world will convert and be saved. Good-bye! An-nyoung!

Even before I had a chance to respond, the light disappeared and the appearance of the Blessed Mother became that of the statue.

May 8, 1990
—Parents' Day

It was Parents' Day, but I could not go to the Blessed Mother because of intense pains all over my body. When even a hair touched me, I felt as if I were pricked with a needle. So, my husband, Julio, went to the Chapel alone and pinned a carnation to the Blessed Mother's dress. I felt so sorry. I was offering pains in bed saying, *"Mother! I am sorry. I will send you a bouquet of my heart and prayer."*

At about 10:40 p.m., I heard the distant voice of the Blessed Mother.

THE BLESSED MOTHER:

Daughter! I feel frustrated. Aren't you anxious to see me?

I listened eagerly, but couldn't hear her any more. So, I got up despite the pains and went to the Blessed Mother. When I stepped into the Chapel, I smelled a strong, indescribable fragrance filling the whole Chapel. There was also a fragrance of lilies. The Blessed Mother was shedding tears and her face looked pale.

As I was praying and asking for forgiveness, the beautiful voice of the Blessed Mother came from the statue.

THE BLESSED MOTHER:

Daughter! It is Parents' Day, but there hardly are any children looking for their Heavenly Mother. I feel lonely, because even you, whom I chose, do not seek me because of pains. Please do not leave me as a lonesome Mother. I have called and saved so many souls with my tears of mercy, but how many have followed me in gratitude for that love?

I am sad. So many of my poor children, who are usually forgetful of me, seek me only during hard times, as if try-

The Blessed Mother shed tears of blood even on Parents' Day (Korean equivalent of Mother's Day). (May 8, 1990)

The Blessed Mother: "I am sad. So many of my poor children, who are usually forgetful of me, seek me only during hard times, as if trying to grab a life buoy. . . ." (May 8, 1990)

ing to grab a life buoy. . . . How can I work in such change-
able hearts?

Once they receive the grace they have asked for, they return to their miserable lives, forget about my love and live
in a despicable, ungrateful way. But, my daughter, my
mercy prompts me to call them again. I am shedding tears
of blood like this because of the poor children who are
ungrateful for the blessings they have received, do not give
love to others, and think that the graces they have received
are their own and something that they were going to receive anyhow for their own merit. Comfort my Immaculate
Heart that is suffering.

This Mother of yours, who has not been approved yet, is
indeed above all creatures and all heretics. A fast approval
is necessary to save the poor souls who are even insulting
God with their pride and sacrileges and are joining hands
with the devils.

What a dear price has to be paid to defeat the devil! I feel
anxious when I see you. Daughter! Take courage and offer
up your sufferings more gracefully. Also pray harder for
unity. As my messages are spreading to the world and are
being put into practice, the devils are becoming more and
more active. The Red Dragon is employing all kinds of means
to promote division, even among priests. Make our enemy,
Satan, powerless with your faith and love. By doing so,
help me save many souls. Offer to me even what you think
are miserable things. My motherly Heart gets wounded, as
I watch all this.

Daughter! You must become strong by opening the door of
your heart widely to God the Father, Who is coming to you.
I will stay with you so that you can fight the devil and
achieve unity in the deep and mysterious Love of God. Isn't
unity a truly beautiful fruit? As there are many souls who
fall into the cunning traps of the enemy, I must ask you for
extreme sacrifices to the extent of offering your life.

Daughter! Follow me, the Mother and the Helper in Redemption, entrusting everything to my immensely wide Immaculate Heart. Do not forget that I, Mother Mary, am preparing a home where you can relax. Follow me without being discouraged. I bestow the same merciful grace on all the souls who trust and follow me and testify for me.

My Son Jesus will bestow the cup of blessing on you through the loving benevolence of me, who is the string that ties Heaven and earth together. Good-bye! An-nyoung!

When the Blessed Mother finished her words, someone was touching me gently. I was wondering if it was the Blessed Mother comforting me in my sufferings, but, when I looked, it was my husband, Julio. *"Julia! The Blessed Mother is shedding tears of blood."* At Julio's pressing words, I looked at the Blessed Mother's statue and saw her shedding tears of blood profusely. She also had much blood under her nose. It was about 11:20 p.m. She continued shedding tears of blood until about 1:20 a.m., when the tears of blood began to dry. After that, she was shedding some tears only.

"Mother Mary! Forgive this poor and miserable sinner and may the Mother's will be accomplished victoriously on this earth. Amen."

June 30, 1990

During the overnight prayer service commemorating the fifth anniversary of the Blessed Mother's first shedding tears, I received pains in my ribs and entered an ecstasy. With a bright light, the Blessed Mother appeared. She looked more beautiful, kinder, friendlier, and more graceful than before. She was wearing a blue mantle, holding a rosary in her left hand, and was radiating light from her right hand on all those who were present at the prayer service.

At that time, Jesus appeared in the sky wearing a red mantle, looking down at us lovingly and kindly, and pouring down light upon us with His open arms. This light was spreading like sunlight over all the people at the prayer service. At that moment, the Saints and angels were also seen praying in great joy. The angels were also dancing and praying with us. The Blessed Mother began speaking with a very gentle and kind voice.

THE BLESSED MOTHER:

Daughter! Thank you.

My Son Jesus bestows special blessings by shining light on all those who came to this meeting remembering me. Also through the pains and love you have experienced, many children will receive the grace of conversion today.

Love leads us to victory. Strive for it with all your heart. Then, the precious grace will be allowed for the salvation of many souls. Because the sins of the world are excessive, the love of my Immaculate Heart alone is not sufficient and that is why I am calling you. Even at this time, I am also showing signs at other places to spread the messages of my love so that the Lord will be praised.

As God is Three Persons in One, I am the one Mother of Heaven for all of you. As the Father, the Son and the Holy Spirit are One, you must also all become one.

I am asking you, because there are many children who come here for curiosity and are seeking miracles and signs. Offer more sacrifices and reparations so that all the children, upon hearing my eager voice of love, may live the messages actively and follow me with confidence. Bring them to me, and, when they follow me completely, I will embrace them with love and let them receive the heavenly joy.

Daughter! Do not forget that I am always close to you at your side.

Julia: *Oh, Lord and my Mother Mary! You have called all of us. May Your Will alone be done on earth. Let all of us approach Your altar with the gifts of thanksgiving and the offerings of sacrifices.*

At that moment, the Holy Spirit appeared from Heaven in the shape of a dove and shed light on all those who were attending the prayer service. Soon, the Blessed Mother and the light disappeared. Jesus also disappeared with the Saints and angels.

July 21, 1990

When I was in the middle of a deep meditation after praying fifteen decades of the rosary in front of the Blessed Mother's statue in the Chapel, I heard her beautiful voice. "Daughter! Hold my hand." I stepped forward and held her hand. I felt a live pulse in her hand. There also was a strong fragrance of roses. The statue turned into the live and beautiful Blessed Mother.

THE BLESSED MOTHER:

Daughter! Offer up more sufferings. Offer up your pains more gracefully as sacrifice and penance. I am calling and gathering many children for the conversion of numerous sinners who love the things of the world. What you are trying to do now is not your idea, but what I want.

Therefore, daughter! My house *(the Chapel)* is a house of salvation for the conversion of many souls, and, so, the expansion of the house is not a luxury, but to gather more of Mother's children with love.

Thus, when you observe the First Saturdays and spend the nights praying with me for the salvation of the world and enter through the small gate carrying the cross in unity, the devils will retreat and sinners will receive the grace of conversion.

The world will pass away, and so will all the passions. But you will surely be saved, if you hold the hands of this Mother who is the string that ties Heaven and earth together and who eagerly desires your salvation. You will live forever, if you try to live according to the Will of God.

Daughter! Consult with Father Spies about everything and prepare my house. Remember that your refuge is my Heart.

Entrust yourselves completely to my will with love, faith and trust.

Shortly, I entered an ecstasy. The Blessed Mother was wearing a crown and holding a rosary in her hand. While standing with a gentle appearance, she melted the vicious devils with her light. At the same time, three men wearing traditional white Korean clothes were seen praying with the Blessed Mother. I think they were the three persons who were martyred at Muhak-Dang in Naju in the 19th Century.

July 30, 1990

At about 10 a.m. on July 27, the Blessed Mother's statue was moved to the video room because of construction work in the Chapel. She began shedding tears at about 10:15 a.m. on that day. From about 11 a.m., the tears began to dry. Father Spies asked me to find out why she was shedding tears. I kept asking her, but she did not say anything. At 9 a.m. today, after she had shed tears for three days, I heard her voice from the statue while I was meditating after praying the rosary.

THE BLESSED MOTHER:

Display the power of love more vigorously and give devoted service in a heroic manner.

I was waiting for her to speak further, but she did not say any more. She looked very sad.

"Oh, Mother of love! I will serve you loyally and heroically."

August 15, 1990
—Feast of the Blessed Mother's Assumption

While offering the devotion and love of a little soul to the Blessed Mother and crying and praying with him, I entered an ecstasy at about 4:15 p.m. The Blessed Mother appeared wearing a sparkling crown and a blue mantle and holding a rosary in one hand. She looked so beautiful, but her face was filled with anxiety.

THE BLESSED MOTHER:

Daughter! I am suffering even today, because there are too many sins in this world.

It was heartbreaking to hear the Blessed Mother say these words. She needs to be comforted and praised by her children on this great feast day of her Assumption, but she is suffering pains even today. I felt so sorry.

THE BLESSED MOTHER:

Daughter! How wonderful it would be, if all the children think the way you think. Now many children are following me superficially by compromising with the corruptible flesh and the world permeated with errors. I am very sad, because there are only very few children who are following me truly with their hearts.

As she sounded choked with tears, I looked at her and saw her weeping. I said to her eagerly.

Julia: *Mother, I am sorry. Please forgive me. I have been unworthy. I will try harder to follow Mother's will.*

THE BLESSED MOTHER:

Right now, the devil is using all kinds of methods to defeat you and to strike down priests and many children whom I have chosen so that the messages may not spread. The flowers of evil look pretty on the exterior and confuse and seize even innocent souls in cunning ways. Such evils hide even behind innocent-looking appearances. This can be discerned only by the souls who are in the state of grace. Can you offer sufferings, if these sufferings are needed for the proud and selfish souls who claim to know the ways of Heaven and sound very knowledgeable, but do not put what they know into practice?

Julia: *Yes, Mother. I will do anything, if you help me.*

THE BLESSED MOTHER:

Thank you, my daughter!

At that moment, there was a loud noise like an earthquake and a strange object appeared before me. Its upper body looked like a grey horse and its lower body like a human. It was the devil of division. He was promoting division among many countries and, as a result, a war broke out among three of them. I saw one of them running away after fighting for a while. The devil was laughing gleefully at this scene.

The head devil dispatched the small devils to the world and was looking for more countries to drag into wars. While he was smiling with an ugly appearance, I said to him that he had better stop now what he had been doing. The devil said to me in a friendly way that, if I joined him, he would give me one country. When I refused flatly, he attacked me and said, *"If I get rid of you and Father Spies, my work will proceed better. You are our big enemy. So, we'd better get rid of you."* While attacking me, he demanded my surrender. But, when I refused, he called other devils and said they should kill me. The head devil that looked like a horse knocked me down and pressed me on my neck. The small devils grabbed my legs and tried to break them. I entrusted everything to the Blessed Mother. I prayed that there would be peace in the whole world, even if I got killed. Suddenly, it became completely dark, and I thought I was dying. But suddenly the pressure on my neck eased, and it became bright. Someone was holding my hand warmly and softly. At that moment, I heard a kind, friendly, and yet sorrowful voice.

THE BLESSED MOTHER:

Daughter! My beloved and sweet daughter! I feel sorry that I always give you pains, but this Mother is suffering greater pains because of the extreme insults. Now it is an age of sins and disorder. As you saw, this world is overflowing with disorder and, as a result, a great calamity is looming over the the entire human race. Even if I try to hold it off, what use will it be, if the world does not repent? There has never been another age when so many children of the world strayed so far away from repentance and brought ruin upon themselves in cooperation with the devils and under the control of the devils as now. All of them must listen to my voice of love. But, instead of listening to my earnest voice burning with love, they revolt against me with insults, criticisms and judgments causing great damage to their souls. Because of this, my beloved little souls are suffering pains for their sake.

Julia: *Mother! I am offering up my pains so that they may convert as soon as possible.*

THE BLESSED MOTHER:

Thank you, my little soul! Their sins are many, but I have pity on them and wait for their return. But, if they persist in being indifferent to me and rejecting me, God's arm of justice will soon be raised and the cup of His wrath will overflow. What will be the use of regretting at that time?

My daughter who follows me suffering pains! Even today, I am calling, through your sufferings, my little and weak souls who will fight a difficult fight against the evil force that causes afflictions and temptations day and night. Offer your sufferings more gracefully. I intend to collect the seeds of martyrdom from the sufferings of my little souls, plant them in the Garden of my Immaculate Heart, so that flowers will blossom from these seeds of goodness. Therefore, prepare many good seeds. They will be used in saving many humans and countries at the decisive time of tribulation.

My beloved little souls! Offer yourselves up completely with your faithfulness toward me for the sake of your brethren who are severely insulting and resisting my love and also for the sake of the priests and religious who are going through the pains of labor. You must walk straight forward on the path that the Saints walked, entrusting themselves completely to me with love. There has never been a Saint who has not followed me closely. You were chosen by me for an important mission. Do not have any doubt about my protection and my love. Trust and rely on me and, thus, turn the cup of divine wrath into a cup of blessing with the intense flames of love burning in my Immaculate Heart.

Daughter! Even when all the people of this world desert you, do not forget that I am always at your side and remember the reward in Heaven. Good bye! An-nyoung!

As the Blessed Mother and the light disappeared, my sufferings started. When I opened my eyes, my body was aching so much that I could not even move. I was carried on a stretcher to my home *(which is next door to the Chapel)*. I felt so much pain in my legs, and I had trouble breathing. People who were present there were surprised at the sudden bleeding of my toes. They said that, while I was suffering, my legs were raised again and again, and the women present there lowered them. At that moment, my toes suddenly began bleeding.

October 4, 1990

The Blessed Mother's statue continued to weep. My husband, Julio, and I prayed the rosary from about 10:40 p.m. followed by meditation. As the meditation continued, it turned into crying and lamentation. I felt heartbroken at the thought of the Blessed Mother's anguish over the poor souls who are following the false prophets because of their blindness and deafness. In addition, my many current difficulties and physical pains were also making me feel anxious and weakening my soul.

When I looked at the Blessed Mother's statue saying, *"Mother, what should I do?"* the statue began radiating a beautiful light and turned into the live Mother Mary. She began speaking with a very anxious voice.

THE BLESSED MOTHER:

Daughter! Do not worry too much. Your body and soul are now weaker than ever. It is a difficult task to save the world from destruction and misery. I understand well that it is very hard to spread the messages in a way they can be understood easily by all. But follow me even in the midst of your extreme pains. You are participating in my sufferings, because my Son Jesus earned life for the human race through His Blood of extreme pains, and, through this Blood, those who are living in the misery of sins will be led to life. God gave you a garment of eternal life that has been made clean by the Blood of the Lamb. Even so, do you feel so weak? I chose you for an important mission, and you must become stronger.

Daughter! When I was on earth, many people called me the mother of a mad man. I should be respected as the Queen of Heaven, but have to implore with many sacrifices, pains, and tears because of the division and disorder among the children on earth. Help me.

Major calamities are about to fall upon the world, but there are too many people who are self-centered. Those who love God and make me known will receive eternal life and will stand by the side of this Mother of Love. The world will change, but the Laws of God will not. Pray and pray again. Prayers of deep love are needed now more than ever for the Holy Catholic Church. This current age is extremely important for the whole human race.

The Blessed Mother was silent for a while and resumed speaking while shedding large drops of tears.

Oh, all the children of the world! It is not too late yet. Come to me in a hurry. Come to me without delay and suck the spiritual milk from my breast that is flowing out like a spring. I will make a flower garden where you can grow beautiful souls. I have left my Heart wide open to accept your pleas and requests.

When you return to me renouncing yourselves, you will find the happiness that you have been longing for, but have not been able to find, in the bosom of this Mother of Peace, who can embrace all of you. Come to me, all of you, and let me not shed tears and tears of blood in vain. Be a comfort to my wounded Heart. By doing so, sinners will recognize

The Blessed Mother: "All the children of the world! It is not too late yet. Come to me in a hurry. I have left my Heart wide open to accept your pleas and requests. . . . However corrupt your souls may be, you will be forgiven with powerful flames of love when you repent." (October 4, 1990)

my voice of love and seek the justice of God by repenting their sins in my bosom. However corrupt the souls may be, they will be forgiven with powerful flames of love when they repent. But those who sin against the Holy Spirit will not be able to avoid the fires of justice at the time of judgment.

After she completed these words, her appearance returned to that of the statue, but more tears were flowing.

Julia: *Oh, Mother Mary! I am sorry and thank you. May Mother, who is Love itself, bring the Kingdom of the Sacred Heart of Jesus and your Immaculate Heart to this world with your immense Love. Amen.*

November 11, 1990
—From 3:00 a.m.

I was crying because of my unworthiness. How can I better fill the Hearts of Jesus, Who anguishes over sinners, and the Blessed Mother, who is weeping? While I was experiencing great waves of agony in the depths of my heart, I began hearing the sorrowful voice of the Blessed Mother. Her voice was also very warm, soft and filled with love.

THE BLESSED MOTHER:

Daughter! My beloved daughter! Daniel was put into a lions' den, but was rescued by God's angel and prophets. Likewise, God will surely save those who seek His justice. Therefore, do not worry or feel too anxious. God is attentive to the sacrifices and reparations by those who were saved from death, and He will not ignore their deep lamentations. But the bloody sacrifices and reparations by my little souls are necessary to save those who persist in their betrayal, as God leaves them in ruins. Even the most fertile soil turns into a wilderness, if neglected. Likewise, the water in a pond decays, if it stays there. You understand this well. Therefore, remove the stones from your heart, pull out all the weeds from it, and arm yourself with con-

version, prayers and the Words. In this age, the devils corrupt numerous peoples' consciences, making them commit sins of impurity, even leading to murders; destroy human dignity by abortions; drag them into errors and all
kinds of sins such as corruption, injustice, curses, violent
words, hatred and revenge; and make them walk the way
of selfishness. How sorrowful my Son Jesus feels when He
sees all these children!

Now, come closer to me with love and entrusting everything to me. Spread my messages of love vigorously to all
the children so that the lost Love of God may be restored in
every corner of the world. The storm is already becoming
violent. I want to rescue this world into my Immaculate
Heart, as it is facing the grave danger of being swept away
by the storm and being destroyed.

My dear children! Come back in a hurry to this refuge,
which is I, Mother Mary, your shield. I call you and call
you again until my throat bleeds, but only very few of my
children respond. So, my Heart is hurting intensely, and I
am calling you shedding tears without ceasing.

Therefore, my daughter! I, Mother of Love, will become the
ark sailing toward Heaven. Help me by forming the Order
of Mary's Ark of Salvation so that all the children may come
aboard. I am your comforter and refuge. I am the Ark of
Salvation that sails toward Heaven. To those souls who
follow me holding my hands, accept me and put the messages of love into practice, I will become the Ark of Salvation for safe arrival at the heavenly harbor. I will hold their
hands in all their tribulations, poverty and adversities.

Now, all my children! Come aboard this Ark which I made
for you, and let's sail toward Heaven sharing love.

Oh, my daughter! Tell my dear son, the Bishop. He has
such a deep filial love for me. Now is the time to announce
Mother's will without any delay. Since I put your hands

The Blessed Mother: "Come closer to me with love and entrusting ev-erything to me. Spread my messages of love vigorously to all the chil-dren so that the lost Love of God may be restored in every corner of the world." (November 11, 1990)

The Blessed Mother sheds tears on December 7, 1990.

together, form a unity now. There will be many sufferings in gathering my numerous children together, but, through your sufferings, the sorrows and lamentations of so many children will turn into a joyful dance, and the tears shed at night will turn into joys in the morning as the souls who have been falling into the deep pit will be rescued.

January 29, 1991

I had been struggling with pains since last night, but, at about 5:30 this morning, I was called by the Blessed Mother and went to the Chapel. The statue turned into the live Blessed Mother.

THE BLESSED MOTHER:

Daughter! My daughter who entrusts everything to me even while suffering pains! I want you to follow me with a greater love and without agonizing too much over your unworthiness. This world is decaying with corruption and degradation. The human race is facing a crisis under black clouds, and sins are spreading like a horrible cancer. The storm is already becoming violent. This world is exposed to a grave danger, as the storm rages on. How would this Heavenly Mother feel in her Heart, as she watches all this?

Follow me with courage even when faced with serious tribulations and threats of violence, wars and destruction. There isn't much time left before incredible punishments will fall even upon those countries which have been protected and intensely cherished so far. Many people are inordinately rejecting God, and the iniquities and corruptions are increasing everyday, causing more violence and more wars.

The darkness is even infiltrating the Church in coldhearted and elaborate ways. Thus, the last hour of bleeding for purification is waiting for you. If you do not live according to the Words of Truth, you will soon suffer calamities and will surely regret it. What is the use of regretting after the justice of God is realized? I am imploring like this to my children, who have been called, as the time permitted for conversion is approaching its end. Be awake and pray without procrastinating. Also become simple like a child. Nobody knows the exact date and hour of the Lord's coming to you. Preparations are in progress to defeat His enemies, destroy them and establish His Kingdom on this earth. He will come to you on clouds, displaying His Power to build His glorious Kingdom. Prepare to greet Him with trust, love and faith. He is coming to you through me, your Mother. As He was sent to you by God the Father through my virgin body, Jesus will be using my Immaculate Heart in returning to you as the King.

Therefore, all the children of the world! Open your hearts widely without delay and return to me. Rekindle the fire in your hearts that has been extinguished, achieve a unity among all and practice my messages of love. Spread the messages all over the world fervently and filled with hope. When the messages are practiced by the little souls in the form of prayers of a deep love, it will become a fragrant oil washing the bleeding wounds of the Lord.

If you do not reject my motherly love and practice love, my Immaculate Heart will achieve a victory in the face of the threat of a new, terrifying war, and there will be love and peace in the world. I will stretch and open my mantle and hide and save in the safe refuge of my Immaculate Heart all those souls who follow my words even in the midst of a huge darkness. But those who do not accept my words and reject the Lord will be thrown into the sea of an intense fire. Therefore, have trust in me, the Mother of Peace, and rely completely on my Immaculate Heart.

March 10, 1991

I entered an ecstasy while praying in the Chapel. The Blessed Mother appeared shedding tears and spoke sorrowfully, almost as if lamenting.

THE BLESSED MOTHER:

Daughter! It is too hard to look at the disorder brought about by so many of my dear children in collaboration with our enemy, the Red Dragon, because of their blindness and deafness. The world is like a desert. The big calamities that occur here and there are warnings. I feel so sad and anxious, as I watch human sufferings under the warnings and punishments. Therefore, daughter! I implore you with sorrows in order to protect you from the traps laid by the devils.

Julia: *Mother, please tell me.*

THE BLESSED MOTHER:

Do you want to see how wicked and vicious the devils' violence is?

Julia: *Yes, Mother.*

At that moment, the head devil, Lucifer, and the smaller devils, whom I had seen on August 15, 1990, appeared and were eagerly talking with each other. A while later, they were laughing loudly and looking around at the world. They entered one country, spread out in the country and promoted division. Then, they gathered and talked again and entered a different country, causing division and fights. They were so delighted and amused. There were flames here and there, sometimes turning into seas of fire. They clapped their hands with joy and looked around again to drag more countries into war. I was watching this and began to cry. The Blessed Mother continued weeping and spoke.

THE BLESSED MOTHER:

All the children of the world! How sad it will be if the fire falls upon you from the sky! Pray and pray again. This current age is extremely important for the whole human race. Shouldn't you find ways to protect yourselves from the many calamities? Your God looks down at your acts and is about to punish you. But He is still forgiving you. Repent hurriedly. Repent sincerely and come back to God

Who can save you. You must repent, because the sins of this world have reached an extremely high level. The world is mired in evil habits and delinquency. As order is disturbed, chaos is increasing, and the spiritual world is being destroyed. All things are collapsing, provoking the wrath of God.

My beloved children! Become little persons and follow me humbly and with hope and courage. When you follow me wholeheartedly in response to my messages of love, new buds will sprout even from the burnt ground, my love will flame up on the ruins, and a cup of blessing instead of a cup of wrath will be bestowed upon you by God.

March 25, 1991

The Blessed Mother's statue had shed tears since February 18 and, this morning, shed much blood from her eyes and nose. Her cheek, dress and the cloth under the statue became very wet. Her voice came from the statue, which looked so sorrowful.

THE BLESSED MOTHER:

Daughter! Pray more. This world should not be left to be destroyed because of the violence by the devil, the enemy of the Cross, as Sodom and Gomorrah were destroyed despite the fervent wish by Abraham, because there were not even ten just people. Too many children are rejecting my eager pleas made with blood and joining hands with the Red Dragon, enabling him to promote errors and moral slackness among people and make them live in sins. Thus, they destroy human dignity by inducing people to commit murders through so many abortions. I implore you, because I cannot look at or listen to these anymore.

Accept me warmly with prayers, sacrifices, reparations and the offerings of consecrated hearts and sufferings. Thus, wipe away my tears and tears of blood shed for you by letting me live in your everyday life. By doing so, you will

The Blessed Mother: "Too many children are rejecting my eager pleas and destroy human dignity by committing murders through so many abortions. I implore you, because I cannot look at or listen to these anymore." (March 25, 1991)

be preparing a place where Jesus, Who will be coming in glory, can reside.

You must also remember that, as birth comes nearer, pains will intensify. Because governments, peoples and societies are resisting the God of Justice, they become surrounded by a huge darkness. Because they are not opening their doors widely to Christ Who is coming, various tribulations and agonies are resulting.

Therefore, all the children of the world! Become even lowlier souls and follow me with confidence. As the difficulties intensify, I will stay closer to my little souls and become their strength. When all the children accept me well and put the messages of love into practice, the darkness of disorder will be defeated through the light of God's great mercy. I hope my urgent pleas will reach all the corners of the world through you.

The Blessed Mother continued to weep.

April 21, 1991

The Blessed Mother called me saying, "Daughter, let us pray together." I went to the Chapel despite the pains and prayed for the conversion of sinners in front of the weeping statue of the Blessed Mother. A while later, I saw a vision and the Blessed Mother.

There were countless people in a dark world. The earth began shaking as during an earthquake or like a boat in the middle of a storm. There were also flames of fire here and there. People were falling in all directions, and the sounds of their screams were reaching the sky.

I cried with a loud voice, *"Oh, God! My Lord! Forgive the poor sinners generously. Save those who call upon Your Name."* Then, many people were repenting with tears and anxiously seeking God. There was a bright light in the sky and the extremely beautiful Blessed Mother appeared above the people. She was wearing a shiny crown with twelve stars, a white dress and a blue mantle. The hems of the mantle were sparkling gold. She was holding an ivory-colored rosary in her right hand and a brown scapular in her left hand. Her beauty was beyond human description.

THE BLESSED MOTHER:

You will be saved, if you live not according to your flesh, but with the Bread from Heaven, and follow me, your Mother.

At that moment, a shiny, white cross appeared above the Blessed Mother and soon turned into an image of the Holy Eucharist. At the same time, the dark world became bright and the trembling stopped. The Blessed Mother spoke kindly but anxiously.

THE BLESSED MOTHER:

All the children of the world! Darkness can never defeat light. The devils are trying to strike down many of my children who are following me. But do not forget that the Lord does not refuse the pleas of those who call upon His Name with love and follow me.

Daughter! You cannot win the victory without going through the cross. You must understand the amazing mystery of the Holy Eucharist by which God comes down from Heaven through priests in order to be with you. Therefore, make frequent Confessions to receive the Lord more worthily; open your heart widely, keep it clean and organized, and love one another so that it will become a palace and a tabernacle where the Lord can dwell. Then, the Lord will live in you, who are unworthy, and set a fire in you.

My beloved daughter! Tell all the children of the world. I want all of you to wear the scapular with the intention of being with me; pray the rosary fervently with all your body and mind and with love; live a completely consecrated life of prayers, sacrifices, and reparations; renew your life with the spirit of self-renunciation and poverty; and, thus, repel the violence of the devil.

I am imploring you again and again, because I want to save you all from this dangerous world. Therefore, renounce your ego and follow my wishes well. Then, darkness will retreat from this world, and the Kingdom of the Lord will come.

All the children of the world! In this age when the lives of my beloved priests and my consecrated children are being drained endlessly, return to my warm bosom of love, which is the refuge for sinners, and let us pray with a greater love. May the peace of the Lord be with you always. . . .

The Blessed Mother smiled kindly and waved her hand. Then, she disappeared together with the light. Her statue was smiling and shedding tears.

May 8, 1991

It was Parents' Day in Korea and I went to the Chapel and pinned a carnation on the Blessed Mother's dress. I said to her, *"Mommy, I love you. You have been suffering so much pain to save many souls who are wandering in darkness and walking toward hell. So, have a restful day today. Be comforted and receive admiration and praise from many children. I am offering this flower on behalf of all your children."*

The appearance of the Blessed Mother's statue did not change, but she spoke with a kind and friendly voice.

THE BLESSED MOTHER:

Daughter! Thank you. I rejoice more over a heart filled with love and devotion than over flowers or deeds. Even the smallest thing can become a great good work for you, if it is done with love. Come closer to me so that you can unite more intimately with my burning love. To soften God's anger, become an even lowlier person. Become a more humble person, offering sacrifices and reparations of the cross, and entrust all your imperfect thoughts, daily life and sufferings to me. Those souls who are accepting me with love and are approaching me will be bathed in my love. Follow without a doubt the wishes of this Mommy who wants to perform miracles of love by using you as an instrument, despite your unworthiness.

Julia: *Yes, Mother! I am always unworthy, but will follow your wishes.*

THE BLESSED MOTHER:

Daughter! Make haste. Should the cup of God's wrath over-flow onto this dark world which is like a desert? Events are unreeling already, but there are too few priests who are following me. The whole world is filled with dangers and is going through pains of labor. There are countless souls who need spiritual and physical help. Right now, God's work of salvation stands on nothingness and worthless-ness. I want to gather all the children, who are struggling with weakness, poverty and fierce battles with evil, into my burning Immaculate Heart.

"Mary's Ark of Salvation"—this is my bosom of love, greater than the universe, which will take children from the whole world to the heavenly harbor. Now I intend to embrace chil-dren from the whole world in my wide bosom. Therefore, construct a basilica. I will embrace them all in my bosom so that they may be reborn with love and I may pull out all their weeds. This way, I can become the guide for the blind; give energy to the poor and hungry; wipe away tears of the children who are sad, agonizing, and weeping; become a comfort to those who are hungry and thirsty for Truth; and become a refuge for those who are insulted, perse-cuted and criticized with all kinds of groundless accusa-tions while doing their just work.

Therefore, build the Basilica of Mary's Ark of Salvation hur-riedly. If you follow my messages of love and put them into practice, great treasures will accumulate for other souls and yours. It will also be the way of saving the souls who would otherwise be lost with certainty. To the burning Sacred Heart of Jesus and my Immaculate Heart, it will become a comfort.

Daughter! Now we must make a chain with the souls who are burning with love and make their flames of love known to the whole world. When you follow me without doubting that this is the perfect shortcut with no danger of slipping and falling off the cliff, my flaming Immaculate Heart will burn away all your sins. Thus, even falling into sins can be utilized for a greater good. Now, bring all those things that you think are worthless, miserable and weak and gather around my great banquet which has a sacred value. There will be a great blessing on all the children who are rushing to my bosom of love. Good-bye! An-nyoung!

She finished speaking. Her lips on the statue were open for a while, and then closed.

May 16, 1991

There was a Mass at 6 p.m. in the Naju Parish Church, celebrated by two priests from the Philippines. Some parishioners of Naju and 33 pilgrims from the Philippines participated. When I received the Holy Eucharist, I immediately tasted blood in my mouth. When I came back to my pew and showed it to Rufino, who was sitting next to me, he saw the Host on my tongue being of a yellow-to-light brown color at first and, soon, turning into a blood-red color starting from the edge. This was reported to the priests and all the faithful present there were able to see it. They were surprised and began crying. The two priests also prayed and cried in front of the tabernacle. The Host continued bleeding, and soon my mouth was filled with Blood.

At that moment, I saw a vision. The weeping Blessed Mother of Naju was wearing a blue mantle, holding a rosary in her right hand and smiling beautifully. With tears in her eyes, she embraced the two priests. Soon there was the merciful but anxious voice of Jesus.

JESUS:

Daughter! Offer up more reparations for the insults by sinners. The world keeps offending, despising, insulting,

On May 16, 1991, Julia attended Mass at the Naju Parish Church, together with 33 pilgrims from the Philippines. After Julia received Communion, the Sacred Host in her mouth turned into visible flesh and blood.

scourging and bruising Me, but the burning Love of My Sacred Heart bestows the grace of mercy, forgiveness and reconciliation on so many souls who provoke the just anger of God, through the precious Blood from the Five Wounds opened on the Cross in order to save this sick and dark world from eternal death and to give sinners eternal life. Because I love you so much, I manifest that Love by coming to you in the form of bread, hiding My Divinity, dignity and even human appearance. I come to you in person in the form of bread because of My great Love for you. But many souls pay little attention to My Real Presence, insult Me with sacrilegious Communions, and neglect Me with ingratitude.

Daughter! Teach the Mystery of the Holy Eucharist fervently to the children who do not understand it so that the numerous people living in ingratitude may be saved through your bloody sacrifices combined with My Love. However hard I may try to give Love to them, I cannot force them to accept it, as I gave them free will. I, Who am present in the Mystery of the Holy Eucharist, am a spring that never dries, a medicine that can save the sick souls, and a doctor to the patient. I love even those souls who have become so sordid and distorted because of sins, because I am Love Itself. So, when they come to Me through the Sacrament of Confession, I will wash away their sins that made their souls dirty and allow them to stay in My Love.

My Heart is hurting intensely, because so many people in this world bow to and flatter the worldly rulers, but only extremely few children kneel in front of the Lord of the Heavens and the King of the Universe, adore Him and ask for graces from Him. Time is running out, because there are so many sins in the world.

All the children of the world! You must fear the chastisement that is approaching you, constantly pray, make sacrifices and reparations, and live a consecrated life. By doing so, you can avoid falling into the devils' cunning temptations that allure you to sin, resentment, violence, corruption, and a selfish life; alienate you from God; lead you to hatred, division, delinquency and disrespect; and, thereby, thoroughly control your mind and make you intemperate. In this world which is being covered with errors and darkness, stay close to the Bible, which contains the Sacred Truths, lead a life according to the Gospels, and put into practice the words of My Mother who has been appearing and imploring with tears at many places in the world in this urgent time. Tell everyone that accepting My Mother's words is the same as accepting Me and that holding her hands and following her is the shortcut to Me.

The time of my Mother Mary's victory is approaching. Make haste in repenting and get on board Mary's Ark of Salvation. My Mother came into this world as the Heavenly Prophetess and My Helper who will lead you to My brilliant and glorious revelations. Follow her words. I will always be with you.

May 23, 1991

At about 4 p.m., I went to the Chapel and began praying together with a priest and a layman who love the Blessed Mother and had decided to consecrate themselves to her. While we were praying, the Blessed Mother's eyes became teary. Suddenly, there was light, and the Blessed Mother began speaking with a soft, quiet and loving voice through her statue.

THE BLESSED MOTHER:

Yes, my dear children! . . . I have called you as my instruments to give an eternal refuge to those souls who are thirsty and starving for love and are wandering around. Hold my hands more humbly and offer up your sacrifices and reparations, following me for the conversion of sinners.

Now, the time for victory is approaching. Follow me without delay. I will use you, through my beloved little soul, as guides for numerous souls who are repaying so much love with insults and are committing sins against the Lord.

When you renounce your ego and follow me completely by practicing my messages of love and by making my Immaculate Heart that is burning with love known to all the children in the world, you will experience pains. But your souls will be purified and made stronger, as gold becomes purified in fire. If you follow me in unity among yourselves, what you have lost in the world will turn into eternal joy by gaining me. . . .

I wish to accomplish miracles of love through you who are unworthy. With all your strength, strive to realize my love with unity among yourselves. I will always be with you.

August 27, 1991
—Morning

After the morning Mass, I entered the Chapel at about 6:40 a.m. The Blessed Mother's statue looked very sad with her eyes congested with blood. I thought she might begin weeping.

At about 7:40 a.m., when a priest, my husband and a brother* were offering candles, tears began flowing on the statue. The priest held the Blessed Mother's hand and cried loudly. Then, it became bright, as rays of light were coming from the Blessed Mother's crown. A loving voice came from the statue. (*In Korea, the lay people are often called brothers and sisters.)

THE BLESSED MOTHER:

My chosen children! Now is the time for purification. Hold my hands of burning mercy tightly. Actually it is not you who are holding my hands, but it is I who have called you and am holding your hands. Now renounce everything, follow me completely and practice and spread my messages of love. Then, through you, who think you are unworthy and poor, great miracles of love beyond anyone's imagination will be accomplished.

On June 8, 1991, an image of the Eucharist appeared under the sun and came down upon the roof of the Chapel. The inside of the Chapel became filled with the fragrance of roses.

Oh, my beloved children! Thank you so much for offering yourselves totally. But many children are dispersing. To assemble them again with the love of my Immaculate Heart, you must build the Basilica in a hurry. Make haste with faithful hearts. I, who am the Helper in Redemption, sincerely wish that all the dispersed children repent, become purified and offer themselves up with sacrifices and reparation. Then, I will make you the Lord's glorious garlands of flowers.

As she finished speaking , the light disappeared and it became quiet.

August 27, 1991
—Afternoon

I was praying with the priest, the brother (both of whom had prayed together with me in the morning) and about twenty other pilgrims. At about 12:30 p.m., the Blessed Mother began admonishing us anxiously—with a soft loving voice.

THE BLESSED MOTHER:

My beloved children! Listen well. I implore you. Now is the time for purification, but many children are confused because of the words that are not from God. My enemy, the devil, is promoting confusion and division at many places in the world by deceiving people with tricks and even by using supernatural phenomena. He performs many unusual tricks that can confuse even the good people. To promptly recognize the devil's violence in his attempts and to come to the refuge of my Immaculate Heart, you must build the Basilica of Mary's Ark of Salvation quickly. Help me.

You must pray and love more fervently so that everyone may avoid condemnation and be saved. I will help you. Just as Daniel, facing death in the lions' den, was rescued by God, as he had sought God's justice and entrusted everything to Him, the devil attempted to topple Gorbachev of the Soviet Union and lead the world to destruction, but he was rescued by God from the devil's hands, and the world was saved from the crisis of destruction, because he sought God's justice and walked the just way and because the little souls offered constant prayers and sacrifices.

Do not worry, but follow me with full trust in me. The Lord will rebuild upon the destruction by the devil and will cure the wounds. The world is going against me, offending me and hurting me, but there are faithful little souls who are praying by my side. Therefore, combine your prayers and achieve unity. When fervent prayers of poor souls reach Heaven, God's just anger will be appeased. Pray and pray again.

I came to this world as the Lord's Helper to save you in this age fallen into danger. When you renounce everything and follow me completely, my role as your true Mother and the Lord's Helper in saving the world will soon be manifested clearly.

The reason that I was chosen to be the Lord's Helper was to give the opportunity of salvation to everyone. Keep in mind that you were also chosen to be my helpers. Accept my words well so that all may be saved together. Offer yourselves up completely, remembering my Son, Jesus Christ, Who was offered as a living sacrifice. I will give you the garment of my fragrance with the love of my burning Immaculate Heart.

At that moment, there was a strong fragrance of roses, and the Blessed Mother's statue was smiling happily.

September 17, 1991

I started praying in the Chapel at about 11 p.m. with brothers and sisters who had experienced a special love from the Blessed Mother. We fervently prayed to the Blessed Mother for the corrupt world, for priests and religious and for the many souls who had fallen into disorder because of their indiscreetness.

Suddenly a black object appeared above us. Then, light radiated from the Crucifix above the Blessed Mother's statue and enveloped the statue. At that moment, light emanated from the statue, melted the black object and shone on all those who were praying. The light was so intense that I fell down and heard the soft voice of the Blessed Mother filled with love.

THE BLESSED MOTHER:

My beloved children! Follow me without worrying. The Lord, Who is listening to you because He wants to help you, will bestow His Love on you. When you follow me, believing my words completely, everything will be accomplished. From Korea, which is my youngest child and which I love so much, I will make my love and victory spread to the entire world.

Now is the time. Stay awake and pray. Many souls are walking toward hell because of the cunning violence of the devil, the enemy of the Cross, but I stretch out my mantle and am waiting for their return, because I love them all.

My dear children! Listen to my words well. Look back at history, when people did not listen to the many warnings given by God. What will happen to this age, if people, like those of the past, remain indifferent to or reject the Words of God and my messages of love? Keep in your heart the words of this Mother, who is the Helper in Redemption, and offer up even the pains that cause bleeding inside of you.

In this age of aridity—an age of an endless desert, the victory can be won only through love. When you love, you must also shed some tears. Tears will help the seeds to bear good fruit and also help the absorption of heavenly nutrition by the souls who are hungry and have been deprived of vitality because of delinquency.

Children! All the souls reaching the Bosom of God will enjoy eternal love, peace and joy in the Lord's Love. But those who betray the graces, are ungrateful and insult the Holy Spirit will be cut off from the Lord forever.

Satan is striving with all his power to promote a tendency of despising the Holy Laws of the Lord, but my burning Immaculate Heart will achieve victory, when the sounds of little souls' prayers to my Immaculate Heart soar high to Heaven. You will surely see my victory.

Now, daughter! Cry out. The victory of my Immaculate Heart is close at hand. You will soon see the day when I will, through you who are unworthy, convert the children who do not know me, open the eyes of the people who do not believe, and silence those who criticize.

Suddenly, in front of me, it became bright, and there was music by a military band. I saw many angels dancing in a circle holding garlands of roses. I heard the music, but couldn't see the band. The angels looked like young girls and had wings on their shoulders. These wings were not like those of birds, but seemed to be made of beautiful, sparkling, blue cloth. The angels' dresses and wings made waves as they moved their shoulders. They were beautiful beyond description.

Then, I saw a man with an angel on his right and a black, hard-to-recognize, object *(devil)* on his left. When he prayed sincerely from his heart, the angel offered a fresh rose to Heaven, whereas, when he prayed superficially, the angel offered a wilted rose. The angels stored the fresh roses and the wilted ones separately. When the man made sacrifices and reparations, forgave and reconciled with others and offered all his life with a joyful heart, fresh roses were offered, but when he was only enduring (difficulties) and lacked love, wilted roses were offered. When he did good works, roses accumulated in Heaven, but, when he did evil and criticized others, the devil was overjoyed and threw the roses, which had been accumulated in Heaven, into the flaming fires of hell, one after another.

God can do everything Himself, but He acts through priests and lay people. Likewise, the devil also does his work through humans. Thus, he employs all kinds of methods in using people around us to make us angry, resentful, unable to forgive and commit many mistakes.

THE BLESSED MOTHER:

Daughter! Did you see that? Good and evil always coexist inside you, because your guardian angel and the devil confront each other: the angel helping you to do good works and the devil afflicting you and tempting you to do evil all the time. The guardian angel stores roses one by one in the treasure warehouse in Heaven. Thus, when a soul offers many good works by offering prayers and making sacrifices and reparations, many roses accumulate. When that soul rises to Heaven, the angels make a garland with the roses and dance holding it. The Saints also welcome the soul with majestic music.

But, even if good works have been accumulated, the devil will burn the roses in the fire of hell by taking the roses out of the treasure warehouse, when evil deeds are committed. Because one goes to hell only when there are no roses left at all, the devil strives with all the available methods to win even one more soul over to his side and, thereby, to form his army.

Therefore, daughter! Do not give a chance to the devil. Arm yourself with love and win the victory. Do not forget my bloody merits and the power of the Lord's Sacred Blood, and knock at the door whenever your cross is too heavy. I will open the door for you with joy.

The souls who are elevated high on the Cross and offer themselves gracefully as victims to the Lord are truly the souls who glorify the Lord and are the little souls who are closest to me. I want all the children to become completely humble and to be tightly embraced in my bosom of love like the Baby Jesus. I will make you spread the strong fragrance of my Motherhood to all the corners of the world.

October 19, 1991

There was an overnight prayer service commemorating the fifth anniversary of the Blessed Mother's first shedding tears of blood. At about 10:50 p.m., I saw a vision. There was a large crowd swarming in one direction, as a man dressed in white and riding a white horse was chasing after them holding a sword about 25 inches long in his hand. The sword looked like a white feather. As he wielded the sword among the crowd, everyone hit by the sword fell down. They struggled to stand up, but couldn't. There were some people who did not fall. They had a mark of the cross on their back resembling the letter "T". Angels appeared and led them to a beautiful church-like place decorated with roses. At that moment, there was the beautiful and kind voice of the Blessed Mother from the statue.

THE BLESSED MOTHER:

I am your Mother who has been elevated to Heaven. Because the devil knows well that I came to this world to help you, he is becoming more active, employing all the available methods to alienate you from me, the Mother of Love, and attacking you fanatically using all kinds of cunning schemes. But the Lord intends to advance the date of purification to separate good and evil in response to the prayers by the little souls who are working for the Lord and following me.

Soon it will become the Age of the Apostles of the Sacred Heart of Jesus and my Immaculate Heart. At that time, there will be many who will regret and wail. Therefore, make haste. The souls who follow the Lord carrying the Cross, spread and practice the Gospels and accept the messages of my burning love will be saved and receive and enjoy eternal life.

It became quiet, when she finished her words.

November 4, 1991

We *(Fr. Aloysius Chang, three helpers and myself)* visited Father Raymond Spies in Anyang. We had long talks and offered Mass. (Throughout the talks and the Mass, we smelled a strong fragrance of roses. Fr. Spies later told us that the fragrance continued there for three days.) After Mass, I sang a hymn: *Mary's Ark of Salvation*, with Father Spies' accompaniment on the organ.

As soon as the hymn was over, I fell down. I could not see anybody, but heard the head devil, Lucifer, whom I had heard before: *We cannot leave this one alive who is interfering with our activities. Let's hurry and kill her. Do not leave any visible scars on her. Do you understand?* Then, there were many voices in response: *Yes, sir.* Right away, they began striking, kicking, trampling and strangling me, and I was struggling and screaming.

"Lord! I am offering up my suffering. Be glorified through this suffering and may the Blessed Mother be comforted, too." Before I completed these words, the devil lifted me up and threw me down saying, *"A stubborn one! I am not going to let you get away this time."* He strangled me again and hit me all over my body. I was bleeding much and felt extremely cold.

Lucifer said, *"I will give you a chance. What are you going to do?"* I was near death and could not even speak, but prayed inside. *"Lord! I am Yours whether I am alive or dead. I only want the Lord to be glorified."* So many devils attacked, struck and trampled me that I lost consciousness. Soon there was a light from Heaven like sunlight warming me. There also was the warm, kind and anxious voice of the Blessed Mother.

THE BLESSED MOTHER:

Daughter! You won a victory over the devil by gathering the seeds of martyrdom and growing them into blossoming beautiful flowers in your just heart. Now is the time for a struggle between Good and Evil. The evil forces will soon perform enormous wonders, seducing numerous people. For this reason, I selected a priest *(Fr. Aloysius Chang)* who is a humble soul, and called him to work in unity with Father Spies. I intend to save many children from the desert of evil and sin through my priests, whom I can put into my eyes without feeling any pain. Therefore, I am holding your hands today. With confidence, display the power of love more vigorously and offer a totally dedicated service heroically.

Let's brighten the road ahead together with this Mother of Love for the souls who are falling into temptations. For that purpose, build the Basilica of Mary's Ark of Salvation by joining hands together. There, I will reveal the secrets of my Immaculate Heart to you so that it may become a sign of joy, love and peace to everyone who visits it.

Let even those who are in despair, depressed, full of wounds and in tribulations suffering under the heavy pressures from their arid hearts, sins, hatred, violence and impure habits come aboard the Ark of Salvation of my Love. I will wrap them with my warm mantle and help them even in the midst of a bitterly cold snowstorm.

My beloved children! Now offer even those trivial things in your life to me gracefully. I will give you the power to transcend even the most trivial things. When you offer up everything and drink the painful cups of the cross and martyrdom with love, even those who are deserted in the middle of pains of death will repent and see the light in darkness.

From this small land, a land made fertile with the blood of so many martyrs, the light will shine upon the whole world through my little, poor souls. My Immaculate Heart will surely triumph in the midst of the glorious victory by Christ.

When the Blessed Mother ended her words, the light disappeared and it became quiet.

November 25, 1991

I was called by the Blessed Mother and had a strong feeling that she would select for us the site for the Basilica of Mary's Ark of Salvation. I went with seven of my helpers to the mountain indicated by the Blessed Mother. We offered a Mass there according to her wish. During the Mass, there was a light from the sky. I could not see the Blessed Mother, but heard her voice, which was so beautiful, kind and anxious.

THE BLESSED MOTHER:

There are as many children in the world as stars in the sky and grains of sand on the beach, but only very few follow me. My beloved children! I called you today for a special purpose. As Satan's violence is increasing rapidly, I called you to participate in the Lord's work of salvation in order to save all. Participate in it by helping each other.

My beloved son (*Fr. Aloysius Chang who celebrated Mass on the mountain)*! A priest whom I can put in my eyes without feeling any pain! Through my little chosen soul *(Julia)*, I will bring you up like an infant wrapped in swaddling clothes, in order to perform amazing miracles of love. I will manifest the great glory of God through you at this place prepared by me.

As there are many children who do not understand the Infinite Love of God and are wandering among superficial things, I will gather children from all over the world and reveal to them the amazing miracles of love. I want my beloved daughter and you, who are her brothers and sisters, to join hands and give me devoted service in unity.

After she finished these words, I cried aloud and offered a prayer of thanksgiving for preparing the site for the Basilica of Mary's Ark of Salvation. My helpers also cried together with me and offered a prayer of thanksgiving.

November 26, 1991

At about 10 a.m., severe pains started and I could hardly move myself or open my eyes, but we went to the mountain that the Blessed Mother showed me during a vision *(the same mountain we went to yesterday)*.

On the way there, I kept my eyes closed because of pains, but suddenly felt that it became bright with yellow and gold in front of us. When I opened my eyes, there was a miracle of the sun. It was about 4 p.m. We could see the sun without straining our eyes. The sun became like the Host and was spinning, surrounded by red, blue, yellow, gold and purple colors. These colors looked like flames around the Host. Also, there were balls of gold-colored light formed on the mountain and floating up toward the sky again and again. We were watching all this cheering with joy and praising and giving thanks to the Lord. My pains eased somewhat after watching the miracle of the sun and I could climb the mountain without much difficulty. We had to go through some thorny bushes, but could easily find the valley which I had seen in the vision. I was shedding tears with joy. At that moment, I heard the warm and kind voice of the Blessed Mother.

THE BLESSED MOTHER:

Dig a spring here so that children from all over the world may drink from it. I will call the children from all over the world to wash away the dirt from their souls and bodies. Because I do not want even one soul to be condemned and go to hell, I will invite all to come and drink from the Miraculous Spring of Mary's Ark of Salvation in order to convert even the most evil sinners. Make haste. While the world is rushing into moral decay, all the children of the world will soon know that I am the Mediatrix of Graces.

I began crying aloud, as I got the answer from Mother which I had been awaiting for a long time. We drank the water from the spring on the mountain. At that moment, all my pains were gone and I felt as if I could fly. We gave glory to the Lord and sang praises to Him. A while later, we began climbing down the mountain filled with joy, even though it was already very dark.

November 28, 1991

At the Blessed Mother's call, I left Naju with my helpers at about 10:30 a.m. First, we arrived at the location of the Miraculous Spring of Mary's Ark of Salvation and prayed there. Then, we went to the site for the Basilica. As promised, the Blessed Mother showed the miracle of the sun from 3 p.m. The Mass started at 3:15 p.m. and the miracle continued throughout the Mass, with the sun looking like the Host and spinning and shedding light upon us. At the time of the consecration of the bread and wine, the light from the sun was reaching us. After receiving Holy Communion, I received a strong light and entered an ecstasy.

In a vision, I heard many screams. I was astonished, when I looked in the direction of the screams,. So many people were struggling in a swamp-like place. Then, there appeared a large ship with the Blessed Mother on board. She was wearing a blue mantle and holding a rosary. As people were swarming and struggling around the ship, the Blessed Mother rescued them one by one. As soon as they came aboard, they became clean! The flag on the ship said "Mary's Ark of Salvation." While we were watching all this, the Blessed Mother looked at us and called us.

THE BLESSED MOTHER:

Hurry up! Come and help. I chose you from the dangerous storms of the world, because I needed your help.

Immediately, we got on board the ship and began rescuing people together with the Blessed Mother.

THE BLESSED MOTHER:

Oh, my beloved children! Thank you. Now that you are holding my hands, you will get to Heaven with Faith, Hope and Love. Let's hurry and begin our work. The beginning is important. Once begun, there will be difficulties, too, but the Lord will protect you from the beginning to the end. Humility, love and consecration are the foundation for all good works. Begin more humbly.

If you believe that good seeds will bear fruit hundredfold and work entrusting everything to my Immaculate Heart, the Basilica of Mary's Ark of Salvation will be built. You must really hurry. This is because we need to turn even one more soul, who is falling into wars, greed, and selfishness, away from the way of hell to the just way of God. If you follow me with complete trust in me, you will have the key to my Immaculate Heart.

Follow my words quickly. I cannot wait any longer. You will see the flames of my Immaculate Heart blinding Satan and performing miracles of love in union with you, who have been called, just as the Lord turned water into wine at the wedding in Cana.

Now, I will ask the Lord to give you a miraculous spring here so that I may wash your soul and body. Soon this place will become a kingdom of love and a place of salvation under the combination of the Sacred Heart of Jesus and my Immaculate Heart, an equivalent of which will be hard to find anywhere else in the world. Soon there will be continuous rays of light coming from the Sacred Heart of Jesus and my Immaculate Heart here. People will smell the fragrance of roses and drink the water of eternal life from the Miraculous Spring. I will let all stay in my love.

But however eagerly I may call you, it will be of no use, if you do not respond, as the Lord gave you free will. The beloved children who respond to the Lord's call will enjoy eternal heavenly happiness and will be given a beautiful garment of Sanctifying Grace. Stay awake and pray, following the Lord Who offered the most noble sacrifices for us. Those who are walking proudly will soon bow their heads and become more respectful, following your example.

December 5, 1991

The Blessed Mother wanted a Mass at the site for the Basilica at noon today. Ten people went to the mountain, but we were all looking at the miracle of the sun from noon and began the Mass fifteen minutes late.

The sun was radiating many colors upon us and upon the site for the Basilica. The sun turned into an image of the Host and was spinning with many colors around it: red, blue, purple, yellow, orange, light green, violet, and so on. Then, there was a column of strong light emitting different colors and connecting Heaven and earth.

After the priest's blessing, the Blessed Mother, holding the Baby Jesus, appeared near the sun. It was so amazing, because it looked as if the column of light connecting heaven and earth were erected there by the hands of the Baby Jesus and the Blessed Mother. At that moment, there was the kind and soft voice of the Blessed Mother from the sky.

THE BLESSED MOTHER:

My beloved little souls! The sun is light. The Lord Who came as Light is shedding light on you by opening Heaven. These signs from Heaven signify the Mystery of Salvation. They also mean that the Lord is with you and is blessing you and this land. It means that my victory is being accomplished in you, who obey me in a simple way, on this land of love illuminated by the Lord's Light according to God's Will. This way, the darkness of evil permeated with errors, with selfishness that prevents your self-renunciation, with passions and with all kinds of sins and uncleanness will be driven out.

My dear children! The glorious day of victory for my Son Jesus is approaching in the midst of the Sacred Love of Mercy. For this reason, the heavenly light will become brighter day by day through you who have responded to me. Trust me completely and unite with each other to save the world.

The light continued radiating upon us, even after the Blessed Mother ended her words. The miracle continued until sunset. *"Lord! Glory, praise and thanksgiving to You!"*

The Blessed Mother wept for the last time through her statue in Naju on January 14, 1992. Since June 30, 1985, she wept for a total of exactly 700 days.

February 11, 1992
—Feast of Our Lady of Lourdes

There was a message from the Blessed Mother after the evening Mass in the Sacramento Church in Manila. I had arrived there on February 7 to spread the Blessed Mother's messages in the Philippines. The Mass was celebrated by the Pastor in a most fervent way. I received Holy Communion and began meditation. At that time, I smelled a strong fragrance of roses and incense and heard a kind, loving and soft voice of the Blessed Mother from Heaven.

THE BLESSED MOTHER:

Achieve unity in love among all of you.

I looked in the direction of her voice, but could not see her.

Julia: *Yes, Mother! We are children of one God and one Mother. We speak different languages, but surely are brothers and sisters loving each other. We are now close brethren.*

THE BLESSED MOTHER:

Yes. You have become brethren through the Lord's Precious Blood. I, your Heavenly Mother, will always be with you to help you love one another more deeply like dry land thirsting for rain. Do not worry about results, but follow me like a child. Then, I will embrace each one of you in my Immaculate Heart and bless you by pouring down fragrant oil of love upon you.

The Blessed Mother ended her words and it became quiet. People said that there had been the fragrance of roses in the church since that morning.

Julia visiting Cardinal Sinn in Manila. (February 1992)

Julia: *Mother of Love who is everywhere in the world! I pray that the Lord's Kingdom will come and the triumph of your Immaculate Heart will be achieved soon.*

May 27, 1992
—In the Holy Land

While I was doing the Stations of the Cross at the Via Dolorosa in Jerusalem carrying a cross, my heart was aching so much as if it were about to burst.

Jesus was suffering not only because of the weight of the Cross, but because of the pains and exhaustion from so many scourgings and the crown of thorns. When He fell, He had to stand up again for the conversion of sinners. He carried the Cross to the end in love, shedding blood and sweat.

Jesus loved us so much that He became our Food and stays with us even at this time.

Julia and her husband, Julio, renewing their marriage vows in the Church in Cana, Israel. An unexpected image of the Holy Eucharist appeared on this photograph. (May 24, 1992)

I was carrying the cross in order to comfort Jesus even a little. My face was covered with sweat and tears. I wept so much that I did not know which Station we were at. Someone gave me Kleenex tissues and I wiped my face with them. Suddenly, my husband and others shouted, *"It's blood!"* and began crying. When I looked at the tissues, there was blood.

Somebody gave me a handkerchief, with which I wiped my face again. There was blood on the handkerchief, too. I asked others if they could see any blood on my face. They said they only saw sweat and tears. The blood marks on the handkerchief were spreading like tree branches. It was the Sixth Station *(where Veronica wiped the Face of Jesus with a cloth)*. When we reached the Twelfth Station, I heard the voice of Jesus.

JESUS:

My beloved children! I am Love. Didn't I give you all of Me? If you know that I am shedding blood, sweat and bloody tears for you even at this moment, wipe away my blood and sweat with your life. Your life should be one of conversion. There was Judas, too, who insulted Me. But, like Mary Magdalene, all of you must convert and walk toward Me holding the hands of Mary, My Mother, tightly in this dangerous world.

When Jesus finished His words, I noticed that my side was swollen a lot, which others could see, too. There also were bruises all over my body.

Glory and praise to the Lord! Amen. Alleluia.

May 31, 1992
—Feast of Our Lord's Ascension in Korea; In Lourdes, France

Together with the Korean and Filipino pilgrims who accompanied me on the trip, I attended Mass, which was celebrated by Father Jerry Orbos from the Philippines at 3 p.m. in a small chapel at the Cathedral in Lourdes. While I was in meditation after receiving Holy Communion, I heard the loving, kind, and yet sorrowful voice of the Blessed Mother.

THE BLESSED MOTHER:

Daughter! Look at those numerous children. The children who try to wipe away tears that flow from my merciful eyes in order to soften the just anger of God are so few. Tears cannot dry in my eyes, because so many compromise with their selfishness and not with the holy heavenly matters.

That is why I called all of you specially, asking for your prayers and reparation for the conversion of sinners. If you unite with each other in love and follow me, you will become a large net of love. The Lord will use you as a net that catches people and, thus, will accomplish salvation.

My beloved daughter! Spread my messages of love courageously in all the corners of the world. You will experience many difficulties, but do not forget that I am with you always. Offer up sacrifices and reparations without ceasing for the sake of my poor children. Your pains that cause bleeding inside of you will certainly not be fruitless. Annyoung!

June 1, 1992
—*In Rome*

I could not even stand up today because of severe pains since yesterday. They were pains of pregnancy, pains that paralyzed one side of my whole body and pains that made me unable to lift or turn my head. I offered up these pains for the conversion of sinners.

The Mass had been scheduled in a church, so, I thought I would not be able to go to Mass today. But I had a strong desire to attend Mass and thought, *"How wonderful it would be, if Mass could be celebrated in the hotel."* What a surprise! Someone told me that Mass would be celebrated in the hotel.

So, I attended the Mass, supported by others. When I received Holy Communion, I smelled blood. My husband, Julio, the priest and others saw the Host bleeding in my mouth. I heard the gentle and merciful voice of Jesus at that time.

JESUS:

Do not worry, but follow Me with complete trust in Me. I will be with you all as I am with you now wherever you may be. When you come to Me always through Mary, My Mother, you will receive the light of blessing.

When Jesus finished speaking, all the pains in my body were gone. Everyone was clapping hands in joy and praised the Lord.

June 2, 1992
—In Lanciano, Italy

We attended Mass in the church in Lanciano, where a miracle of the Blessed Sacrament had occurred during a Mass about 1,300 years ago. The Host changed to heart muscles and the Blood of Jesus in the Chalice in the form of wine also changed to the form of human blood. They are being preserved in that church.

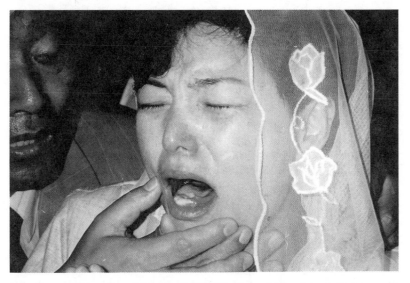

The Sacred Host turned into visible Flesh and Blood in Julia's mouth in the Church of St. Francis in Lanciano, Italy. (June 2, 1992)

Father Jerry Orbos (center) introduces Julia and Julio Kim to the Holy Father. (June 3, 1992)

When Father Orbos consecrated bread and wine and lifted them up to God the Father, there was light pouring down upon him and, then, upon me and everyone else attending the Mass. I prayed after receiving the Eucharist.

"Too many people are committing sins with their tongues, causing wounds to each other. Give special blessings on their tongues so that they may praise the Lord. . . ."

Then, I swallowed the Host. But a tiny piece of the Host remained on my tongue and was becoming larger. I was so surprised that I showed it to my husband, Julio. Other people also came and saw the small piece of the Host growing bigger and becoming bloody. They were crying loudly. At that moment, there was the warm but stern voice of Jesus from heaven.

JESUS:

I am Light. I am the Light of Love that chases away all the darkness. I intend to let all of you receive my Light of Love and, thus, to repel the darkness from this world that is turning into a vast desert.

December 8, 1992

—Feast of Our Lady's Immaculate Conception; Fifth anniversary of moving her statue to the Chapel

We were praying the rosary during the overnight prayer service. During the Fifth Decade of the Joyful Mysteries, it suddenly became bright around the Blessed Mother's statue. The statue turned into the living, beautiful Blessed Mother. The time was about 11 p.m.

A while later, I entered an ecstasy and saw the Blessed Mother shedding tears and tears of blood. At that moment, I began hearing the kind, loving and yet solemn voice of Jesus, although I was not able to see Him.

JESUS:

My beloved children! Today is the Feast commemorating My Mother Mary's Immaculate Conception in preparation for My Incarnation into this world. It was part of My Father's plan of salvation. But, as I said before, if she did not say, *"I am the servant of the Lord. Let it be done to me as you say,"* My Father could not have done anything about it, as He gave her a free will. Therefore, all of you must also say a humble *"Yes"* following the example of My Mother Mary.

Admitting your sins in a simple and humble way and in obedience, aspire ever more strongly for the little person's way of Love, loving and trusting My Mother. Then, your attachment to pleasures, reputation, social status, power, material goods, pride and face-saving will be replaced by heroic deeds.

Do not lay down your cross, even when it feels too heavy. If you lay it down, evil will enter your heart right away and take control of it with an explosion of passions. Wake up in a hurry and pray.

Too many of My children loiter outside the door and are unable to meet Me, because they do not accept My Mother's messages of love while insisting upon their own way of faith that they have received and are giving to others.

Fragrant oil began flowing from the Blessed Mother's forehead on November 24, 1992, and continued for 700 consecutive days until October 23, 1994. She said that the oil and the fragrance represent her presence and her love and friendship for us.

My dear children! Listen well. Keep in mind that My Mother only leads you to a life of intense love inside My noble Heart. Come to Me hurriedly through My Mother, who is the short-cut to Me.

My Heart suffers intensely, because she receives so much pain for you and calls you again and again to spread My Love even until her throat begins to bleed, but she is not respected by her children in the world even on this great Feast of hers. Wipe away her tears of blood in a hurry with your life, consoling her with love and respecting her.

My Mother prepares a safe refuge in her Immaculate Heart for all of you and leads you to Me. The hour of the pains and chastisement of Gethsemane and Calvary is approaching the children of the world. But the gate to Heaven will open through the prayers, graceful consecrations and bloody efforts by you, My little children. Do not fear. Entrust everything to Me with faith and trust. I will be with you always.

When Jesus finished these words, the light disappeared and the live Blessed Mother turned back into the statue. During the prayer service, oil continued flowing from the statue. The fragrance from the oil filled the Chapel.

December 14, 1992
—Feast of St. John of the Cross, Priest and Doctor

From 6:30 p.m., I relayed the Blessed Mother's messages to those who gathered in the Greenbelt Church in Manila, the Philippines. In the middle of the prayers, there was a bright light from above. When I looked, I saw it coming from a picture of Jesus, Who was opening His arms. The light was radiating like sunlight and shone upon all those who were in the church. At that moment, the Blessed Mother appeared near the Crucifix, smiling warmly and wearing a white dress and a blue mantle. When she opened her arms, a strong fragrance of roses filled the church. The Blessed Mother spoke in a very friendly and gentle manner.

THE BLESSED MOTHER:

My beloved children! Come to me in a hurry and entrust yourselves to me completely with faith and trust. I, your Heavenly Mother, will be with you always.

I am Mother to all of you. Come closer to me, overcoming different nationalities and national borders. When you believe my words and follow me totally, my protection and love will be with you and great blessings by God will be bestowed upon you.

Then, the Blessed Mother dropped some roses on us. Almost all the people present there, except some who were closing their eyes, saw the light and the Blessed Mother. Even those with closed eyes testified that they felt the light and the presence of the Blessed Mother. Some people picked up fresh rose petals.

January 23, 1993
—New Year's Day (Lunar Calendar)

I had much pain, but went to the Chapel to pray before the Blessed Mother's statue and to offer New Year's Day greetings to Jesus and the Blessed Mother. I offered my greetings in union with the loving hearts of the Holy Father, Bishops, priests, religious and all the helpers in the world for the Blessed Mother in Naju. Suddenly, it became bright around the statue and the statue turned into the beautiful, living Blessed Mother. She spoke with a warm, friendly and yet anxious voice.

THE BLESSED MOTHER:

My beloved daughter! Thank you for your loving heart and offerings. I bless all of you. I want you all to stay in my peace and become instruments of peace among all your neighbors.

How numerous are false prophets these days! They have fallen into the devil's deception and are spreading all kinds of untrue information as messages from me. That way, they are confusing my children and promoting disorder to neutralize and dilute my messages. This causes me much pain. You are also being persecuted and criticized with so many preposterous accusations. Despite such misunderstanding, have no fear, but follow me, entrusting everything to me.

Daughter! I am always with you. Why are you so worried? The devil is so violent that he is even mobilizing some of my priests in driving my messages into a whirlpool of confusion. For this reason, a terrible danger is pressing down upon the world, and the hour of apostasy and betrayal is drawing near. The degradation of the human race is worsening every day and the world is standing on the edge of a cliff. Humans are bringing about their own destruction.

Because they are not following the Lord's Words and my messages of love, many chastising warnings are falling upon them: earthquakes, floods, droughts, traffic accidents, fires, hunger, disease, major destructions, many kinds of ecological disasters, abnormal climates. . . . Even so, they do not wake up, making my Heart burn and burn so much that I shed tears of blood.

Daughter! Let's pray more fervently for the human race which is bringing about its own destruction and for the Church and the Pope. The whole human race must convert in a hurry, before it cries out in fear.

There will be persecutions, as the Church gets wounded and divided, but offer up this hour of death agony well. I want all of you to stay in warm kindness to each other and in prayers of deep silence.

Respect the dignity of humans and practice true love by helping those who have nothing instead of helping the lofty, and by finding and giving love to those who are poor, hungry and sick and becoming their friends. Prepare a place where you can welcome those who wander around and suffer; give clothes to those who have no clothes; give a warm and merciful parental care to the handicapped; and give comfort to those who have been hurt.

Your inner suffering and bleeding is severe, but follow me, remembering that the Lord of Love is preparing a place of sacred joy and satisfaction for you in the Heavenly Garden. I will always be at your side and encourage and help you. So, do not lose hope, but entrust everything to me. Good bye! An-nyoung!

When the Blessed Mother finished speaking, the light disappeared, too. Her appearance returned to that of the statue, but the fragrant oil streamed down the statue. The fragrant oil had been flowing since November 24, 1992.

May the fragrant oil that Mother gives us wash away dirt from the whole world and make it clean!

January 26, 1993

At about 5 p.m., I was in deep meditation about the Holy Father under the Crucifix in my room. A while later, I was startled at hot air suddenly blowing at me. My body became hot and was sweating very much. At that moment, the room became filled with the fragrance of roses. I was wondering if the Blessed Mother was coming. But there was the warm voice of Jesus! It was a voice overflowing with a warm, merciful Love.

JESUS:

Daughter! I feel the love of a little soul in your heart, as you think you are poor, unworthy and weak. That is why I have entrusted the work to you. So, do not worry too much.

My little soul! I will embrace you in My Heart of burning Love, as you cry out for having nothing but your shamefulness and for being so unworthy and unqualified.

Who can save this world where the devils are spreading so many errors and sins? I can. Then, who am I? I am Power

to the little and weak and the King of Love. Can you understand this?

My beloved little soul! I do not forsake your praying heart.
Didn't I guide Peter's small boat to safety? Do not place
your trust in human power in accomplishing anything. You
will suffer much amidst numerous hidden rocks and enemies' traps, but will achieve the final victory in My burning Sacred Heart.

When you feel humble and weak, you resemble My Mother.
Now, pray harder for the Pope. He always stands alone on
Calvary, tired and lonesome. He is My Father's beloved
son, Peter's successor and my Vicar whom I have chosen.
My enemies are becoming more active by employing all the
available means to topple him. All of you must display the
power of love by following him and uniting with him in
prayer and loyalty and sharing his cross, as the devil is
planning violent attacks on him by deceiving humans in
cunning ways through those who are close to them and,
thereby, making them disobey the Pope, who is the shep-
herd of the whole world.

If you live according to the Father's Will, live a life based on
the Gospels, and put My Mother Mary's messages of love
into practice, My beloved Vicar, the Pope, chosen from the
whole world, will be safe and peace will come to the world.
Listen to My Words and keep them in your hearts. If you
refuse to live a life based on the Gospels and reject the
messages of love that My Mother gives you so anxiously
imploring with tears of blood, this desert-like world will
experience a crisis.

It is not too late yet. Come to My Bosom of Love in a hurry.
Didn't My Mother Mary also remind you that if you repent
hurriedly and come back to me saying *"Yes,"* I will not question your past, but will embrace you in My Sacred Heart
burning with Love and will bless you in the Name of the
Father, the Son and the Holy Spirit?

February 6, 1993

I had much pain today, but went to the Chapel to attend the over-night prayer service in observance of the First Saturday. At about 10:30 p.m., we began praying the rosary. When we reached the Fifth Joyful Mystery, it became bright around the Blessed Mother's statue and I heard a baby sucking its mother's breast. Even though I could not see the scene, it was evident that the Blessed Mother was feeding a certain soul spiritual milk. This sound continued until the end of the rosary prayer. When the prayer was over, the Blessed Mother's face looked very wet with tears. She began speaking with an anxious and sorrowful voice.

THE BLESSED MOTHER:

My dear children! There are many children who observe First Saturdays and yet do not know the reason for doing so. Therefore, I want to tell you today the reason for observing First Saturdays.

It was a day of cruel suffering for me—a long, long day when I was left alone, having lost my Son Jesus. I always had sufferings from the day I conceived Jesus my Son, but, on that Holy Saturday, I expressed sorrows externally for the first time and cried so miserably all night praying for my Son Jesus and for sinners. Those painful hours were also the time for transition from my Son's Death to His Resurrection, a day for going from death to life. This is the reason that I asked you to pray with me tonight.

Didn't the Lord say, *"Come to Me, all who are weary and find life burdensome, and I will refresh you?"* I will help you so that each one of you may find rest in the Holy Spirit and live in the Mystery of the Passover, singing the Lord's Passover with me, who is the Mother of Passion and Agony and the Mother who entered the glory of her Son's Resurrection.

This Mother, who loves you all and loves especially those children who pray with me on First Saturdays, will stay with you always, as I was with the Apostles, praying with them in the Cenacle in Jerusalem, and will feed you my spiritual milk of love. Those of my children who accept me and drink the spiritual milk will receive the grace of repentance and will find peace and a great comfort in my love, and, thus, will be able to withstand any difficulties.

If you continue observing First Saturdays well and put what I have requested of you into practice, this Mother, who is the Mediatrix, will acquire all the graces for you that you ask for, will give you a special protection and the grace needed for eternal salvation at the time of your death, take you to the Heavenly Harbor in Mary's Ark of Salvation and offer you to the Lord.

So, on First Saturdays, unite with the Lord by making a sincere Confession, attending Holy Mass and receiving Holy Communion; approach the Sacred Bible and contemplate on the Gospels; with love, do reparations for the betrayals that have hurt the Lord's Heart; consecrate yourselves to my Immaculate Heart; pray the rosary sincerely and fervently, meditating on its Mysteries; accept everything with complete trust, humility and meekness; and live as a little person in my burning Immaculate Heart.

My beloved children! Believe like a child my words that I give you through my little soul who thinks that she is the poorest and least qualified in the world. I give these words to all of you.

There has never been another time when the world was so filled with Satan's temptations and with sins, and afflicted so much pain on the Lord's Heart as now. Look! Even at this moment, people are dying because of droughts, earthquakes and volcanic eruptions. In so many other ways, numerous people are dying.

As nobody knows the time of the Lord's Coming, no one knows when God will take your soul. Therefore, stay awake with love, praying with me. If you accept the Lord's Words and me well, you will see even greater miracles in my garden and enjoy eternal life in the Lord's Kingdom of Love.

February 18, 1993

At about 11 p.m., near the end of the Holy Hours prayer meeting *(held every Thursday evening in the Chapel)*, I fell down on the floor because of a sudden bright light pouring down from above. With the light, the Blessed Mother appeared as the beautiful Mother of Mercy. She was wearing a white dress and a blue mantle and was holding a rosary in her left hand. With her right hand, she touched everyone in the prayer meeting. Her beauty was beyond human description. After touching everyone, she began speaking with a friendly and yet anxious voice.

THE BLESSED MOTHER:

My beloved children! Thank you for responding joyfully to my call. Do not be concerned about how many of you are gathered here. What is important is that you become sanctified in the Lord and offer up your prayers with a sincere heart. I came down from Heaven as the Queen of the Universe enwrapped in a brilliant immaculate light in order to nurture you.

Become children. Know clearly that Satan leads you to judge with your own ideas and behave as adults, feeling self-confident, and, thus, makes you fall into a trap. You must gain Heaven by offering yourselves up with a child's heart.

I will be with you every time you gather together to observe the Holy Hours so that your prayers and sacrifices may be united with mine and offered to the Lord. You must combine your little devotions and offer them up together with mine so that they may soothe the Lord's Wounds.

A multitude of souls are moving farther away from God and rushing toward perdition, and the whole human race is faced with an unprecedented danger to their lives and freedom. My Son Jesus is looking down at this poor humanity, lamenting over the sinners' indifference and betrayals, and aspiring that all of you would offer the Holy Hours devotion sincerely as sacrifices and penance.

The Holy Hours prayers that you offer compensate for the indifference, sacrileges and insults committed against the Sacred Body and Blood of Christ, Who loved the whole human race so much that He became their Food. These prayers console the pains of death He experienced at Gethsemane and the sorrows He felt because of His disciples' desertion. They also make up for numerous children's sins of violating God's Sacred Dignity and for their ingratitude and betrayals.

The prayers, sacrifices and devotions offered for the conversion of sinners during the Holy Hours become reparations for their sins and sacrificial offerings to God's Justice. This will soften God the Father's just anger. For this reason, the Lord is pleased to accept the reparations and devotions offered during the Holy Hours. The Lord promised a plenary indulgence to those souls who make a sincere Confession, receive Holy Communion, and observe the Holy Hours well, by pouring down His Spirit into them and bathing them in His Sacred Blood. This promise will surely be kept.

My children, whom I love so dearly! Do not try to calculate the outcome in human ways and out of curiosity. You must know that the Lord's ways are so different from human ways. Do not view anything with human eyes or think in human ways, but keep and follow the Lord's Laws faithfully. The new light of grace will be bestowed, and a Resurrection and Pentecost filled with joy will come down upon all the souls who pray in the Lord's name and observe the Holy Hours before the great storm begins, wherever they may be in the world.

After finishing these words, the Blessed Mother became invisible and the light also disappeared.

April 8, 1993
—Holy Thursday

At about 7:40 a.m., I felt the Blessed Mother's call and went to the Chapel. The fragrant oil continued flowing on her statue. Her expression was particularly beautiful today. As the area around the statue became bright, the Blessed Mother began speaking through her statue.

THE BLESSED MOTHER:

My children, whom I love so intensely! Today is the day for priests whom I love most. Pray for them. It is a blessed day when my Son Jesus offered all of Himself and made a covenant by establishing the Sacraments of the Holy Eucharist and Holy Orders. It is a day when priests received the precious task of baptizing you, forgiving your sins through the Sacrament of Confession, teaching you the Gospels, celebrating the Holy Sacrifice of the Mass and, in doing so, renewing the Sacrifice on Mt. Calvary and ministering graces through the Sacraments instituted by Jesus. Also, Bishops bless oil today.

What is the Last Supper? It is a feast of love and sharing. In order to give the totality of my love, which is so high, deep and wide, to my beloved Pope, Cardinals, Bishops, priests, religious and all my children in the world together with my Son Jesus, I am squeezing all of myself and giving you fragrance and oil. The fragrance and oil that I give to all are gifts from God. They represent my presence, love and friendship for you.

If a grain of wheat falls to the ground and dies, it produces much fruit. But if it does not die, it remains just a grain of wheat. Salvation came to this world, only because there was the painful Sacrifice of Calvary by my Son Jesus. Repent hurriedly and become a floral crown of joy for Him.

I make a special request to all priests. Imitate Jesus, the Teacher, Who sacrificed all of Himself, and give all the chil-

In April 1993, images of the Holy Eucharist appeared many times in the Blessed Mother's hands in the photographs and videos taken in the Chapel.

dren in the world the Love He showed to the disciples at the Last Supper. Do not look to the world, but to Jesus Who suffered the agony of death on the Cross. Then, you will become faithful priests.

All the children in the world! As John did together with me, all of you must stand at the foot of the Cross with all your love, meditaing on those hours when Jesus offered sacrifices. You must help priests so that they may carry their heavy crosses well. Do not fear the world, even if it does not understand or accept you when you try to practice justice. My burning Immaculate Heart will always be your home and your refuge.

April 14, 1993

At about 7:20 a.m., I went to the Chapel in response to the Blessed Mother's call. She spoke with a warm and kind voice from her statue.

THE BLESSED MOTHER:

My dear daughter! Today I will give you a special sign for my beloved priests who have responded to my call.

My little soul! . . . I am Mother to all of you and the Queen of Heaven. I have called many priests in order to save the souls who are wandering in darkness. But they have neglected me and distanced me because of the eyes of the world and face-saving. . . .

My beloved priests! Get closer together and hold each other's hands hurriedly. And achieve unity in total love. The devil will cause more confusion employing many different methods, but do not fall into his cunning schemes and stop spreading the messages. If you do not help me, I cannot do anything, either. Hurry up and bring those numerous sheep, which have been lost and are wandering, to the refuge of my Immaculate Heart. I need you, because I want to save all the children through you.

What will be the use of regretting at the time of chastisement? Now is the designated hour for you and the time to enter the battle. Do not worry about tomorrow or be concerned about the future in human ways. The place that I have prepared for you, the irreplaceable place for you. . . It is the great task that the love of my Immaculate Heart has chosen for you. I want you to understand this and to respond to my call without reservations. When you humbly walk a little person's way of love toward holy virtues according to my wishes and follow me in obedience, the Lord's miracles of love will be wrought through you.

Now the plans of my Immaculate Heart are about to be realized. Therefore, help the little, unworthy soul *(Julia)* whom I have chosen and spread my wishes to the whole world so that they may be put into practice. When the messages of love that my Son Jesus and I give you are realized in this world, the greatest victory of establishing the glorious Kingdom of Christ will be won and you will see the glory by my side.

When her words ended, drops of fragrant oil streamed down from the forehead of the Blessed Mother's statue. I took several photographs and also did some videotaping. Clear images of the Holy Eucharist appeared on the Blessed Mother's hands in the photographs and video.

May 27, 1993

Fr. Raymond Spies, who loves the Blessed Mother, came to Naju and was praying in front of the Blessed Mother's statue in the Chapel. I was also standing before the statue. At about 11:30 a.m., I almost fell down because of a strong light from the Immaculate Heart of Mary and knelt. At that moment, the Blessed Mother, who was shedding fragrant oil, began speaking softly with a very friendly and kind voice.

THE BLESSED MOTHER:

My beloved daughter! Why do you hesitate at this hour

when you should enter the battle? God's mercy will take root at this fertile place, which will be prepared with love, and accomplish miracles of love through you, my children. Therefore, hurriedly invite Fr. Spies and Fr. Chang, who have accepted my call, to the mountain chosen through you. Following the Will of God, Who gave you free will, I am going to make that place a shrine of mine and wash numerous souls who are walking toward hell.

Because the light was so strong, I fell down on the floor. Then, I heard some whispering sounds. There was something that I could not see clearly, but it looked like the devil. Suddenly, he began attacking me and pressing me down hard on my chest many times until it became badly bruised. It was difficult for me to breathe. Soon, the Blessed Mother appeared and the pain and tension on my chest eased. She was wearing a blue mantle as usual. She opened her arms and looked down. A bright light was surrounding her and shining upon the people below. Everyone whom I saw in the vision received the light from the Blessed Mother. Nearby, there was the stream of water that the Blessed Mother gave us. She resumed speaking with a kind voice.

THE BLESSED MOTHER:

My beloved priests! Do not forget my wish to bestow upon all of you the combined love from the Sacred Heart of Jesus and my Immaculate Heart that are burning, but follow me energetically and courageously, united in complete trust and love and with the faith that has been entrusted to you.

All the priests in the world! How corrupt and polluted this world is! Promotion of dissensions through intrigues and contradictions, sacrilegious activities, irresponsible behaviors, slanders because of jealousy, greed—the desire to possess all instead of sharing with others, corruption through avarice, and the attempt to justify all kinds of moral disorders through pride—all these are the cunning enemies that make souls decay.

Because people join forces with the devil through their pride, they, even without realizing themselves, become wolves that

wear sheepskin and plunder habitually and drive numerous sheep mercilessly into a whirlpool of confusion.

For this reason, I want to call the souls who have been
contaminated with these evils and are walking toward hell
to my bosom of love and fill all their deficiencies. When you
forsake yourselves totally and follow me trusting my words
that I give you through the little, poor soul whom I have
chosen, God of the Blessed Trinity will give His bright light
to all through you, who are His little workers, and there
will be a new Pentecost.

When Fr. Spies heard about the Blessed Mother's call and was leaving the Chapel for the mountain, a rainbow-like circle of light appeared around the sun. This light became stronger when we arrived
at the mountain. The Blessed Mother appeared in the sky above the
Miraculous Spring. She looked the same as in the vision I saw in the
Chapel. She said with a beautiful voice, "The bright light that
surrounds the sun represents my love and my presence."
Soon, she disappeared.

June 27, 1993
—Sunday celebrating the establishment of the Papacy

At the Blessed Mother's call, I went to her statue, which was exud-
ing fragrant oil, and prayed together with pilgrims. At 3 p.m., the
Blessed Mother's statue seemed to be completely wet with the fragrant oil and the area around the statue became bright. I heard her
loving and kind voice.

THE BLESSED MOTHER:

Daughter! My Son Jesus gave Peter the Keys of Heaven.
Isn't the Pope the successor of Peter? Pray and offer sacrifices for the Pope. Support and protect him. As the Vicar of
My Son Jesus, he is carrying a heavy cross. He has been
consecrated to me, loves me so much and accepts me so
well. . . . He already understands my words that I am giving to all with tears and tears of blood in Korea.

To the Pope, who is my son, whom I love without limit and whom I can put in my eyes without feeling any pain, I will give a special love and sign.

So many children in the world are mired in the secular spirit. They continue committing sins, driving more nails on the Lord, pressing down the crown of thorns harder on His Head, and, thus, making Him shed more Blood. However, the Lord does not bleed in vain, but drops His Blood into a chalice and gives It to all His children through the priests whom He has called. But how many of the children are accepting Him?

The Lord saved you through His Passion and Death on the Cross. He saved all of you with His Precious Blood, Wounds, and painful Death and is leading you to the Life of Resurrection through His Body and Blood in the Blessed Sacrament. Now all priests must teach the importance of the Holy Eucharist to all the children in the world, as they celebrate the Sacred Mass with true love and sincere participation. Thus, today I make this request to my beloved son, the Pope.

I have manifested the images of the Holy Eucharist in various ways so that all my children may understand the importance of the Holy Eucharist. Hurriedly become blazing flames of love, reparation and adoration toward the Lord Who is in the Holy Eucharist.

I will always stay close to the Pope, help him, protect him from dangers, and be with him in the Heavenly Garden. If my words are well accepted and practiced, the chastisement which is to fall upon all of you will turn into a Second Pentecost, and the Church will be renewed by the irresistible power of the Holy Spirit and Love.

When she finished speaking, the light disappeared, too. Some of the pilgrims and I took some photographs of the Blessed Mother's statue. We were amazed, because all of us present there saw the statue

In this photograph taken in the Chapel on June 27, 1993, clear images of the Sacred Host and Chalice appeared beside the Blessed Mother's statue. There also were images of a Cross and the letters "A" and "Ω".

Another photograph taken on June 27, 1993. This time, there were images of five blood marks on the Sacred Host. Small pieces of cloth were at the foot of the statue to absorb the fragrant oil exuded by the statue.

move to the left. Images of the Sacred Host and a Chalice appeared in the photographs.

May the Lord bestow His Infinite Love and Mercy on the Holy Father! Amen.

January 21, 1994

I was violently attacked by the devil for two hours from about 11:30 p.m. I could not see him clearly, but it was the black devil who said, *"We cannot let you live any longer. We are going to kill you, because you are our enemy who takes away armies from our side which we have raised with much toil."* Then, he said, *"Come quickly and beat her up!"* The devils began beating, trampling on and strangling me. While I was struggling with the devils, it was impossible for me to get away, and my whole body was stiffening. I rolled about in the small room, suffering from extreme pains in my head and chest as if they were breaking apart. Blood was flowing out of my throat and nose. I offered up the indescribably severe pains for the conversion and salvation of the numerous poor souls who have been so contaminated with sins and are rushing toward their perdition. I prayed, *"Lord! If You need my body, I entrust it to You so that it may be used according to Your Will."* At that moment, with a bright light, the Blessed Mother appeared and the devils ran away in a panic. I was totally exhausted and almost unconscious, but began feeling more comfortable when I saw the Blessed Mother.

The Blessed Mother was wearing a crown of twelve stars, a white dress and a blue mantle and was holding a rosary in her right hand. The light from her was so strong that I could not continue looking at her. She began speaking with a friendly, kind, soft and yet anxious voice.

THE BLESSED MOTHER:

My beloved daughter! Thank you. You offered the extreme pains for the conversion of sinners well. The devil afflicts you, but do not forget that I am always protecting you at your side.

My dear children! In this age, so many children are being enveloped in a huge storm, while walking toward their perdition. Now is a precious time for your repentance. Do not ignore, but accept well my earnest appeals that I send to you in many different ways, while you are in the middle of an extreme danger. Even among the children I love so dearly, only a very few respond to my call in a genuine way, saying, *"Amen."*

In this time of purification, so many children forget about the graces they have received, listen to the false testimonies concocted by Satan, are sidetracked from my way, and judge, criticize and condemn it. Because Satan is employing all the available means like false testimonies and even some supernatural phenomena, even many innocent people are being misled.

At this time when the devils are trying to conquer the whole world, I am calling you so that we can confront them together. So, I want you to offer yourselves up well. When you help my little soul who works for me, you are helping me.

My beloved children! Even if you suffer from persecutions and pains that are beyond imagination, I will help you at your side by amazing methods and will carry through my plan to the end and accomplish it. The devil will afflict you with violent and persistent attacks, but I am protecting you at your side from the devil in an invisible way to accomplish my plan. I will protect you; so, stay awake. When you confront the devil and lead many souls to my Immaculate Heart, you are leading them to my Son Jesus. This will become the most beautiful floral crown of glory in my Immaculate Heart.

Children! I chose you for my plan. Therefore, carry out your mission in obedience and as a martyr. The time has come when you must accomplish your mission.

Remember the Apostles, because you are like them who were gathered in the cenacle before they carried out their mission until martyrdom. Do not imitate Judas. Both Peter and Judas were the Lord's Apostles. But Judas went the way of perdition, because he betrayed the Lord and did not repent. Peter denied the Lord three times, but repented with tears, earning Heaven after testifying for the Truth, following the footsteps of the Lord.

In this dangerous age, so corrupt with many kinds of sins and permeated with errors, you must spread my messages of love courageously to the entire world. Console me by combining your strengths and achieving a closer unity in love among all of you and with your spiritual directors.

In this age when numerous children are mired in errors and being swept away by the tides of evil without even knowing it, hurriedly bring the herds of sheep, which have been trampled upon and scattered around, to my side. I will guide them to my Son Jesus. However heinous their sins may have been, my Son Jesus will become a wonder medicine of balsam for all their wounds that have been caused by hatred, anger and sins and will save them, if they open their hearts widely and rush to Him.

Courageously and hurriedly spread my messages of love to the whole world so that all my children may respond to the words I give them shedding tears and tears of blood and that they may repent. If you accept my words without reservation and follow Jesus Christ in this world which is becoming more and more miserable, you will experience my presence filled with motherly love in this age of danger-ous trials; this world will become purified resulting in the softening of God's just anger; the victory of my Immaculate Heart will certainly be achieved, bringing the Lord's King-dom into this world; and you, who are working for me, will surely stand by my side. Good-bye!

The Blessed Mother made the Sign of the Cross after finishing these words. She disappeared, as I was also making the Sign of the Cross. When I woke up from the ecstasy, my helpers were weeping at my side. It was about 3:30 a.m. on January 22, 1994.

February 3, 1994

At about 2:30 p.m. in my room, I began feeling severe pains in my whole body from the head to the toes. Offering up these pains to the Lord, I entered a deep meditation on the messages that the Blessed Mother gave us recently. A while later, when I was still suffering and weeping, it suddenly became bright and an image of the Blessed Mother's weeping statue appeared above the clothes chest, where she had begun weeping in 1985. Then, the image of the Blessed Mother's statue became larger and turned into the live Blessed Mother. She stepped down from the top of the clothes chest. She was wearing a shiny crown, a white dress, and a blue mantle and was holding a rosary in her right hand. She was also wearing a blue sash around her waist. She was so beautiful. She began speaking with a warm, loving and somewhat anxious voice.

THE BLESSED MOTHER:

My most beloved daughter! Tell the children in the world that they should respond to the Lord's call in a hurry, if they want to be saved. How blind and deaf they are and how stubbornly they are refusing to follow me! I have been screaming until my throat bleeds, asking them to repent quickly before the cup of God's wrath, which is already filled, starts overflowing. But because so many children in the world are not listening to my words and are ignoring them, the cup of God's wrath is now beginning to overflow little by little.

Therefore, all the children in the world! Come hurriedly to me so that we can go to the Lord together. Do not think that the many disasters that are occurring all over the world are just random accidents. You must wake up quickly and divert God's wrath from you.

As I told you before, the natural order is now being disturbed and abnormalities are occurring frequently. Thousands and thousands of people are dying because of floods, fires, famines, earthquakes, droughts, tidal waves, traffic accidents, large-scale destructions, many kinds of environmental disasters, and unusual weather. Also, many people are dying because of wars, incurable illnesses and contagious diseases. When snow falls and cold wind blows, you know winter is beginning. When new buds sprout, you know it is spring. Then, why do you still not understand that these disasters are the signs of the beginning of great calamities? Through these many signs, you should know that the time of great calamities is close at hand. Those who suffer most in this world are the innocent babies who are being killed in their mothers' wombs. Why should there be such cruel, inhuman evils?

All the children in the world! My beloved sons and daughters! Do not bring about the chastisement of darkness, fire and blood upon you. People were eating, drinking and marrying until the very day Noah was entering the Ark. They were all swept away by the flood. If you do not listen to my voice with which I am imploring you so ardently, you will be putting yourselves in the same situation.

Depending on whether you accept my words well or reject them, the time of the Second Pentecost and Purification can be advanced or delayed. Therefore, become simple and innocent babies, listening to your Mother and rushing to her. Then, you will be saved through a new Resurrection and a new Birth, and this world will surely be saved through the Lord's Resurrection.

My beloved children! Didn't I tell you that, when the sounds of prayers by little souls are combined together and soar high into Heaven, the cup of blessing instead of chastisement will be bestowed upon you? Now, I want to combine all of your prayers, sacrifices, penance, consecration, self-denial, poverty and sufferings together, put them in the cup of my Immaculate Heart, and offer them up to God's Justice that demands reparations.

Therefore, all the children in the world! Hurry up and vigorously spread to the entire world my words which are based on love. You must not hesitate.

(You have already seen) internecine conflicts and major events that have changed the world drastically. Freemasonry is leading this cruel world to destruction and, by spreading heresies in the Church, is causing division and confusion and is promoting a major apostasy in the Church. Meanwhile, some Bishops, priests, religious and many lay people are leading sinful lives, having been trapped in the snares laid by the cunning and wicked Satan, and yet do not realize that they are in sins. They are walking toward hell, thinking that what they are doing is good and of true value. They are totally ignorant about this, because they are not awake. This is why my Heart has been burning so intensely that it is gushing out blood.

In this age, I am going through the hours of death on the Cross in Gethsemane and Calvary together with Jesus again. My little soul! You are participating in the Lord's Passion together with me. So, have no fear and be strong. And have courage.

There have already been numerous warnings, but (my children are not responding). Therefore, daughter! You need to offer up your bloody sufferings for the sake of the children in the world, meditating on the Mystery of the Passion of my Son, Jesus Christ. You have already been invited to Calvary; so, meditate on the life of Job and unite your tears, sighs, sweat and every drop of blood with the Lord's sufferings and mine and offer them up so that they may not be in vain.

My beloved daughter! My burning Immaculate Heart is being pressed down hard by extreme pains caused by the people in the world who have betrayed God and are being controlled by the wicked devil. Daughter! You are taking part in saving this world through your severe sufferings. Therefore, offer them up well. Leave all your worries and concerns to me, your Heavenly Mother. Then, I will become the mark that indicates my working within you together with Jesus.

When the Blessed Mother finished her words, she disappeared and the light was gone, too.

February 16, 1994

While I was suffering pains, I felt the Blessed Mother's call at about 8 a.m. and went to the Chapel and began praying. Soon, it became bright around the Blessed Mother's statue, and I heard the kind, gentle and beautiful voice of the Blessed Mother. There was also a strong fragrance of roses.

THE BLESSED MOTHER:

My dear little souls! Walk with me in the light of holy virtues by holding each other's hands tightly in the Love of the Lord and me. Then, you will become the light that repels all the darkness of evil and sins. Now, look at me with eyes that are not just human.

In this age, my Immaculate Heart is covered with a crown of thorns, which are so sharp and hurting. Make me known hurriedly with greater love and sacrifices. This Mother feels extreme pains in her Heart, as she looks at more and more souls who fall victim to Satan's temptations every day.

Support and give courage to my poor little soul *(Julia)* who has to suffer pains all the time and is hated so intensely by the devil, because she has to testify for the Lord. She is now offering up her pains in reparation for the sins in the world, while being pressed down hard by a crown of thorns and covered with wounds all over herself. Isn't she a piece of live flesh torn off humanity?

My dear sons and daughters! When you help her, you are helping me and consoling my Immaculate Heart. The Lord will bestow graces whenever needed. So, support her so that she may spread my messages of love all over the world courageously and completely.

She has little knowledge of this world, because it has been

taken away from her so that she may participate better in the Lord's Work of Salvation and may work in me only. She often feels helpless because of this.

When you help my little soul well and achieve unity, I will pour down fragrant balsam on you. It is a symbol of humility, faith and reliance. Do not expect to receive from each other, but give to each other.

Also, stay awake all the time. The devils fear and hate you so much now. They will try furiously to topple you with all kinds of wicked schemes, but do not forget that I am always at your side guarding and protecting you.

Become simple like a child and live a consecrated life. Then, I will breathe my spirit into you so that you may be nurtured with my life and become my sons and daughters who manifest the Heavenly Mother's presence. Also, you will receive floral crowns of glory in Heaven and enjoy eternal happiness at my side.

When the Blessed Mother ended her words, the light disappeared and more fragrant oil flowed down from the Blessed Mother's forehead, making her whole statue wet.

August 12, 1994

At about 8:20 a.m., I strongly felt the Blessed Mother's call and went to the Chapel and began praying in front of her statue. Soon, I saw a vision. The sky was clear and bright. Then, suddenly, clouds came and blocked the sun. The whole sky was rapidly being covered with clouds turning the world into a darkness. I began screaming with a choked voice:

We are going to perish, unless we repent. Hurry up! Let us repent, amend our lives, pray properly and follow the Lord through the Blessed Mother!

Then, many people came from different parts of the world and began praying together. Soon, the clouds that had been covering the whole sky disappeared, and Our Lady of Victory appeared, radiating a bright light of beautiful colors. This light from the Blessed Mother was so strong that it was reaching and warming the ground. On the ground, there were Fr. Raymond Spies, other priests, Sisters and many lay people. A while later, I saw them walking into the Blessed Mother's House *(the Chapel)* while receiving the light from the Blessed Mother. Even inside the Chapel, the light of different colors was penetrating the roof and brightly shining upon everyone. The light was especially strong upon Fr. Spies and Fr. Aloysius Chang, who were tightly holding each other's hands. At that moment, Our Lady of Victory turned into the weeping Blessed Mother and began speaking with a loving, gentle and kind voice.

THE BLESSED MOTHER:

My beloved priests! My beloved children! Listen to the loud screams from the world. So many people are rushing toward their perdition. . . . How numerous are the children who have become blind and deaf because of the darkness that is spreading all over the world!

Severe typhoons were prevented, as I anxiously implored my Son Jesus to remove them in response to your prayers and little sacrifices. How can the blind and deaf people understand that this was a warning? (Note: Julia says that the Blessed Mother was referring to the two typhoons that caused severe damages in some areas in the Western Pacific and were approaching Korea in early August. To everyone's surprise, these typhoons suddenly lost strength and only brought rain to Korea, which had been suffering from a drought.)

If the children in this world do not wake up and do not accept my earnest requests, God can take away His favors from them, as He did from King Saul when he misused his free will. However, I prayed to God not to remove His Love from those who have responded to my call and are following me. So, follow me without worrying. As God did not forsake Moses, He will not abandon you.

My priests and children who have been invited to my love! As I will help you with my power that can crush the serpent, spread my messages of love to the entire world with a hundredfold increase in your courage so that the messages may be practiced in everyone's life.

God can pluck, tear down, demolish and destroy (what stands in this world), but wills to shorten this time of internal death agony by using you as His instruments chosen by me to apply fragrant oil to the wounds of those who need your help while wandering on their sinful roads in this dangerous age.

Therefore, come closer to me and help me with your united strength. How numerous are the poor children who have fallen into the devil's wicked temptations even after experiencing my love. You will be encountering many difficulties while spreading my messages of love for the purpose of helping people to follow the Lord. However, by spreading my messages, you will be following me and applying fragrant oil to the wounds of those who are crying and screaming in the middle of the swamps of sins.

So, hurry up! I will always be at your side and rescue you from dangers. Even when you are persecuted while following my words and spreading them, do not forget that a great reward is being prepared for you in Heaven.

Priests and children whom I have chosen! Today I will build you up like a well-defended castle and like iron pillars and brass walls. So, rapidly spread my messages of love to all the children so that they may live according to the messages. When my messages of love are practiced properly, I will bring back even those who have been taken away by the devil to the end of the earth and will sustain them forever. Then, you will be embraced and fondled in my Bosom of Love and will regain spiritual and physical vitality by drinking my milk.

When the Blessed Mother ended her words, she smiled beautifully and then disappeared.

August 15, 1994

While attending Mass from 10 a.m. at the Naju Parish Church celebrating the Feast of Our Lady's Assumption, I saw a vision after Communion. I was so astonished, because fireballs were falling from the sky upon people and burning them. Fr. Spies was shouting and trying to rescue people, and he was being helped by Fr. Aloysius Chang. Soon, fire was spreading and endangering the priests. Suddenly, there was a bright light from the sky, and the Blessed Mother came with her blue mantle widely stretched. She rescued the two priests, covering them with her mantle. She said to the two priests.

THE BLESSED MOTHER:

My sons who have been nurtured to become my apostles! Today I bestow upon you the light of my mercy and love. Even when darkness covers everything, you, who are following me with trust, will receive light and help from me. Even when my enemy seems victorious, I am protecting you from the devil by means of my presence, which is invisible to you, for the purpose of accomplishing my Plan.

This world, filled with sins and covered with darkness, is approaching destruction through many kinds of disasters and loss of faith. The activities of the Church also are becoming paralyzed because of the Freemasons. Many children and even the majority of the shepherds who set out to work for the Lord are not awake, see the things of this world from a human standpoint, and carry out their activities in a superficial way. How great the harms to the sheep who are following them will be! I am trying to warn you, who are responding to my call, that the moment of death is drawing near because of their apostasy and disloyalty and to ask for your help.

Send my little soul to the world so that she can spread my intentions in a hurry and correctly. I will turn my messages of love that are being spread through my little soul into fragrant oil for the wounds of the children whose souls are sick.

As I said before, I will build where Satan has destroyed, heal where Satan has hurt, and achieve victory where Satan appears to have won. This word of mine will surely be accomplished. For that purpose, I need your help so urgently.

In this age of the most extreme divisions, Satan wishes that fire fall upon this world. He is even employing the means that transcend time and space in order to destroy the world as his last attempt. Thus, his battle against me has begun already. But I will prepare an armor for you, who are my soldiers, so that you may wear it during the war and I will protect you with my shield. Therefore, follow me with a greater trust in me and fight courageously and loyally with the spirit of a martyr.

My beloved priests! My most beloved priests! You are my babies. Babies recognize their mother's voice promptly and follow her joyfully. Console this Mommy by applying the fragrant oil of love to the wounds in her sorrowful Immaculate Heart.

After she ended her words, she embraced the two priests tightly and held their hands lovingly. She smiled and disappeared.

September 24, 1994

Fr. Jerry Orbos from the Philippines celebrated Mass at the Naju Parish Church from about 11:40 a.m. About 40 pilgrims from the Philippines, 20 from the U.S.A. and 10 Koreans attended the Mass. During the Elevation of the Eucharist, I saw the merciful and smiling Jesus in the Sacred Host and felt an indescribable joy in my heart. I offered up an earnest prayer.

Oh, Lord! The King of Love, Our Savior, Who truly came to us by lowering Himself to the extent of becoming our Food in order to save us! Have mercy on Your children so that they may repent hurriedly and be able to avoid the approaching calamity of fire.

After receiving Holy Communion, I came back to the pew and began meditation. At that moment, I clearly smelled blood in my mouth and asked Rufino and Andrew sitting next to me to take a look. They were surprised and hastily informed the priest. Fr. Orbos and others gathered around me and some began crying loudly after witnessing what was happening. They saw the Sacred Host becoming yellowish brown from the edge and, then, thin blood veins appearing all over the Host. The blood was filling my mouth. After a while, Fr. Orbos told me to swallow the Host, which I did. Soon, I entered an ecstasy and saw a vision.

Numerous people were on board several large ships which were sailing in the ocean. I was in one of them. The ship I was on board was simpler than others, but had a large image of a dove at the head of the ship and, a little behind it, two banners. The banner on the right had the image of the Eucharist and a Chalice, and the other on the left had a large "M" on it. Between the two banners was Our Mother of Mercy wearing a blue mantle. She was so beautiful and filled with love. She was guiding the ship.

Other ships, on the other hand, had an image of the Red Dragon erected on board and were brightly and luxuriously decorated in different colors: red, green, yellow and so on. There were large crowds of people in those ships eating, drinking and noisily enjoying themselves. At that moment, several people in our ship looked at the people in other ships with envious eyes. Immediately, those in other ships noticed this and helped them cross over to their ships. The Blessed Mother implored them not to go, but they ignored her and left. The Blessed Mother was weeping silently and sadly.

Some time passed. A big storm was approaching and the sky was turning black. Soon, fireballs were falling from the sky. The Blessed Mother promptly stretched out her mantle and covered us. We were safe. But those in other ships were burning and screaming. They fell into the sea and drowned after some struggle. It was a terrible scene that one could not even look at with open eyes. The Blessed Mother was watching this shedding tears and with so much anxiety. She rescued several people who were approaching our ship, calling the Lord and asking for the Blessed Mother's help. They were people who had been blind and fallen into the devil's deception, but repented and sought the Lord at the last moment.

When the Blessed Mother finished rescuing them, the storm ended, and the ocean became calm. The sky became clear and blue again and a bright light was shining upon us. There were sounds of the angels singing: *Ave, Ave, Ave Maria.* . . . At that moment, the Blessed Mother began speaking to all of us with a kind and gentle voice.

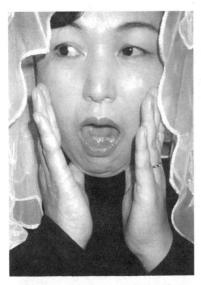

The Fifth Eucharistic Miracle to Julia on September 24, 1994

Fr. Jerry Orbos praying over Julia during the Eucharistic Miracle

Julia with pilgrims from the Philippines after Mass (September 24, 1994)

THE BLESSED MOTHER:

My most beloved children! In these end times, I called you to be my apostles and placed you in the refuge of Mary's Ark of Salvation, which I prepared for you, as a hen gathers her chicks under her wings. Keep this in mind and do not look back or get off the Ark. I clearly tell you that, in this age of purification, I love not only your soul but also your body and walk with you holding your hands on the perilous road. This place is the shortcut to Heaven where you can fully participate in the glory of my Son Jesus. I guide you all with my love so that you may become children and little souls. That is the only way my Son Jesus and I can converse with you and live together.

In this time of purification, numerous children on vast continents join hands with the devil, think and speak with an adult's mind, mobilize all the human knowledge and wisdom and, as a result, make wrong judgments and behave accordingly. Because of this, they loiter around outside the Sacred Heart of Jesus and my Immaculate Heart and do not understand the words of their Heavenly Mother. This gives me much pain in my Heart.

These days the tricks of the devil are so deceptive and sometimes even involve supernatural phenomena. For this reason, even good souls and many shepherds are being misled taking many sheep to calamity and perdition. I ask you, whom I have called, to spread my messages of love to them and, thus, wake them up so that they may truly understand the Lord, as they are now blind and deaf spiritually and are inviting their own chastisement and walking toward their perdition. My Son Jesus spread the Good News of Salvation saving numerous souls and performing many miracles of love during His short public life. Likewise, I have prepared you for this extremely important moment. So, help all others convert, heal their illnesses, treat their deep wounds, spread the graces, peace and love, and forgive them regardless of their offenses.

If all my children in this world transcend national bound-
aries, racial barriers and factional differences, form a unity
and harmony with each other, and display the power of
love, the Church will be revitalized, a shining new Pentecost will be realized, and this world will be saved through
the Lord, Who is present in the Eucharist.

Martin Luther tried the Reformation, but he, too, was a
beloved son of mine just like yourselves. Humans can make
mistakes, but remember that the Lord can turn evil into
good and use even our mistakes. Therefore, do not ever
judge and criticize others in human ways. The smaller separated churches have not accepted me, but will gradually
accept me as the Mother of the Church. My beloved little
souls! As I was together with the Apostles in the cenacle in
Jerusalem, I will always be with you, who are following
me. So, spread my words of love not only to Catholics but
also to all my children in the world. You, who are spread-

Father Jerry Orbos (front, second from right) and others who witnessed
the Eucharistic Miracle on September 24, 1994.

ing the words that the Lord and I give you, may experience internal death agonies; but remember that your Heavenly Mother has prepared a refuge where you can relax forever. Continue your strenuous efforts, spreading the truth about the Lord, Who is truly present in the Eucharist.

How ardently has the Lord desired to share this Mystery of the Passover with you! My Son Jesus, Who shed His Precious Blood through the Five Wounds on the Cross for the salvation of His children in the world, is still coming to you as the Transfuser through the Blessed Sacrament, administered by priests, and will stay with you and live among you always. As I told you before, keep your hearts open widely all the time and make frequent Confessions so that you may receive the Lord with a clean heart. Meditate deeply on the Mystery of the Holy Eucharist and stay awake. Then, instead of the terrifying chastisement of blood and fire which is to fall upon this world, the Lord's infinite mercy and blessings of salvation will be bestowed upon you.

When she finished speaking, the vision ended, too.

October 23, 1994

At about 8:30 a.m., I felt the Blessed Mother's call and went to the Chapel. Her statue was smiling and looked especially beautiful. While I was in deep meditation before the statue, it suddenly became bright around the statue, and two beautiful angels appeared—one standing on the right side of Our Lady and another on the left. The statue turned into the live Blessed Mother. She began speaking in a friendly and kind manner.

THE BLESSED MOTHER:

My beloved daughter! As I shed tears and tears of blood for the conversion of sinners for 700 days, I have given you fragrant oil for 700 days until today by squeezing all of myself with all my love, for the salvation of the children in the world, after preparing and showing the fragrant oil on my head for 400 days. But how many children have returned to my bosom so far?

Daughter! I could wash myself or have angels wash me, but want you to wash me with the water that I have prepared for you. I, who am your lonesome Heavenly Mother deserted by many people, wish to receive a deep filial love, devotion and comfort from all my children.

But daughter! The world is being placed in a grave danger because of the escalating sins. In this extremely important age when the cup of God's just anger is overflowing, you must display the spirit of martyrdom and hurriedly inform all the children in the world of the wishes of this anxious Mother as the final effort to save this world. The human race is going through agonizing moments at many places around the world. Members of the same family are striking each other, nations are confronting one another, and people in the same nation are cruelly killing each other. Isn't this a time of terrible sufferings?

As the pains of labor continue at many places in the world, I will call the representative of the Pope *(the Apostolic Pro Nuncio in Korea)* through your spiritual director. I called you *(plural)*, who are experiencing spiritual and internal difficulties, to the decisive battle between me and Satan. Therefore, increase your courage and cry out loudly the messages of love from the Lord and me. I will always be with you. I am going to call him *(the Apostolic Pro Nuncio)* so that you may work with him to prevent the human race, which is living in a barren wilderness and facing a crisis, from building a second Tower of Babel and being destroyed as in the time of Sodom and Gomorrah. Hurriedly and more vigorously spread my messages of love to the entire world. Shouldn't we rescue all the people who are bringing about their own chastisement and bloodshed?

My beloved children! The hour of apostasy and betrayal in the Church is seriously approaching, due to the work of the Freemasons, but even many of the clergy and religious are spiritually blind and deaf, are not faithful to their vocations, become corrupt internally, and do not recognize my words. This Mother feels so anxious.

The Pope, who is the Vicar of my Son Jesus and the first son of the Church, is groaning under the death agony at Gethsemane at this time. His heart is being pressed down with deep sorrows, as he climbs Mt. Calvary carrying a cross of cruel pains. As he is human, he suffers from the weakening of his body and the pains and fatigue in his body. But he feels more pains and a deep loneliness, because many, who used to support him and love him dearly, are betraying him like Judas, disobeying him, blocking him and not supporting him any more. However, I am always supporting him at his side with my motherly love. Therefore, you must remain loyal to him, support and protect him, listen to his words, be united with him and pray for him continuously with a loving heart.

When all of you, who are following me, live a consecrated life, offering up your sacrifices and penance for the conversion and salvation of sinners, I will guide you all on the road that surely leads to Heaven. When you say "Yes" to my words and follow me completely, you will see a new daybreak upon a new world that has been purified.

When the Blessed Mother ended her words, the two angels, as well as the light, disappeared. The appearance of the Blessed Mother returned to that of her statue.

November 2, 1994

There was a Mass celebrated by Fr. Martin Lucia at St. Anthony's in Kailua, Hawaii. Fr. Lucia has been promoting Eucharistic devotion all over the world. During Mass, I saw an image of Jesus in the Holy Eucharist. He was nailed to the Cross and bleeding. When I received Communion, I heard the voice of Jesus, filled with dignity and love.

JESUS:

My little soul, who humbles herself constantly, thinking that she is unworthy! Today My Mother arranged your meeting with the priest who is spreading the Mystery of the Holy Eucharist so that I, Who came down from Heaven to shed Blood and become a sacrificial offering for the salvation of all the children in the world, may spread My burning Love to all of you.

As Fr. Jerry *(of the Philippines)* responded to My Mother's call, My beloved priest here has also responded to her. So, all the priests, religious and lay people who have accepted My Mother's call must unite with each other and with your spiritual director, forming a chain of love, and unceasingly spread all over the world the Mystery of the Holy Eucharist and the intentions of My Mother who is imploring you shedding tears and tears of blood to save the whole human race.

Many shepherds may appear to have faith in Me, but their souls are closed and locked and do not truly accept Me. When they celebrate Mass in a superficial way, they are closing the door to God, while opening it to the devil. Thus, the devil is causing confusion even among the shepherds and is making them become insensitive to and unaware of their sins and is making them become defenseless. Because of this, numerous children who say they are believers are treating the Eucharist carelessly. How can I work in them?

I wish to work miracles of love for all My children through the Eucharist because of My boundless Love for them, but they do not prepare themselves for receiving Me, do not realize My True Presence, insult Me with sacriligeous Communions, and, thus, neglect and betray Me. Because of this, I am deserted by numerous children and left alone in the tabernacles, waiting anxiously for them to return to Me and give love to Me.

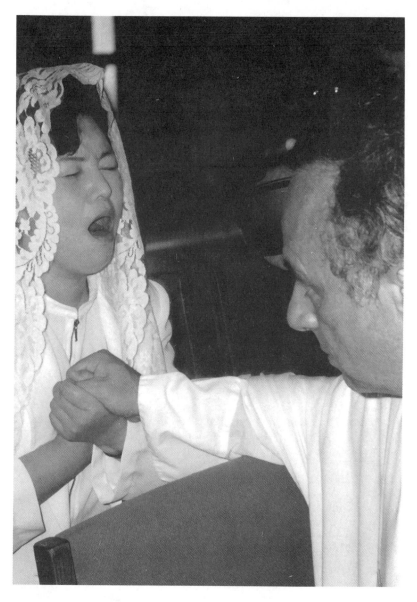

Father Martin Lucia looking at the Sacred Host bleeding in Julia's mouth. (St. Anthony's Church, Kailua, Hawaii, November 2, 1994)

My beloved children! Clearly tell everyone that the Mystery of Salvation is being realized through Me, Who is present in the Holy Eucharist.

Also have complete trust in and reliance on My Mother who is also your Heavenly Mother. My Mother, who is united to the sufferings of My Sacred Heart and is weeping tears and tears of blood and praying constantly so that all the children in this world may leave their sinful ways and return to My Bosom of Love, is the only one who can turn the just anger of God the Father away from you.

When Jesus ended speaking, the Sacred Host in my mouth was melting and was giving off a strong smell of blood. The Sacred Host turned into visible Flesh and Blood. Those who were at the Mass saw the Blood and the Flesh which was moving. They were shedding tears and praising the Lord, Who is truly present in the Holy Eucharist.

"Oh, Lord! Praise, gratitude, glory and adoration to You. Amen."

November 24, 1994 (1)

The Apostolic Pro Nuncio, who represents the Holy Father in Korea and whom the Blessed Mother had called *(see her message on October 23, 1994)*, came with Monsignor Peter *(his secretary)* and Fr. Raymond Spies. Fr. Sang Chul Oh, other priests and lay people were also there. We placed a queen's crown on the Blessed Mother's statue in the Chapel and began praying at about 10:20 a.m.

It was about 11 a.m. when I saw a bright light from the Crucifix above the Blessed Mother's statue. I said to Fr. Spies, *"Father, there is a bright light radiating down from the Crucifix."* Shortly afterwards, the Blessed Mother told me, **"Receive blessings from the Pope's representative and your spiritual director so that your hands may become clean."**

Immediately, the Apostolic Pro Nuncio and Fr. Spies blessed me. They blessed me for the second time on my forehead and hands with the fragrant oil (from a small bottle) that I had given to Fr. Spies about two years ago. Then, I got closer to the Blessed Mother's statue and began praying on my knees. The statue was also radiating a bright light. The Blessed Mother spoke with a kind, loving, soft and yet anxious voice.

THE BLESSED MOTHER:

My beloved daughter! I have a request to the representative of the Pope, my son, whom I love so dearly that I can put him in my eyes without feeling any pain. Ask him that a tabernacle be prepared beside me.

I feel so lonely, because many leaders are ignoring me for the sake of face-saving and the eyes of the world, paying no attention to my ardent request to look after numerous sheep that are walking toward hell. . . .

Now, look! . . . Some of the souls who used to be flower gardens for God are falling into the devil's mire that covers everything with thick mud and corrupts it.

So many priests are offering Mass unfaithfully. As a result, the Lord is unable to perform miracles of love in them through His Real Presence. He is suffering pains and is unceasingly calling the priests who are in sins to be faithful to their duties and become united with the Lord's Love.

Nowadays, errors are being taught even by some of my priests and are spreading all over the world. The Gospels are being promulgated by false prophets in such a way that the Gospels might become more acceptable to modern society under the pretext of civilization and innovation. But these are being promoted unfaithfully and are not the Gospels of my Son Jesus. While many kinds of sins multiply, they are being justified as if sewage water could be claimed to be pure water. Many blind people are believing such claims. The devil, who has led them into such deceptions, is overjoyed.

My beloved sons! Today I called you, whom I love most dearly, in a special way to this place where you will experience the Lord's Presence and mine as heroic and faithful witnesses so that the Mystery of the Holy Eucharist may be made known all over the world. So, help me hurriedly to save the sheep that have been lost.

I have said repeatedly that the Mystery of the Holy Eucharist, which is the Bread of Life from Heaven, is a spring that never dries and a medicine that gives you salvation. But only very few are making preparations before receiving Him. If my numerous children only knew that the Eucharist is truly the Life, the Everlasting Spring, the Manna and a continuing miracle that is no less than the miracles of the Creation of the Universe and of the Redemption, they would not be walking toward hell. . . .

The Holy Eucharist is the center of all the supernatural events, but is being trampled upon by so many children through sacrilege, insult and humiliation. Therefore, my messages of love must be spread all over the world more vigorously so that the time of the Lord, Who is present in the Eucharist, and of the New Pentecost may be advanced.

My beloved priests! When you spread my messages of love which I give you shedding tears and tears of love, you will experience pains, too. But I will elevate you, who have been called from all over the world, to a high level of sanctity so that you may reveal the true identity of the errors and promote the Truth with your mouths which will be like two-edged swords and thus may spread the fragrance of Christ. All the falsehood, plots, tricks and cunning slanders will disappear in the presence of the light from God the Father, just as fog clears under the sun.

Therefore, do not worry, but have complete trust in and reliance on me. As you are now staying in my Immaculate Heart, no one will be able to harm you. As I will clothe you with garments of all the virtues, you will be living as little souls who are being led by my fragrance at every moment of your lives.

My beloved daughter! A certain priest living in sin was about to receive the Eucharist, but the Lord was not able to live in him and is having St. Michael the Archangel bring that Eucharist to my beloved Papal Representative and your spiritual director through you. So, stretch out your hands.

I was hesitant because of awe, but the Blessed Mother said, "Do not worry. Hurry up and receive the Eucharist." *"Yes, Mother."*

As I stretched out my hands, St. Michael the Archangel, who was not visible, brought the Holy Eucharist in the middle of a powerful light. When I received the Eucharist, I fell down to the floor because of the strong light. When I regained consciousness and got up, I saw the Apostolic Pro Nuncio, the Monsignor, Fr. Spies, my husband and others around me.

The Sacred Host in my hands had the images of a cross and the letters "A" and "Ω" on it and was already broken into two. One was in my left hand and the other in my right hand. I gave the Eucharist in my right hand to the Apostolic Pro Nuncio and the one in my left hand to Fr. Spies. The Apostolic Pro Nuncio and Fr. Spies gave Communion to other priests and about 70 lay people who were in the Chapel. Fr. Spies placed a piece of the Sacred Host in a pyx.

November 24, 1994 (2)

At about noon, I stood up to go home next door. I walked supported by Julio, my husband, and Rufino, as I had fallen down on the floor because of the strong light from above and was feeling tired. When I was about to open the Chapel door, the Blessed Mother called me in a hurry.

THE BLESSED MOTHER:

Julia! Hold the hands of the Apostolic Pro Nuncio and your spiritual director and come to me in a hurry!

I immediately held the hands of the Apostolic Pro Nuncio and Fr. Spies, approached the Blessed Mother together with them and knelt before her statue. The Blessed Mother continued with a kind, pleasant and loving voice.

THE BLESSED MOTHER:

Giovanni! Thank you for responding to my call. You are truly my beloved son who has received special graces. You had such a perfect faith as to completely trust my merciful Immaculate Heart and respond to me. Today you are specially invited to this place as the representative of the Pope, who is the first son of mine and of the Church.

My beloved son, Giovanni! Be united with my poor daughter who is weak and in pains and who considers herself the most unworthy and least qualified person in the world and, thus, help save the children in the world who live in sins. . . .

My Heart is burning so much that I am throwing up blood, because I wish to spread my voice to the world through my daughter in this urgent time, but this is being blocked because of narrow-minded insistence on habitual ways by human thinking. I cannot wait any longer, because a total disaster is possible due to the schemes of the Freemasons.

My most beloved priest! Even many of the leaders in the Church are rejecting my messages of love and committing the sins of sacrilege by concocting many lies for the simple reason that my messages have not yet been approved. How great the damage will be to the sheep that are following them! Help me so that my messages of love may be approved soon. By doing so, you will be comforting the Lord Who is present in the Holy Eucharist.

In this current age, numerous children are hastening on their way to hell, making this world like Sodom and Gomorrah. The cup of God's just anger is full, and the chastisement is so close. That is why I gave special graces to my unworthy daughter so that she may go out to the world and spread my messages of love, but even this is being criticized. Hurriedly arrange a meeting between the Pope and my daughter who has offered up everything to spread the Lord's Words and mine. I will surely be in that meeting.

From left: Apostolic Pro Nuncio in Korea, Julio Kim, Fr. Raymond Spies and Julia Kim in the Chapel in Naju. (November 24, 1994)

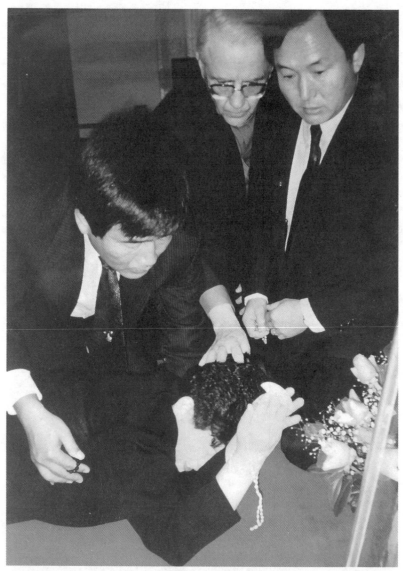

Julia fell to the floor because of powerful light from above. Then, St. Michael the Archangel brought a large-size Eucharist to Julia. The Host was already broken into two when Julia received It between her fingers. (November 24, 1994)

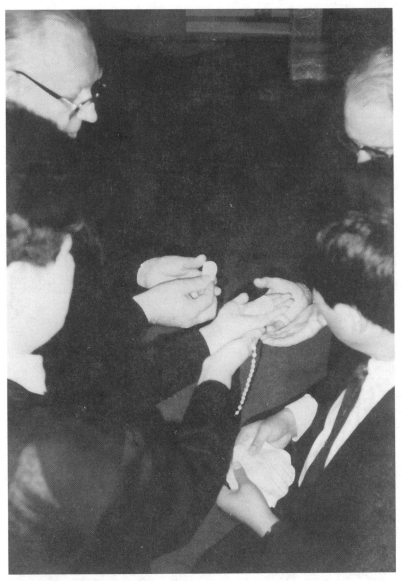

After receiving the Eucharist from the Archangel, Julia gave the Host in her right hand to the Apostolic Pro Nuncio and the one in her left hand to Fr. Spies.

The Apostolic Pro Nuncio and Fr. Spies broke the Eucharist brought by the Archangel into smaller pieces and gave Communion to about 70 people in the Chapel.

Then, the Blessed Mother asked Julia to hold hands with the Apostolic Pro Nuncio and Fr. Spies.

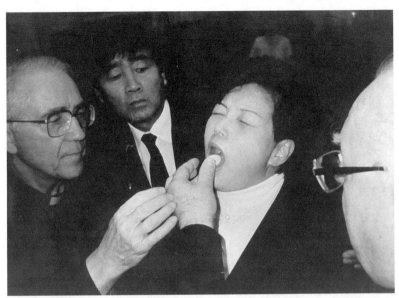

Suddenly, a small-sized Eucharist came down and landed on Julia's tongue almost vertically. The Apostolic Pro Nuncio took the Host from Julia's tongue.

The Apostolic Pro Nuncio holding the small-sized Eucharist in his hand

Therefore, do not worry about possible reactions, but sow the seeds of the Holy Spirit. If even one tiny seed falls on fertile soil, you will be rewarded in Heaven and give joy to Heaven. You will be showing the way to Heaven to all peoples and giving a great joy and comfort to me, who is in pains.

My beloved sons! I will be with you so that you may spread the messages courageously and wisely. Therefore, hurry up! Now, together with the Lord, I bestow upon all of you the light of my boundless love and mercy. Good-bye! Annyoung!

When I said, *"Amen,"* a small Eucharist came down enwrapped in light. The Blessed Mother said, "Receive the Eucharist in a hurry." As I was using both of my hands to hold the hands of the Apostolic Nuncio and Fr. Spies, I hurriedly received the Eucharist with my tongue, because I was afraid It might fall on the floor. Seven priests and about 70 lay people in the Chapel witnessed this.

January 18, 1995
—9:20 – 9:40 a.m.

While I was suffering pains, I strongly felt the Blessed Mother's call and went to the Chapel supported by a helper, as I was not able to walk alone. As soon as we opened the door of the Chapel, we smelled a fresh, sweet and powerful fragrance of roses filling the Chapel. Light was also radiating from the Blessed Mother's statue. I offered up a candlelight to her and began praying. Then, I heard the beautiful and friendly voice of the Blessed Mother from her statue.

THE BLESSED MOTHER:

My beloved daughter! Even in this current age, my Son Jesus is suffering on the Cross shedding much Blood and covered with Blood to save this world permeated with sins. This Mother who watches this is also bleeding from her torn Heart.

Offer up your current pains of delivery gracefully so that all the children may repent soon. I feel so anxious when I look at you suffering pains while following me. But come closer to me, filled with the hope that the joy of birth will surely come. Do you know how I am comforted by your effort to prevent even one soul from perishing? Have no fear and try harder to help all the children come aboard the Ark of Salvation.

Now is the best opportunity for you *(plural)* to repent. When God sends a warning, sufferings accompany, too. But if you repent and comply with my requests, the cup of God's blessings will be bestowed upon you. So, do not waste this precious time and opportunity. I have already indicated several times through Fr. Gobbi and you, who *(Julia)* is unworthy, that this current age is extremely urgent.

My most beloved daughter! How can I be unaware of your heart that agonizes with sufferings, even though you have asked for them! I am anxious, too. I could let you stand up right away, but you continue suffering extreme pains, because too many children in the world are falling into sins and I need souls who offer sacrifices in order to save even one more soul. The lotus flower does not blossom when the water is changed repeatedly, but it blossoms beautifully in a dirty pond. Likewise, remember that you can arrive at glory only through sufferings. Offer them up well for the conversion of the children in the world.

All the children in the world! I ask all the souls not to listen to the sounds of evil. The devils rejoice so much when they take joy away from you. They cause division among people and press down their hearts with darkness and sorrows. So, be watchful all the time and carry your cross well, even when it feels too heavy. If you lay down the cross thinking that it is too heavy, evil, which has been waiting for that moment, may enter you right away. I implore you ardently.

As water flows to lower and lower places, my Son Jesus went down to lower places again and again. All of you must imitate my Son Jesus and become lower and lower. The bodily matters belong to the world, while the spiritual matters belong to Heaven. Following this Mother's wish that you pursue the heavenly matters only, offer up your sufferings totally and gracefully.

After a brief pause, the Blessed Mother continued, weeping.

Now, look! They said, *"The Shinkansen (the bullet-train railway in Japan) has been built so solidly that it will withstand any natural disaster."* (Note: There was a major earthquake in the Kobe area in Japan on January 17, 1995.) What was the use of saying that? I love that country and that nation so much that I have given them an opportunity to repent, imploring them with tears. But most of them have closed their hearts, have failed to live according to God's Will and have not accepted me, who is their Heavenly Mother.

Pride can ruin not only individuals but the whole world. God broke their pride with which they trusted human power, without realizing that God can destroy iron pillars and brass walls so solidly built by humans in one moment, and that He can erect them in one moment, too. But I love that country and that nation so much that, in response to the prayers of the little souls who are practicing my messages of love and following me, I will gather them under my mantle and help them to be saved by returning to God, repenting their sins truthfully and living a sincere life with all their hearts.

Do not think that all these were random accidents, but wake up hurriedly, throw away pride and selfishness and come closer to me with a humble heart. Then, I will offer you up to the Lord; the Lord's blessing instead of His chastisement will come down upon you; and my Immaculate Heart will surely triumph, which will give you a great joy, love and peace and fill your faces with happy smiles.

My dear children! Many children were sacrificed, not because they were at fault, but because there only were extremely few children who were accepting the Lord's Words and me. Do not think complacently of this as a matter of people far away, but pray. If you do not live according to God's Words and do not go to the Lord with me, there may be more and more natural disasters, depletion of natural resources, wars, communicable diseases, many kinds of environmental pollution, and other calamities. Therefore, you must stay awake, pray and live a life of conversion and, thereby, enter my Immaculate Heart.

All the children in the world! It is not too late yet. Accept my messages of love that I give you through my little soul and come back to my bosom which will be your refuge. As I told you before, I will let the triumph of my Immaculate Heart and the light of mercy spread to the entire world from Korea. Let all the children in the world know this so that they may wake up and pray.

February 2, 1995
—*Feast of the Presentation*

For some time, I had been staying at a relative's house because of severe pains. So, on New Year's Day *(according to the lunar calendar)*, I was not able to be with my family or the Blessed Mother('s statue). But I was so anxious to see the Blessed Mother on this Feast Day of the Presentation that I went to the Chapel. There I grasped the feet of the Blessed Mother whom I had been so ardently longing to see and prayed, *"Mother! You told us, 'I will help you with my power that can crush the serpent.' Please help this endangered world to be saved with your power that can crush the serpent. . . ."* At that moment, I heard the loving and beautiful voice of the Blessed Mother from her statue.

THE BLESSED MOTHER:

My beloved daughter! This is the day when I presented my Son Jesus to God the Father and also the day when it was foretold by Simeon that I would experience the pains of my Heart being pierced with a sharp sword. As Simeon predicted, I have received numerous pains from my beloved children, but, at the same time, I am being comforted by souls like you who are participating in my sufferings.

My daughter who is so exhausted! With renewed courage and energy, march ahead bravely. There is no time to waste by hesitating. Do not worry even when you hear all kinds of insults. Know that all the insults that you hear are actually insults to me and offer them up well.

Numerous children, who have gone far away from my Son Jesus and me, have been swept away by storms and have fallen into errors and, because of the resulting lack of faith, are not able to accept the Dogmas and are causing a great disorder in the Liturgy and the Church Laws. Even many shepherds have fallen into this disorder and are walking along the way to hell. The gate of hell is wide open to receive them.

I have already told you again and again what the remedies are against the many disasters that are striking many places in the world. . . .

The Blessed Mother continued with a voice filled with sorrows and almost crying.

As I told you before, daughter, fire can fall from the sky upon the souls who are blind and deaf and are wandering without knowing the way. But there are not enough little souls yet who can soften the just anger of God. Therefore, help me by moving to the place which I have prepared (the mountain where the new basilica will be built), holding hands with the priests whom I have chosen with love.

Remember that, with a great thirst and anxiousness, I am inviting all the children in the world to come aboard my Ark of Salvation so that I can take them (to Heaven). And prepare a most joyful place with the pure love from my Immaculate Heart. Hurriedly spread my messages of love to my children who do not know the way to Heaven and, by doing so, comply with the wish of this Mother who wants to save them from danger.

All my beloved children in the world! My messages of love will be the brake that suppresses disorder. All the children in the world must hurriedly understand my messages of love and accept them. If the children in the world do not follow the Will of God and do not accept my words, God will respond with severity, and they will not be able to escape from the fire of justice. A safe tomorrow cannot be promised.

But if you comply with the wish of this Mother who wants to carry out through you the Plan of Love and Salvation that God of the Most Holy Trinity has entrusted to me and answer with an *"Amen,"* the blazing flames of the Holy Spirit will renew this world and make it shine and you will be saved in that light.

May 9, 1995

I attended the 7:30 p.m. Mass at the Parish Church. While I was in deep meditation during Mass in order to be united with the Heart of the Lord, I saw a vision. The Holy Father was celebrating Mass together with many priests. Jesus, Who was wearing an ivory-colored mantle, was standing by the Holy Father and the Blessed Mother, who was wearing a blue mantle and was so beautiful, was also there. She began speaking with an anxious voice.

THE BLESSED MOTHER:

My beloved daughter! I am so anxious, because even the shepherds who have responded to God's Call are not following the Will of God the Father completely and are not able to enrich the souls who are thirsting for Love. . . . The Lord wishes to perform miracles of love through the Pope, Cardinals, Bishops and priests who have responded to my call, but the clergy who are following my Son Jesus are so few.

"Now, look," said the Blessed Mother. I saw that the clergy who are truly following the Lord were so few. Many priests were compromising with the world and were becoming demoralized. Some, including even a Cardinal and a Bishop, were deserting their vocation. The Blessed Mother was watching this and was shedding tears.

THE BLESSED MOTHER:

Daughter! My enemy's fury is increasing rapidly and he is crying out with joy and victoriously over the fall of many priests. This Mother of Heaven cannot help weeping continuously because of the heretics who have deviated from the true and traditional Church. Many priests, who should look after the sheep which have been lost and are wandering about, are facing the danger of losing true faith. They even sometimes forget about the Resurrection of Jesus, because they are immersed in the spirit of the world which is permeated with disbelief and errors. Thus, the tide of a great apostasy is spreading extensively inside the Catholic Church. Therefore, try to become signs of my love filled with my Motherhood. . . .

Even if the land dries up, I will become like the sea with powerful tides, if you become united and practice my words. I will always be in the deepest corners of your souls, if you do not fear anything but trust me completely. Pains of delivery may be great, but they are signs of a great joy that is approaching. If you believe my words and put them into practice, you will be singing joyfully in the garden of God's Kingdom, where there is not even a trace of darkness.

Sons and daughters who have been called because you are so dearly loved! This Mother, who is the Mediatrix of Graces and the Co-Redemptrix, will transform you through the little soul whom I have chosen. So, do not fear but settle down. Today, this Mother in Heaven is accepting your little hearts into my Immaculate Heart. Bravely become apostles of my Immaculate Heart in unity so that my Plan may be realized well. When you follow me walking a little person's way of love with humility, faith, reliance and trust,

I will enwrap you with the armor of the Holy Spirit so that even the arrows of fire that the devil throws at you may not dare hurt you.

After the Blessed Mother ended her words, I saw the Holy Father and many priests celebrating Mass together with huge crowds of people from all over the world.

June 11, 1995
—The Feast of the Holy Trinity

I was in bed because of extreme pains. I could not open my eyes or move my body. The nails from close helpers go deeper and cause greater pains. They must be hurting the Hearts of Jesus and the Blessed Mother even more. I wept thinking about my unworthiness. I had so earnestly wanted to lead a hidden life. I cried, because my heart was being torn with overflowing sorrows over the criticism and judgment that the Blessed Mother receives because of my unworthiness and sinfulness. What should I do? What should I do? Suddenly, I heard the warm and yet sorrowful and anxious voice of the Blessed Mother.

THE BLESSED MOTHER:

Daughter! Today is the great Feast Day of the Holy Trinity. I feel sadness in my Heart when I see you lying down exhausted, while praying for unity in the whole world. I can raise you up right away and liberate you from pains. But, the world is unable to achieve unity and is filled with darkness because of many sins. The devil has laid traps with thorns, venom and cruelty. That is why your sufferings are necessary. Offer them up well.

Do your best in everything and prepare a book with testimonies from many children who have received love from the Lord through me so that you may not fall into the grave events filled with pains. If they give testimony on the graces they have received, they will receive more blessings. How would it be possible that many people receive graces except through pains? Why are you hesitating and trying to give it up? Execute it without reservation. Do you under-stand this? The current age demands miracles. That is why I prepared a plan. Why are you trying to give it up with your own thinking? Do not follow the wishes of the en-emies, but obey this Mother's words in a simple way.

Through the mercy of God the Father, new days are being prepared for you. In this early stage, there are many priests who persecute you, alienate you and even call you, my little soul, an insane woman. But do not forget that there also are my beloved priests who are following me and sup-porting you. Proceed as I told you without worrying. Then, your doubts will go away, your faith will increase, and the lost children of the world will be comforted.

Numerous people are spiritually blind and deaf and are rejecting my presence, because their hearts are so dried up in extreme poverty and lack of understanding. That is why I am asking your spiritual director and you to publish a book with testimonies on the graces that many children have received. Do not worry about the consequences, but march ahead bravely. . . .

This Heavenly Mother will take care of the results and ac-complish amazing fruits. Those who are walking the way of ruin and destruction, judging and criticizing (me), will come back as simple and good children following this Mother, thanks to the book. Some of those who are dis-tancing me now may still refuse to accept me. A day will come when they will beat their chests for shame.

Make haste. I am asking you, because I want to protect the numerous children who are walking toward hell. Stay alert remembering that my enemy is active, violent and danger-ous and is trying to topple you.

Nobody knows the hour, but God can take your soul early for the salvation of many children. But when the prayers of numerous souls are combined together and soar high into Heaven, your life on earth will be extended and my burning Immaculate Heart will triumph.

Brace yourself with more strength, because my enemy is mobilizing all the available means to block you, beat you up, and destroy you. He is using all his power to discourage you and intimidate you so that you may give up the work and my plan may be delayed.

I will always be with you and perform miracles of love.

June 16, 1995

I offered up indescribably severe pains that had lasted for several days for the conversion of sinners and the sanctification of priests and religious.

On June 30, it will be the tenth annivesary of the Blessed Mother's shedding tears for the first time. During the past ten years, she has revealed her presence by shedding tears, tears of blood and fragrant oil for the salvation of all the children in the world. She has brought miracles directly or indirectly to numerous people on countless occasions. Despite all these, she has not yet been approved. Instead, she has been receiving misunderstanding, criticism, and accusations. I felt so sad when I thought about the Blessed Mother, who had been suffering so much.

I had an appointment to see Fr. Spies in Anyang. It was difficult to keep that appointment because of my pains, but I went to Fr. Spies praying to the Lord, *"I am Yours, if I am dead. I am Yours, if I am alive. I am Yours always. Your Will be done."* I attended Mass celebrated by Fr. Spies. During Mass, I was lying down because of the pains. Soon, I entered an ecstasy and began trembling at the sight of people who were being purified in the fire of Purgatory. Then, I heard the voice of Jesus.

JESUS:

Are you hesitating and trying to lay down the cross saying that you are unworthy and unqualified? But you promised to suffer pains and I saved you from death several times in order to make use of you.

I was surprised and looked around.

JESUS:

You make frequent Confessions and do much penance. But you have frequently faltered despite your promise of martyrdom. Will you walk through the fire in order to purify your soul even more?

I was scared, but said, "Yes," and walked through the fire. The heat and pain were beyond human description.

JESUS:

Now your soul has been purified. Go to the Kingdom of God.

Right away, angels took me to Heaven which I had seen before *(July 24, 1988)*. God the Father was sitting on a high throne. The Blessed Mother was also there surrounded by angels.

GOD THE FATHER:

Child. . . *(after a pause)* Do you want Me to chastise the world now?

Julia: *No, please wait a while longer. More souls will repent according to the Blessed Mother's words. There already are many who are repenting.*

GOD THE FATHER:

Then, will you return to the world and spread (the messages) more diligently?

Julia: *But. . . I am not qualified. It is beyond my power. I am so unworthy. So many people do not realize that the end times are approaching.*

GOD THE FATHER:

That is right. If the people in the world knew that the end times were approaching, they would repent. . . . If they do not repent until the end, there will only be ruins. You must go and tell them that I, Who am God and Father, will soon speak with a stern voice. You must protect yourselves with prayers.

If priests, who are ministers of Jesus and were chosen by Me through My Son, do not listen to My Words and continue to judge and criticize them, the sheep which are following them will also continue to walk toward hell. They must keep in mind that My Judgment will be fierce. They are blocking the Gate of Heaven with their knowledge, leaving numerous souls to loiter and wander outside. I cannot tolerate this any longer.

When one priest is ruined, it is not just he who is ruined. Many souls fall together with him. This gives Me extreme sorrows.

My beloved daughter! Many priests, religious and lay people are commiting sins with their tongues. Can you suffer pains in the fire of Purgatory so that they may repent?

Julia: *Yes. If they can repent, I will suffer pains.*

I stuck out my tongue and received the pains of fire on it. Even after the suffering, my tongue remained charred and black. One side of my tongue was red and cracked. I had no saliva in my mouth and felt so painful.

GOD THE FATHER:

I feel so painful in My Heart, and this world truly needs to be chastised. But I see your earnest wish and your loving heart offering up sufferings to save even one more soul. Go to the world in a hurry and cry out.

At that moment, the Blessed Mother who was wearing a blue mantle came to me as if she was flying and embraced me.

THE BLESSED MOTHER:

Now, receive the Holy Eucharist in a hurry which is Heavenly Food and will fill your soul.

I woke up and saw Fr. Spies about to give me Communion. Because my tongue was hardened, I could not swallow the Sacred Host. I made gestures asking for water. Fr. Spies gave me the Precious Blood and I could swallow the Host. At that moment, I saw a vision. The Blessed Mother was sitting wearing a shiny royal crown and was carrying the Baby Jesus. She had a beautiful, peaceful and bright smile. In her front were the Holy Father, the Apostolic Pro Nuncio, Fr. Spies, other priests and lay people who love the Blessed Mother, playing joyfully like children.

After the Mass, I made a Confession to Fr. Spies, while still lying down. The Blessed Mother was sitting nearby. Jesus was standing just behind the priest. While hearing the Confession, Fr. Spies was not aware that the Blessed Mother was sitting beside him. When Fr. Spies touched the place where the Blessed Mother was sitting with his left hand, it slipped because that place was slippery with much fragrant oil. Soon, the fragrant oil dried up. We were so amazed.

June 18, 1995

Today was the Feast of Corpus Christi. Because of severe pains, I could not even open my eyes or go to Mass. On June 5, 1988, which was also the Feast of Corpus Christi, I attended Mass after suffering for two weeks and witnessed the Sacred Host becoming larger and bleeding (in my mouth). I also received messages from Jesus, Who was bleeding. Today also I saw Jesus, Who was bleeding more than before. The Blessed Mother was also feeling more pains in her Heart, because the children who receive transfusions from Jesus were diminishing. She spoke sorrowfully.

THE BLESSED MOTHER:

My beloved and poor daughter! Your bloody sufferings will not be fruitless. Offer them up well in reparation for the sins of sacrilegious Communions. Do not panic even when you face difficulties in the course of your life. Your sufferings have been allowed by God. Tolerate even misunderstandings, criticisms, contempts and slanders. Even when some people intend to do evil to you, they will not be able to harm you. Instead, there will be God's mercy. That is because all the deceptions and slanders will dissipate like fog under the shining sun.

You have frequently said that you are unworthy, weak and unqualified and have nothing to offer to God except your shamefulness. You have asked me why I have chosen you, who is filled with shortcomings and, thus, let many people, including even some priests, commit sins of judging. But your shortcomings are what I want. Why would I have chosen you, if you did not have many shortcomings? To prevent you from becoming proud, the Lord even took away much of your knowledge. All your sacrifices and sufferings will not be vain. Even if you are not in this world, the messages you have received and the works will remain forever. The Lord, Whom you call Abba, Father, has nurtured you and guided you spiritually. This Mother has also nurtured you and trained your soul. Am I not guiding you now together with your spiritual director?

My daughter! Where do you find souls with good will? Mary Magdalene and Zacchaeus were among them. Also, the thief who was dying on a cross screamed, filled with trust, *"Lord, remember me when You enter Your Kingdom."* How did the Lord respond? He saw the truly repenting eyes of the thief and said, *"Amen I say to you, this day you shall be with Me in Paradise."* You make progress when you realize your poverty. You capture my Heart, when you say you are not qualified. You have complained repeatedly that you are not up to the work, realizing your immense poverty. But I have never left you.

Julia: *I am even feeling dizzy. It's not too late yet. I have wanted to live an ordinary and hidden life like a nameless wild flower. But why me? . . . I have thought it over again and again, but I am not worthy to do this work. I have not done anything to deserve rewards, either.*

THE BLESSED MOTHER:

Child! Haven't I told you that I chose you because of that? Don't be stubborn, but entrust everything to the Lord and follow Him. He needs your help, because He is being scorned more and more everyday. That is why He saved you from death again and sent you back to the world. In consultation with your spiritual director, spread my messages of love all over the world in a hurry and more courageously and wisely so that people may not commit sacrileges against the Lord, hidden in the Holy Eucharist.

You must not waste any precious time, in order to prevent everyone from destruction. Do not be discouraged, but make haste to quench the Lord's thirst.

The time when God the Father will speak with a stern voice of judgment is approaching. You must protect yourselves with prayers, sacrifices, penance and consecration. My Heart has already been torn apart into pieces, and my bloody tears and bloody sweat are pouring down on the earth.

I have already told you that the terrifying judgment of God will come down. As you know, that day will come like a thief at night. Destruction will come suddenly, when people are singing of peaceful and secure times. It will be like the pains of delivery to a pregnant woman, which are sudden and yet certain and cannot be avoided. The souls who accept my messages that you are spreading are accepting me. Those who reject them reject me and reject the Father in Heaven.

Little soul! Be more courageous. Become a light in this dangerous world and offer up reparations so that all may come aboard the Ark of Salvation that I have prepared and may not commit sacrilege against the Holy Eucharist. Annyoung!

June 19, 1995

The Blessed Mother has helped many people bear the fruits of her messages and has desired the publication of a book on these fruits so that many people may be able to have the book on the tenth anniversary of her first tears in Naju. But because this work was so difficult, I became worried and, together with several helpers, went to the Chapel and prayed before the Blessed Mother's statue. I entered an ecstasy near the end of the Third Glorious Mystery and heard the Blessed Mother's anxious voice. She was shedding tears of blood.

THE BLESSED MOTHER:

My beloved daughter! How could I be unaware of your agonizing heart? Do not be troubled. Do not be sad. Do not cry. What the Lord and this Mother want is that even one more sinner who has been lost repents. When a sinner repents, God the Father, God the Son and God the Holy Spirit, together with all of God's Saints and angels in Heaven, will rejoice. Doesn't the Bible tell you about a father throwing a big banquet when one of his sons, who had been lost, returned?

Let's compare this to a gold coin. If the gold coin is wrapped and stored, it will be of no use. Likewise, precious writings will be of no use, unless they are made known. Those who have ears will hear and follow this Mother. Make them known in a hurry. Then, you will harvest richly and numerous sheep will return to the Bosom of the Lord.

Listen well. Those who give to others will receive more, and those who hide (what they have) from others will be deprived of what they have. Who can possibly obstruct God's Will? Do not hesitate, as the time left is short. Also, I am the one who is doing the work.

My dear children. On the day when it will have been ten years since the beginning of my crying out shedding tears, with what are you going to wipe away my tears of blood?

Already, the time for preparation is over and, now, you are entering the decisive time of battle. The human race will face the time of a great bloody chastisement. Shouldn't you rescue (people) hurriedly? Do not delay, but hurry up.

This Mother in Heaven is trying to save even one more soul. Why are you calculating and thinking in human ways?

This book that I want will richly fill the hearts of the arid souls. And, because of this book, the practice of the messages will multiply. It will be a precious gift that will help open people's closed hearts and make them seek me. Therefore, do not worry, but comply with the wishes of this Mother who is undergoing a death agony. God has sent angels to His servants in order to show them what is about to happen.

Now, do not delay, but hurry up. I will guard and protect you. What will be written in that book are fruits and living testimonies. Those who walk in the daytime do not fall, because there is light. But those who walk at night can fall easily, because there is no light.

June 21, 1995
—10 a.m.

The Blessed Mother speaks to the priests whom she has chosen.

THE BLESSED MOTHER:

My beloved sons, my priests who are so lovely that I can put you in my eyes without feeling any pain! It is my motherly duty in this age of severe purification to train you, whom I love and cherish, to suffer pains. Therefore, offer everything up well. . . .

Keep in mind that all the large and small pains that you experience in this difficult time may not be in vain but may turn into gifts of perfect love, because I, your Mother, am helping you. Do not worry or feel lonesome. Instead, push my work ahead with courage and tenacity.

Priests who have received my love and my special graces! Know that, as I did for Jesus, I always stand under your cross, do not leave you even for a moment, and watch you with my eyes filled with motherly love and mercy. I will help you so that you may blossom in all virtues and exude fragrance.

Therefore, trust my words like a child and follow them. When you encounter difficulties, I will cover you with my heavenly mantle which has been prepared specially for you and will protect you. The Heavenly Father will also bless you.

June 21, 1995
—3 p.m.

I felt the Blessed Mother's call and went to the Chapel where she had wept through her statue. The Blessed Mother had a very sad expression, as she knew well about my sorrowful heart. Because she could not go to the place *(the mountain, the site for the new Basilica)* where she had wanted to go, she was so anxious and sad, almost crying, as she was looking in the direction of that place. A while later, she spoke with a sorrowful and yet warm and kind voice.

THE BLESSED MOTHER:

I ask all the children who work for the Lord and help me. For the conversion of sinners, pray, offer sacrifices, do penance and live a consecrated life. Turn your life into prayers. The human race has already come to the brink of a cliff of destruction because of its degradation. The ongoing battles are the signs of the approaching great chastisement that will befall the human race. From now on, how many countries will be turned upside down and how many people will have to be sacrificed. . . . If those who pursue evil persist in contradicting God the Father's Will, how can I continue preventing His Hand of Justice (from striking)?

The thorns in this end time are particularly hurting. How can those who denounce and disobey God understand anything but the preposterous fury! I am now tired of those who do not try to learn the truth but oppose me unconditionally. This age when pride and lack of love among the pessimists and the disobedient are surging is a time of misery and, to the Church, a time of painful delivery.

Whatever traps laid by the forces of evil you may face on your way, you must follow me, your Mother, who is the shield that will protect you from all kinds of attacks in my battle. Then, this Mother will rescue you from any trap and protect you.

My beloved children! The Freemasons have already laid plots of darkness and are paralyzing even key activities in the Church through their followers. So, the Church should recognize my messages fast, but it is indifferent. If, as a result, even my children for whom I took great pains to rescue from the marsh fall back into the whirlpool, what will happen to them at the end of the world, and who will be responsible for that? What will be the use of regretting and beating one's chest at that time? Ah! I am sad. All the roads are becoming blocked.

At that time, the Blessed Mother looked extremely sad and continued with a choked voice.

THE BLESSED MOTHER:

My beloved children! To console me and help the messages be spread and practiced, offer up your sufferings gracefully. All the children in the world who are helping me! Entrust all your difficulties to me. Your peace should not be shaken. The devotion in a burning heart manifests itself as unlimited love and a firm and courageous determination. When you live according to the rules of love, you will not be taken over by fear, nor will your spirit be broken by despair. Now, with one ray of hope, I again ask you, whom I love. It is not too late yet. Make haste and give me a hand so that all my children who are in sins may repent. If they only repent, many sheep who are following them will obtain Heaven. . . . *(after a pause)*

Obedience is the precious key that opens the gate of Heaven widely. What my little soul is doing may sometimes not make any sense to you, but can be precious examples. Follow my words which I give you through my little soul. I will open the gate of Heaven to all of you who are following me and will prepare special places for you. I will always be with you.

Sometimes we cannot do certain things that you and I wish to do, in order to be obedient to the Church. Even so, I will gather you into this poor cradle in order to fill the gap and arm you spiritually. Become beautiful and flawless flowers and enter my Immaculate Heart hurriedly and drink the spiritual milk that I give you. Then, you will receive the blessing of enjoying happiness in the eternal heavenly Paradise as children. Good-bye! I pray for peace. An-nyoung!

June 30, 1995 (1)

It was the tenth anniversary of the Blessed Mother's first weeping. I was so anxious and sad, because I was unable even to see visitors. How much greater the pains in the Hearts of Jesus and the Blessed Mother must be! There were also priests from abroad, but they were not allowed to celebrate Mass even in the Parish Church. I felt so sorry to the pilgrims from abroad. Several of the priests from abroad already returned home, because they could not celebrate Mass.

From about 3 p.m., the shape of the sun was changing gradually. By about 3:30 p.m., it became a clear image of the Eucharist. It was also spinning and pulsating like a heart. It was radiating different colors—blue, green, purple, yellow, red and gold. These colors were reflected on people's clothes. Many people who witnessed this were screaming with joy and some were crying. The light was shining upon the roof of the Chapel and upon the people on the ground. I saw Jesus and the Blessed Mother near the image of the Eucharist in the sky. There also were angels. The Blessed Mother began speaking in a most merciful, loving, kind and soft manner. She was extremely beautiful and looked like her statue in Naju—the Mother of Mercy.

THE BLESSED MOTHER:

My beloved children! I bless you in a special way today, bestowing the light from Heaven on you so that you may now live in the light of the Lord and myself and may become the apostles of the light that radiates from my Immaculate Heart.

If you follow me completely, you will soon see the day when the darkness that is covering the Church will disappear. The light of love from the most merciful and loving Sacred Heart of Jesus and my Immaculate Heart is bestowed upon you so that peace instead of suffering and anxiety may be given to you. In this desolate world, the danger of a new war is turning into a reality. But the power of God's Love cannot be blocked.

You came to me, because it is the tenth anniversary of my first weeping. I, who am God's servant, will enwrap you all with my mantle and bless you. So, follow my words well. Those who say that they are being neutral are blocking my way with a fragile cover-up and cruelty and are walking toward hell. They are leading themselves toward perdition, but do not realize this and still talk about love without practicing it.

My children! You should not refuse this Mother's request that you reconcile with each other so that violence and fear may cease.

Now, all my children! Do not approach me because of curiosity and as spectators, but follow me with complete trust. You may not fully understand my words now, but will some day. If you refuse to believe and follow my words, however, you will surely regret it.

All my beloved children in the world! It is not too late yet. If you believe, follow and trust my words as true messages originating from God, you will enjoy eternal happiness. I bestow heavenly blessings on all of you. An-nyoung!

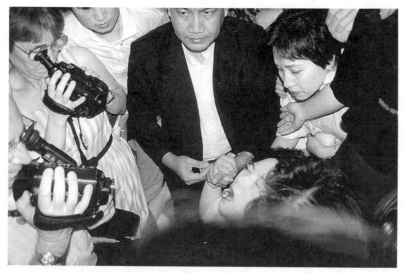

Fr, Jerry Orbos and other pilgrims witnessing another Eucharistic Miracle to Julia in the Naju Parish Church on June 30, 1995

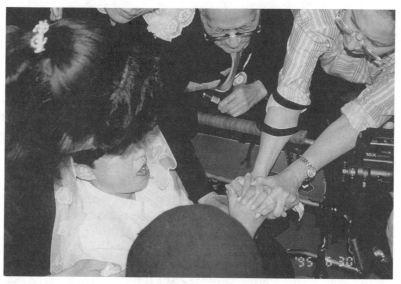

Fr. Shimura from Japan and others witnessing the same miracle on June 30, 1995.

June 30, 1995 (2)

There was Mass at 7:30 p.m. in the Parish Church concelebrated by the Pastor and seven priests from abroad. Tears kept flowing from my eyes. There have been several events recently that have saddened the Lord and the Blessed Mother. The priests and pilgrims from abroad were attending Mass celebrated in Korean, which they could not understand. I felt so sorry and cried a lot.

After receiving Communion, I went back to my seat. As I was about to begin meditation, I smelled blood from the Eucharist and asked a lady beside me to take a look. People around me also saw this and began shouting, *"It's blood!"* A priest from Japan *(92 years old)*, who was holding my hand, also saw it. Pilgrims were totally amazed and some began crying. The Pastor, who was unaware of what was going on, asked people to be quiet, and the Mass continued. Fr. Louis Bosmans from Canada continued to videotape. At that moment, I heard the warm and loving voice of Jesus from the direction of the tabernacle.

JESUS:

My beloved sons and daughters! I will bestow a special blessing on you, because you came here to comfort My Mother despite the long distance.

If you have insulted Me by receiving Communion sacrilegiously, see the signs that I am giving you today and receive and worship Me with a most sincere heart. Then, I will heal your deep wounds, cure your illnesses and give you a generous heart that can love everyone. I will give you the power to liberate yourselves from the powerful army of the devil, I will give you special graces that will be used as undefeatable and secure weapons, and I will give you a strong and tenacious power to practice goodness that can trigger a chain reaction more powerful than a nuclear reaction.

Therefore, hurriedly receive Me Who loves you to the extent of becoming your Food. Today I bestow special graces and blessings on all of you.

July 1, 1995
—*3:40 a.m.*

We had been planning celebrations for the tenth anniversary of the Blessed Mother's first weeping, but, instead, were praying quietly as pilgrims in front of the Blessed Mother's statue. During the prayer, there were flashing lights from the Crucifix above the Blessed Mother's statue. Then, the wooden image of Jesus turned into the live Jesus. He was on the Cross, bleeding. Blood was flowing from His forehead, which was being pressed down by a crown of thorns, His side, two hands, two feet and Heart. Jesus spoke sorrowfully.

JESUS:

My beloved soul! It has been ten years since My Mother Mary began shedding tears and imploring you in order to bring to Me all the children in the world who are filled with pride and hastening on their way toward hell. The Heavenly Mother, who deserves to be respected, is receiving extreme insults and pains instead of respect from the numerous children in the world. Offer up to the Heavenly Mother all of your suffering heart that has desired to comfort her.

My little soul! You know well that the spiritualism that secretly calls on the power of Satan is not from God. Satan can certainly weaken people's free will, but cannot destroy it unless people cooperate with him.

I am watching the insults, ridicules, scourgings, and humiliations by the enemies, the opponents of My Love, in the past, at present and in the future. You know well what will happen to those who are dragged into eternal perdition and also that the devils can be active in many different ways and to different degrees, as they can mobilize whatever means that are available to them. So, make haste so that the numerous children in this world may return to Me, and quench their thirst in the Sacrament of the Holy Eucharist, which is a Mystery of Love, in which I give up all of Myself.

During an all-night prayer meeting in the Chapel, seven Sacred Hosts descended from the Crucifix above the statue and landed on the altar in front of Our Lady's statue at about 3:45 a.m. (July 1, 1995)

The seven Hosts which came down miraculously

Julia: *Lord! I am not able. I am filled with shortcomings and unworthiness.*

JESUS:

Yes. I dwell in your heart that feels your unworthiness and littleness. Do not focus on yourself. I will not take away your shortcomings from you. I can make all of your soul and body perfect in one moment. But, I am leaving your shortcomings as gifts to you so that you may lower yourself further and further and come to me as a little soul. So, you will experience many pains and misunderstandings in following Me and My Mother, but these will not be stumbling blocks.

Julia: *Thank you, Lord. I am not worthy, but will follow Your Will.*

JESUS:

Yes. Thank you, my little soul! This world has become one which is swarming with heretics. In this age which is placed in the middle of a danger, try to imitate Me.

My real, personal and physical Presence in the Mystery of the Eucharist is an indisputable fact. I have repeatedly shown the Eucharist turning into visible Blood and Flesh so that all may believe that the Eucharist, which is a Mystery of the Infinite Love, Humility, Power and Wisdom, is My Living Presence. If certain priests do not believe in this Personal Presence of Mine in the Church, they certainly do not qualify as co-redeemers. When they ignore Me, Who is Christ, true God and true Man, they publicly deny My Divinity while acknowledging My human nature. That is because they have lost the ability to discern between good and evil and between authentic and unauthentic.

My beloved little soul! Never be discouraged. I will always be with you. Entrust everything to Me without worrying. I will send angels to protect you.

Now, look at Me clearly. Today I will give you a Sign of Love, while all of you are looking, with the same love that I had when I gave you the Seven Sacraments and gave up all of Myself. Help Me, all of you, in saving this world, which is becoming sicker and sicker, by uniting with each other and practicing love.

Jesus raised His hand, which was bleeding, and blessed all of us. Then, the Blood that was flowing from the Seven Wounds of Jesus gradually turned into Sacred Hosts and were falling down. I had been listening to the reading of the Lord's message holding hands with Fr. Su from Malaysia. I was surprised and jumped up and tried to receive the Hosts. But the Hosts fell so forcefully that they passed by my hands. I was standing speechless. Everyone in the Chapel heard the sounds of the Hosts falling on the altar before the Blessed Mother's statue. At that moment, Jesus resumed speaking.

JESUS:

My Mother has repeatedly asked for a tabernacle to be prepared (in the Chapel). But because it has not been prepared yet, I am giving you today My Flesh and My Blood in a special way for all of you.

When Jesus ended speaking, His appearance returned to that of His wooden image on the Crucifix.

July 2, 1995

The Archbishop *(of the Kwangju Archdiocese covering Naju)* instructed us to consume the seven Sacred Hosts that came down at 3:45 a.m. yesterday. In obedience, two priests who witnessed the falling Hosts yesterday and five lay people, including me, were selected to receive the Hosts. I could not help crying a lot, because we had to consume the Sacred Hosts that Jesus Himself gave us while bleeding on the Cross instead of preserving Them. I was the last to receive Communion. When I received the Host, I smelled a powerful fragrance of roses from the inside of my mouth and felt that the Sacred Host was becoming larger. Someone sitting nearby asked me to open my mouth. When I did, those around me were so surprised and shouted, *"The Host turned into Blood!"* Many began crying loudly.

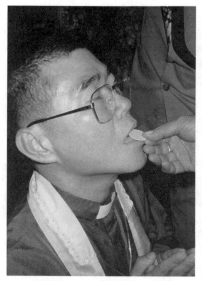

In obedience to Archbishop Yoon's instruction, the seven Hosts were consumed by seven people, including Fr. Francis Su (left) and Fr. Pete Marcial (right). (July 2, 1995)

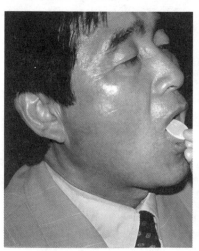

Julio and Julia Kim were among the seven people who received Communion in the Chapel on July 2, 1995. The Sacred Host that Julia received turned into visible flesh and blood in her mouth.

A while later, I entered an ecstasy. I was walking with the Blessed Mother. She was extremely beautiful, wearing a white dress, a blue mantle and a blue sash around her waist. She spoke in a soft, kind and pleasant manner.

THE BLESSED MOTHER:

Daughter! More and more children are falling into the sweet temptations by the devil, who tried to compete against God with a preposterously big ambition. They do not realize in what kind of a situation they are and receive Communion sacrilegiously. They are earning more and more of God the Father's just anger. Do you want to see?

Julia: *Yes, Mother!*

As soon as I replied, I saw a place crowded with numerous people. The Holy Father and many other clergy were celebrating Mass. Many priests were offering Mass while they were in sins. Many religious and the majority of lay people were receiving Communion while they were in sins, without realizing their sinfulness. They were eating up the Eucharist without any hesitation. The Blessed Mother felt so much pain in her Heart and spoke.

THE BLESSED MOTHER:

My beloved daughter! In this manner, they get lost and are wandering in darkness. They cannot even recognize themselves. How can they understand themselves, when they have lost even the sense of direction? First, they walk in fog, then, in darkness, and, then, far away from the source of love, totally forgetful of the Lord's Divine Nature and blind and deaf spiritually. Where would they be going? This Heavenly Mother desires to save all the children who have gotten lost, with your help.

Daughter! My messages of love that I am giving through you, who is unworthy, can be a guide for all the souls. But because only very few are following them, big calamities that Satan wants and is causing are occurring repeatedly. God has not taken away the devils' abilities that they were created with. That is why they proudly came to the world and are reigning. They lead people to sins, instigate them to disobey God, infuse pride, which is a terrible vice, into them and constantly plan evil schemes. Their hypocrisy and malice become combined together and become like a mixture of explosive gases, making the spiritual warfare more fierce. You will not even be able to discern, unless you remain awake.

My daughter who suffers willingly! To save this world which is decaying under the dark curtain of death, it is necessary that priests respect and fear God, lead a holy life following my Son Jesus, and lead the numerous sheep to Heaven. That is why signs were given today so that these priests, who have responded with an *"Amen"* to the invitation to become little souls, may testify.

My beloved priests! My priests whom I love so dearly that I can put you in my eyes without feeling any pain! You were given the power to change bread and wine into the Body, Blood, Soul and Divinity of the Lord in the Church. You were also given the power to forgive sins. Therefore, hurriedly teach the Mystery of the Eucharist to all so that they may make sincere Confessions and receive the Eucharist with clean hearts. Help them follow the Lord.

The Lord gave up all of Himself for your sake. He not only shed Blood two thousand years ago, but even now is squeezing all of Himself on the Cross for you, is coming to you in the form of bread and is consumed by you. If people knew this, they would not have joined forces with the devil. This great power (to change bread and wine into Jesus) in the Blessed Sacrament, a Mystery of Salvation, was not given even to Cherubim and Seraphim but was given to priests. How many of them are truly paying attention and are coming to me?

I ask my beloved priests to help all those who thirst and crave for worldly things to truly repent and return to the Lord through the Eucharistic Signs that have been given through the little soul who professes to be unworthy and unqualified. All these should be for God's glory and for the salvation of souls. Entrust all the rest to me. When you follow me entrusting everything to me, your union with God through His Incarnation will continue in the Mystery of the Eucharist. This union is unprecedented and beyond human description.

Now, entrust the remainder of your life to me with complete trust, pursuing the highest good and walking a little person's way of love. Come to me humbly. Then, you will be removing the thorns of rose bushes for me and will be applying fragrant balsam to my wounds.

Receive the special blessings that God the Father and God the Son in Heaven are bestowing on all of you today. All the children! I relay to you the greetings from all the angels and Saints and also send you my deep love! Then, annyoung!

The Blessed Mother finished speaking and disappeared. I opened my eyes at the sound of many people crying. It was the inside of the Chapel.

July 5, 1995
—Feast of St. Andrew Kim, Patron of Korean Clergy

While suffering extreme pains, I offered up myself to the Lord. I was praying and crying, because I was not able to do all the work that I set out to do. At that moment, I heard the warm, loving voice of the Blessed Mother.

THE BLESSED MOTHER:

Daughter! My beloved daughter! Offer up your pains contemplating more deeply on the Lord's Sacred Heart and my Immaculate Heart that have been torn apart. . .

My sons and daughters! Know that the Light of the Lord's Love is penetrating your lives, souls, hearts and being. Do not fall into despair or lose your hearts. Now is a very important time. If you follow me offering up all your sufferings gracefully, the Lord's help and protection will be bestowed upon you accordingly in your work and hardships. If you humbly live according to my wish, the pains of my daughter whom the Lord has chosen will lighten every moment through your sincere prayers.

My beloved children! Regardless of what happens, do not stop or hesitate but go forward courageously. God has allowed free will to humans. Therefore, if people do not follow God's Will, they cannot be forced. But today I offered up my daughter who has been suffering death agonies, those priests who have been called to work for me, and other children who have responded to my call to God on the altar of my Immaculate Heart. Therefore, remember this offering and follow me, throwing away everything and as more and more humble and little persons. Then, you will become the light that dispels darkness.

Now that I have called you to the Heavenly Garden, entrust yourselves totally to me with faith, trust and fidelity instead of reasoning and theorizing. Respond to me saying *"Amen"* and achieve unity. Nobody will be able to take you out of this place. Therefore, become givers of comfort and joy for me. As the Father, the Son and the Holy Spirit are One, you should also become one. Through the prayers that you little souls offer up fervently and united as one, my burning Immaculate Heart will surely triumph.

September 7, 1995
—Thursday

We gathered in the Chapel for the Holy Hours Devotion to offer reparations for the insults Jesus has received. As we began to pray the rosary, I saw a vision. Many people wearing red uniforms were marching in lines toward us, aiming their rifles at us in a frightening way. However, because of the fervent prayers we were offering, they were losing their power and lowering their hands with which they were holding the rifles. The color of their uniforms also was changing from red to light grey. They were soon turning back. There were tens of thousands of them—no, more than that—they were countless. The color of their uniforms continued to change to light blue. At that moment, light was shining from the sky. I could not see the Blessed Mother, but heard her beautiful voice.

THE BLESSED MOTHER:

My beloved daughter! As you just saw, my enemy's red army can lose power and be turned back by the fervent prayers you offer together during the Holy Hours. Right now, God's just anger is overflowing and God the Father is about to strike (the world) with His right hand that has been raised. But, thanks to the fervent prayers by you, little souls, He is delaying the hour. Therefore, stay awake and pray more fervently. From here *(Heaven)*, I join myself with you, as you offer up ardent and strong responses and fervent and persevering prayers in sincere love and gener- osity.

All my beloved children in the world! In this urgent time, observe the Holy Hours every Thursday well which can compensate for the sins and ingratitude that have trans- gressed the Solemn Dignity of God. About two years ago *(on February 18, 1993)*, I already told you in detail about the Thursday Holy Hours Devotion. Put it into practice by staying awake and praying.

The decisive time that can determine the fate of the whole human race is being prepared. Therefore, hurriedly wake up from sleep and listen to the voice of this Heavenly Mother who is imploring you so ardently.

My beloved children! Wake up and come to me, as I will take you all to Jesus, Who is truly present in the Blessed Sacrament and is silently waiting for you during the Sacri- fice of the Mass.

Offer up little flowers of constant prayers and self-denial for the sake of my numerous children who walk the way of

world-shaking events *(crimes, scandals, wars, etc.)*, persecutions, fratricidal strifes, and unrestricted selfishness and
who are addicted to the things they like and wish to possess, the comforts and the pleasures of senses. Then, the
children who have joined the red army will return to the
Bosom of the Lord, the Kingdom of the Lord will be established in this world, and my Immaculate Heart will triumph.

I send the blessings from the Lord and my love to all who
are gathered here. Good-bye. An-nyoung.

When the rosary prayer ended, the vision ended, too. It became very
quiet.

September 22, 1995

His Excellency (Bishop) Roman Danylak from Toronto, Canada, celebrated Mass on the mountain *(near Naju)* together with Fr. Joseph
Peter Finn from Ontario, Canada, and a Korean priest. Sixteen lay
people attended the Mass. We received Communion in both species.
When I received Communion, the Sacred Host in my mouth turned
into a mixture of Flesh and Blood and became larger. I smelled a
strong odor of Blood. The Sacred Host also began moving. One of the
laymen saw this and reported to Bishop Danylak. The bishop witnessed this phenomenon, followed by other people. A while later,
Bishop Danylak instructed me to swallow the Host. I swallowed the
Host with much difficulty, because it had become a lump of Flesh
and larger. While we were in meditation, crying, I saw light radiating
from the sky and heard the voice of Jesus which was dignified, majestic and yet loving, even though I could not see Him.

JESUS:

My beloved little soul! The greatest treasure in My Church
is My Mother Mary who is most holy. My Mother is the
Queen of the Universe, the Queen of Heaven and your
Mother. Therefore, My Mother Mary can love you, as I loved
you, and can do anything that I can do through the grace
from Me. Today My Mother, who is the Queen of Heaven
and your Mother, is opening and showing My Heart through
my little and unworthy soul to the Bishop who is trying to

Another Eucharistic Miracle occurred during an outdoor Mass celebrated by Bishop Roman Danylak from Toronto, Cananda, and two other priests. The Sacred Host in Julia's mouth turned into a heart-shaped lump of flesh and was bleeding. (September 22, 1995)

follow Me and My Mother like an infant so that he can make it known more widely that I am truly present in the Eucharist, which is a sublime mystery of Faith and Love.

If my priests, who celebrate Mass every day, truly believe and feel My Real Presence and live the sublime and amazing Divine Reality, numerous souls will be purified and live in the grace from My merciful Heart beyond expectations through this Real Presence of Mine. Make My Physical Presence known hurriedly.

This world is now on the brink of destruction because of human degradation, apostasy and infidelity, but too many of my ministers are asleep. Thus, even my ministers are being misled by false prophets. The present disorders are tormenting Me and keep tearing apart My Heart. This also becomes a whip and keeps tearing apart My Mother's Immaculate Heart.

My little souls who have been called! You will experience misunderstanding and persecution in the Church which has been wounded and divided. But I will always dwell in you and encourage and help you at your side. Therefore, do not fear but make known with trust My living Presence in the Holy Eucharist.

I have shown signs several times through my little soul to enlighten the many priests and numerous other children who say that they know My Real Presence and My breathing in the Eucharist with My Body, Blood, Soul and Divinity, and yet do not really know it. But only very few children are following Me. Even many priests forget about the sublime simplicity of the Holy Eucharist, which is My Physical Presence, and of the Gospels which I teach, and they are trying to spread Me with deceptive talk and complicated reasoning. This is like throwing mud at simple people.

My beloved children! Do not reject My pleas which I make in this manner while being truly present in the Eucharist. If people do not want to acquire true understanding, do not follow My Will to bestow Love upon them, deny My Divinity and deny the Divine Origin (of God's revelations), then, they will face God the Father's anger.

Because My Mother's loving and kind words for the past several centuries have been ignored, sin has reached a saturation point, even within the Church.

Hurriedly live a consecrated life, praying and offering up sacrifices and penance so that you may be connected to the Power that is indispensable for the eventual victory and, thus, do reparations for the most abominable sins of blasphemy that have been committed since early times. And if you follow My Mother Mary in order to restore My honor that has been trampled upon, you will not get lost, even in the dark maze of life in this world. My Mother Mary is the shortcut to Me, a shining dawn of My renewed Church, and the ark of a new covenant.

My children who are following Me and making Me known!
Do not worry about what those who criticize you may be
thinking, but pray, pray and spread (My messages). When
God's Hands are upon you, the thoughts of those who criticize will change quickly like the clouds which dissipate in
the sky. I bless you and all those who are dear to you.

An outdoor Mass at the site for the new Basilica to be built on a moun-
tain near Naju at the Blessed Mother's request. (October 19, 1995)

October 27, 1995
—Rome, Italy

I do not remember the exact hour, but, from the middle of night, I
could not sleep because of the devil's attacks. While I was struggling
with extreme pains, light was shining from above. At that moment,
I heard the warm, loving voice of the Blessed Mother.

THE BLESSED MOTHER:

My beloved daughter! . . . Pray in a hurry, because the
devils are being extremely violent to strike you down. The
Pope, who is the Vicar of my Son, the first son of the Church,

and my beloved son whom I love so much that I can put him in my eyes without feeling any pain, is now exhausted with internal and external pains. But ask him not to worry, but to entrust everything to this Heavenly Mother, as I am shining the light that emanates from my Immaculate Heart upon him.

I have already clothed him with a garment of virtues and protected and nurtured him so that everything he does in his life may be attracted to my fragrance. The purpose is to protect him and become his shield, armor and iron covering at every decisive moment so that I may lead him to the Heavenly Paradise. Therefore, all of you must become people who are closest to the Pope's heart. Listen carefully to the words he says while walking on the difficult road of the cross of Calvary and put his teachings into practice and spread them. Also help everyone to love the Pope with a filial love so that all may carry his painful cross with him.

How many priests are willing to walk with the Pope on the road from Bethlehem to Calvary that my Son Jesus walked? Many priests are studying the teachings of the Church superficially, without depth, and behave accordingly. That is why my son, the Pope, is suffering even more.

My beloved son whom I can put in my eyes without feeling any pain! The Pope, who is the Vicar of Jesus, the first son of the Church and the successor of Peter! I have been imploring shedding tears and tears of blood and screaming until my throat begins bleeding, but the blind and deaf leaders do not understand.

I feel so anxious that I wish to spread the messages of love from my burning Immaculate Heart all over the world through the Pope, who is the first son and head of the Church. Help me in a hurry. Take numerous souls, who have lost their way and are rushing toward hell, on board Mary's Ark of Salvation, which I have prepared, and guide them to Heaven.

My son whom I love extremely! The hours of apostasy and disloyalty are afflicting you. But, if you *(plural)* meditate more deeply on the Lord's Sacred Heart and my Immaculate Heart, which have been torn apart, and if the messages that I give you through the little soul are spread and put into practice in the world, you *(plural)* will be guided through me to the high pinnacle of sanctification, offering yourselves up as living sacrifices with a heart of a martyr every day and will experience the Father's Love on the way.

It is in my Plan for God's Work of Salvation that I prepared this meeting of yours. Trust and rely on this Plan of mine like a child and help me in a hurry so that my messages of love which I give you through the little soul may be approved and spread all over the world.

On that road, you *(plural)* will meet the Divine Person of my Son Jesus. And the powerful action of the Holy Spirit, my Spouse of Love, will proceed actively inside you so that all those who have lost their way and are wandering because of errors and sins may repent and that this world may face the time of the triumph of my Immaculate Heart that will blossom like a fragrant flower.

Together with my Son Jesus, I bless you all. An-nyoung!

October 31, 1995
—Rome, Italy

Today I attended the private Mass celebrated by the Holy Father. I could not control my tears, as I was thinking that, despite so much suffering, the Holy Father could not rest while looking after numerous sheep.

When I received Communion, there was a strong fragrance of roses and a strong smell of blood. The Sacred Host in my mouth was becoming larger, too. Monsignor Paik, who was also attending the Mass, saw this and instructed me to go to the back and wait. While I was meditating in the back, I saw bright light shining upon the Holy Father and the area around him. I also saw baby angels in the light, dancing and guarding the Holy Father. At that moment, I heard the loving and kind voice of the Blessed Mother, even though I could not see her.

THE BLESSED MOTHER:

My beloved son, the Pope who is the first son of God's Holy Church! Do you know how much I, together with Jesus, your elder Brother, have loved you and love you?

Jesus loved you *(plural)* so much that He came to you in person as your Food, but, as in the past, He is still being denied, deserted and betrayed by so many children today. For this reason, the hour of bloody ordeals and purification is drawing near and I came to you to rescue the children in the world.

Hurriedly and with a simple heart like a child, accept the gift *(the change of the Eucharist)* that God the Father has prepared and make it known to all. Teach the importance of the Mass, the importance of the Sacrament of Confession and the Mystery of the Holy Eucharist to all the children in the world who do not know them and, thereby, perpetually continue the gift of the Paschal Mysteries of the Last Supper and Resurrection.

The visible change of the Eucharist today was to show that Jesus came to you through the Sacrifice of the Holy Eucharist, which is a repetition of the Sacrifice completed on Calvary, Golgotha, to wash away all the sins in the world with His Precious Blood.

How numerous are the clergy who do not defend truth but keep silent for fear and remain as spectators because of face-saving and the eyes of others, even when they see errors and despite my messages of love that I have been screaming (to you) until my throat bleeds!

Let all know the Sacred Real Presence of the Lord in the Holy Sacrifice of the Mass where He comes as the

Transfuser, help Him wash away the filthy dirt from their souls, and give eternal adoration and praise to the Lord.

My beloved son! Thanks to your faithful love with which you have responded to this Heavenly Mother saying "Amen," no one will be able to separate you from the Love of God or take you away from Him. Your name has already been written in my Immaculate Heart. Therefore, be happy even in the middle of misunderstanding and persecution. Whenever you were in difficulties of various kinds, I defended and helped you and encouraged and consoled you in the refuge of my mantle.

You are my beloved son whom I can put in my eyes without feeling any pain. You are my beloved first son of the Church and younger brother of Jesus. I have led you to participate in the eternal priesthood together with Jesus. Therefore, sing of the Resurrection, living a life of intimacy with Him. Then, you will become the Light of Jesus Christ that comes down through you *(plural)* shining brightly upon the world, penetrating the curtain of darkness that surrounds the world, and you will face the Second Pentecost.

I pray that the Divine Grace and bright Light will be with you always. An-nyoung!

When she ended her words, the light and angels became invisible.

November 21, 1995
—Feast of Presentation of the Blessed Virgin

I attended the Mass celebrated by Fr. Spies. While I was in meditation after Communion, there was a powerful fragrance of roses. Light was also radiating from the sky. I heard the beautiful and loving voice of the Blessed Mother, even though I could not see her.

THE BLESSED MOTHER:

My beloved daughter!

. . . I wish to let the Church know through the Pope, the first son of the Church, about the protection by this Mother and about the great breadth of my Motherly Love for my children.

Hurriedly pray and pray. As the Apostles gathered and prayed together with me in the cenacle in Jerusalem in preparation for the Descent of the Holy Spirit, you, too, should pray with me in my Immaculate Heart as the Apostles of these end times.

In this period of purification, the devils, my enemies, are mobilizing all kinds of deceptions, even showing many supernatural phenomena and miracle-like occurrences. This way, they are misleading not only the innocent and good-willed souls, but also some priests and religious by instigating their curiosity and making them believe (the deceptions), bringing about confusion.

Therefore, in union with the Pope, who is the first son of the Church and has been nurtured by me, and under the guidance of this Heavenly Mother, bring the numerous souls, who are walking toward hell, to the Lord Who shed His Blood for the salvation of the world.

When you follow me believing, trusting and relying on me, I will carry out my Plan at your side through amazing methods; God the Son, Who is my Son, will establish a Kingdom of Glory filled with Love, Peace and Joy through you; and, through Him, there will be a Resurrection and a new Pentecost in this world.

When she ended speaking, the light disappeared, too.

January 6, 1996

At about 10:30 p.m., while praying the rosary during an overnight prayer service in observance of the First Saturday, I heard the loving and kind voice of the Blessed Mother from her statue in the Chapel.

THE BLESSED MOTHER:

Dear children who have been called by me! Pray with a greater sincerity and with love. Through the prayers that you offer together tonight, which has been set aside (for you) to be with me, the devil, who is afflicting you and is causing confusion through deceptions so that even the children who have been called by me may become alienated from my love, can be repelled.

The devil, the enemy, is confident that he has already won the victory in the Church. But, as I am always with you, I, your Heavenly Mother, will offer up the Pope, who is the first son of the Church, and you (plural) to the Lord's temple as (I did to) my Baby Jesus and will pour down the fragrant oil of balsam upon your heads so that you may be saved, if you walk the way of spiritual childhood and reform your lives humbly and as little persons according to the teachings in the Gospels and my messages of love.

The priests and children whom I have called! If you always follow me, who is your Heavenly Mother and the string that ties Heaven and earth together, I will accept you, protect you and prepare a refuge for you which will make you stronger and firmer. Therefore, hurriedly spread my messages of love to the numerous children who are wandering in darkness.

My Son Jesus is in Heaven, but is also present on earth with His Body, His Blood, His Soul and His Divinity, while hiding His Dignity, Humanity, and Divinity. Jesus in the Holy Eucharist will lead you to the pinnacle of prayer.

Children! My beloved children! Realize that the Love of my Son Jesus and me, your Heavenly Mother, is penetrating your souls, hearts and beings and rely (on Us) completely with faith and trust. Your bloody sacrifices, reparations, and prayers of love are necessary for the victory of My Son Jesus and my Immaculate Heart. Therefore, pray and follow my wishes hurriedly. Even if darkness worsens and sins spread everywhere, my burning Immaculate Heart will radiate light more brightly and you will be saved through graces and earn Heaven, if you practice my messages of love.

EPILOGUE

Signs from Heaven for Naju

By Father Raymond Spies
Anyang, South Korea—May 20, 1992
(Translated from French)

Oil flows from the statue. . .

The fragrance spreads. . .

The Messages are translated into English in the United States. . .

Oil has been oozing out of the statue in Naju. The oil began flowing before myself and a missionary (Father Juan-Manuel Martinez) who accompanied me to Naju on May 4, Monday. It flowed again before us on May 5, Tuesday. It is flowing even today, May 20, Wednesday. But from May 17, there has been a change.

This morning, at about 10:30, Rufino Park, who has been working closely by Our Lady's statue and assisting pilgrims ever since 1987, telephoned me, informing me that oil had been flowing continuously, every day, both on the front of the statue and on the back. But, on May 17, Sunday, it stopped flowing on the front, flowing on the back only and reaching the bottom of the statue. They ran out of the small pieces of linen to collect the fragrant oil. Today, I had more white, good-quality linen purchased in Anyang and had it cut into small pieces. Fifty pieces were sent to Naju to be placed under the statue.

On May 5, there were seven small pieces of linen that absorbed oil. They were distributed among my companions on the trip, the pilgrims and myself.

241

On May 12, Julia mailed more pieces to me, which arrived here at about 3:30 p.m. on May 14, Thursday. A very sweet and pleassant fragrance from the small pieces of linen filled the office where two of my assistants, Agnes (74 years old) and Luke, were with me. Luke had been to the post office in Anyang at 3 p.m. as usual, where we have a post office box. Upon return to our office, he handed over to me the day's mail. But, even while he still had the mail in his hands, Agnes and I clearly smelled a very strong, pleasant fragrance coming from the mail that Luke was holding in his hands. Spontaneously, Agnes and myself mentioned it. Luke confirmed it by giving me two very large envelopes from the United States by one same person. On the envelope, it said: *Extremely Urgent.*

Luke said, giving me the envelopes, *"The mailman at the post office asked, 'what is this strong fragrance coming from these two envelopes?'"* Luke did not know what to say. The mailman was very amazed.

When I opened the two envelopes and pulled out the contents, I immediately understood the reason for the fragrance, which was similar to the fragrance from the statue in Naju and from the oil that flows from the statue.

Inside the two envelopes were the complete text of the English translation of the Messages and letters. The fragrance was a sign of the Virgin's satisfaction, approval and blessing.

The translator is a Korean, actually a U.S. citizen. His name is Benedict (Benoit Labre in French) Sang M. Lee. He did the English translation with a sincere devotion in service to the Virgin.

While talking to Mr. Sang M. Lee on the phone on the same day, I told him about the surprising fragrance that was coming out of the two envelopes, the text of English translation and the letters that he had sent me. I told him it was a sign of benediction for him and his work of translation. Mr. Lee was totally surprised and happy about my call and the fragrance.

On May 15, Friday, the same mailman talked to Luke again about the fragrance. Today, May 20, Wednesday, Luke told me on returning from the post office, *"The mailman asked me about the fragrance again. . . . He remains totally amazed."* I suggested to Luke that he give the mailman a short explanation, even if he could not fully understand.

In the mean time, Julia continues spreading the Virgin's messages. In one of the messages, the Virgin told Julia, *"Let me borrow your mouth. . . ."* In fact, Julia has been invited to many places to make known the Messages at the call of the Virgin. The Virgin also said, *"It is this small land* (Korea) *from which my Love, my Light and my Victory will spread in the entire world through the intermediary of prayers and sacrifices of my little souls."*

May 20, 1992

Anyang, South Korea
P. Raymond Spies

The Blessed Mother's larger statue outside the Chapel in Naju

APPENDIX

*Some Practical Information for Pilgrims
Going to Naju, Korea*

I. Schedule of Events at the Blessed Mother's House *(the Chapel)* in Naju

1. Overnight Prayer Service—15 times a year:

- *June 30*—Anniversary of the Blessed Mother's first tears
- *October 19*—Anniversary of the Blessed Mother's first tears of blood
- *December 8*—Feast of the Immaculate Conception
- *First Saturday* of every month

The prayer meeting begins at about 9 p.m. and ends at about 6 the next morning. Rosary prayers, consecration to the Sacred Heart of Jesus and the Immaculate Heart of Mary, songs, testimonies by Julia and others. Julia also prays for everyone who wants her prayers near the end of the service (if she is not suffering pains at that time).

2. Holy Hours Devotion: Every Thursday evening (9-11 p.m.)

Prayer service especially in reparation for the insults, indifference and neglect of the Sacred Heart of Jesus in the Holy Eucharist.

The Chapel is always open for pilgrims. On Fridays, the Chapel office is closed, but visitors are welcome to pray in the Chapel.

The address of the Chapel is:

> The Blessed Mother's House
> 107-28 Kyo-Dong
> Naju, Jeonnam Province
> South Korea

The address of Julia's Spiritual Director is:

> Rev. Raymond Spies
> Centre Pere Damien
> P.O. Box 36
> Anyang, Kyungki-Do 430-600
> South Korea

II. Travel Information

Korean Airlines, Asiana Airlines, Japan Airlines, Northwest, Delta and United Airlines have almost daily flights from the U.S. West Coast (Seattle, WA; Portland, OR; San Francisco, CA; or Los Angeles, CA) to Kimpo International Airport near Seoul, Korea. The flight time from the U.S. West Coast to Korea is about ten and a half hours. The return flight takes only about nine and a half hours because of the westerly wind. The air fare for a round trip (Economy Class) varies between $600 and $900 from the West Coast depending on the season and other factors.

Kimpo International Airport is located about 12 miles west of downtown Seoul. There are buses and taxis available between the airport and Seoul. If you are scheduled to transfer to another flight from Kimpo to Kwangju (a city near Naju) on the same day you arrive in Kimpo, you will not need transportation to and from downtown Seoul. Currently, two airlines—Korean Airlines and Asiana Airlines—serve between Seoul and Kwangju.

When you arrive at Kimpo International Airport, you will first go through the entry procedure and, then, customs. If you have a U.S. or Canadian passport, you will not need a

Pilgrims from Singapore, Malaysia, Australia, Korea and other countries just after witnessing a Eucharistic Miracle to Julia in the Chapel in Naju. (July 3, 1995)

Pilgrims from the U.S.A. with Fr. Francis Su and Julia at the site for the new Basilica on the mountain near Naju. (October 21, 1995)

Korean visa for entry as a tourist for a stay of a month or less. If you would like a Korean visa, you can apply at a Korean Consulate office near your home. There is no inoculation requirement for entry into Korea. After the entry and customs procedures, you can exchange your currency for Korean won at any of the bank offices at the airport. The bank offices are located immediately outside the customs area. As of early 1996, the exchange rate is approximately 750 won per U.S. Dollar. If you have Korean money left at the time of departure from Korea, you can exchange it back into your currency. When you exchange your currency into Korean won upon arrival in Korea, you will be given a receipt from the bank office. You may need to show that to the bank to exchange Korean won back into your currency before departure from Korea. Also, remember that the Korean airports collect airport tax from departing passengers, which is a fee for using airport facilities. Currently, the amount of this tax is about US$15 when leaving Korea. The taxes for domestic flights are less.

Naju is a small city (population of about 80,000) in the Jeonnam Province located about 200 miles south of Seoul. It is almost at the southwestern tip of the Korean peninsula. The beach is only about 20 miles from Naju. Kwangju is the largest city near Naju with a population of about one million and is the capital of the Jeonnam Province. There are several Western-style hotels in Kwangju. If you are not part of a pilgrimage group, you will need to take a taxi or a bus between Kwangju and Naju. The drive time between Kwangju and Naju is about 30 minutes. There also are some lodging facilities in Naju which are in walking distance from the Chapel. They cost less than in Kwangju, but are simpler and probably less convenient than the hotels in Kwangju. Besides Kwangju and Naju, there is another city on the western beach where you can stay—Mokpo. It is a fishing harbor, where you can enjoy the beautiful scenery, too.

If you have enough time, you will get more out of the trip by taking a train or an express bus between Seoul and Kwangju instead of the airplane. Express buses for Kwangju leave the Seoul terminal every 30 minutes. By train or express bus, it will take about 4-6 hours between Seoul and Kwangju instead of just 45 minutes by airplane. Actually, there are express buses between Seoul and Naju, too (one every two hours). The express bus terminal in Seoul is located south of the Han River and is easily accessible by subway.

The climate in Korea is similar to that of the Northeastern and Central States in the U.S.A. with four distinct seasons: a hot and humid summer, a cold winter with some snow, and very pleasant spring and autumn. There is a rainy season in early summer. Most people in Korea cannot understand English, but you will find some English-speaking staff at the airports or hotels. The traditional religions in Korea are Confucianism and Buddhism, but now there are many Christians, too. Out of the population in the South of about 45 million, almost 10 million are Protestant, and about 2 million are Catholic. The crime rate is much lower than in U.S. cities, but much caution is advised when crossing streets in Korea, as the traffic is heavy and drivers are impatient.

III. A Possible Pilgrimage Schedule

(1) Arrival at Kimpo International Airport. Take a bus or a taxi to a hotel in Seoul.

(2) Next morning, take a taxi or subway to Seoul Train Station or the express bus terminal (unless you fly to Kwangju, in which case you have to go back to Kimpo Airport). Arrive in Kwangju in the afternoon. Rest at a hotel.

(3) On the third day, take a bus or taxi to Naju. Visit the Naju Parish Church and, then, the Chapel, which is also called the Blessed Mother's House. The distance between the Parish Church and the Chapel in Naju is about 10 minutes on foot. Pray in the Chapel. Participate in any prayer service held in the Chapel. Attend Mass at the Parish Church. Come back to the hotel in Kwangju, unless there is an overnight prayer service in the Chapel.

(4) Take a bus to the mountain where the new Basilica will be built. It will take about 20 minutes from Naju to the moun-

tain by bus. Currently, the road is so narrow and bumpy near the site for the new church that the bus will not take you all the way. So, you may have to walk for about 20 minutes after getting off the bus. Participate in the prayer service and Mass, if available, on the mountain. It is also the place where two miraculous springs are located. So, you will need to bring a plastic bottle to bring some water home. Many miraculous healings have been reported in connection with this water. Some pilgrims have even smelled the fragrance of roses from the water and even from the soil on the mountain. When English-speaking priests are available, you can make a Confession either in the Chapel in Naju or on the mountain.

(5) When you are finished with your activities in Naju and Kwangju over a span of several days, return to Seoul by air, train or express bus. While staying in Kwangju, you may attend Mass at one of the churches in Kwangju.

(6) Places to visit in Seoul:

a. *Myongdong Cathedral*, located in central downtown in Seoul. The best-known and one of the oldest Catholic churches in Korea. This Cathedral is often viewed as the center of the Catholic Church in Korea. There is a Catholic book and gift store just outside the Cathedral.

b. *Korean Martyrs Church*, which is located between downtown Seoul and Kimpo Airport. It was built on a small but steep mountain near the Han River. Thousands of Korean Catholics were martyred at this location in the late 19th Century. There is a small museum and a bookstore in the same building. Pope John Paul II visited this Church in 1984, when he came to Korea to canonize more than one hundred of the Korean martyrs. In Naju, the Blessed Mother has mentioned twice that her giving signs and messages in Korea is related to the sacrifices by so many Korean Catholic martyrs.

c. *Kyungbok Palace* in downtown Seoul near the Blue House, which is the current presidential office and residence in Korea. There is a small fee to enter this palace. There are many old traditional-style buildings which were used as offices and residences for the Korean kings and their families.

d. If you are intersted in some shopping and have time for it, the best known places are: Namdaemoon Market located between central downtown Seoul and the Seoul Railroad Station; Itaewon, which is located just south of a U.S. military base in Seoul, just north of the Han River; and many department stores like Lotte, Shinshegye and Midopa.

Parishioners of Sacred Heart Church in Auckland, New Zealand, honoring the replica statue of Our Lady of Naju. A sweet fragrance of roses filled the area. (April 1995)

Testimonies on Naju

Since the beginning of the miracle in Naju in 1985, numerous people have experienced amazing changes in their lives—reconciliation in their families which had been thought impossible, returning to a fervent practice of the Catholic Faith, conversion from other faiths to the Catholic Faith, devoting time and resources to spreading Our Lady's messages, experiencing cures of difficult and even incurable physical illnesses, and so on. In deep gratitude to the Lord and the Blessed Mother and filled with joy, many of them have testified during prayer meetings in the Chapel in Naju and some of them have left their testimonies in writing. The following is just a few of the written testimonies on Naju. *(Some of them are translations from Korean.)*

1. Raphael Kim, Youngkwang, Jeonnam, South Korea (May 20, 1992)

On the day we first visited Naju, the Blessed Mother was weeping lots of tears of blood through her statue. We cried loudly for a long time, repenting our sins and our indifference to her, who was actually so close to us all the time. Since then, we visited Naju frequently, filled with the desire to see the Blessed Mother.

On October 19, 1990, we attended an overnight prayer service for the first time. While listening to Julia relay the Blessed Mother's messages to us, I could not control myself and wept so much repenting my sins.

When Julia prayed for me near the end of the prayer meeting, I felt her hand as hot as an iron as it was touching my chest. I also felt an intense pain on the left side of my chest, which lasted until the next day. But, on subsequent days, my health improved visibly every day. My diabetes, which had afflicted me for 30 years, was gone! I stopped all the medication for the diabetes, but felt as light as a feather in my body. Now I can eat anything: rice, candy, chocolate, etc. My 20 year-old arthritis was also cured. Before, I had trouble bending my knees. Excess water had to be taken out of my knee joints. Now, it is all gone.

My mother had her first stroke in October 1991. She was in the hospital for three months. But, on May 1, 1992, she had another stroke. Doctors said it was hopeless. The whole family (25) gathered, expecting the worst. But, because my mother loved the Blessed Mother in Naju so much, we informed Julia. She came at about 10 p.m. on May 3. We were shocked, when Julia began praying for my mother's recovery. Everyone had already given up hope. My mother remained unconscious.

A while later, as Julia continued praying, my mother opened her eyes and, looking at Julia, said, *"The holy water!"* and, *"Forgive me."* Julia prayed so fervently. She prayed for each of us, too. She left a little past midnight. My mother continued recovery and ate some food. By daybreak, she became fully alert and spoke clearly.

All of us were in such a shock that we couldn't even talk well. Our nine brothers and sisters were all married, but had different religions. We had lots of distrust and tension in the family. Now, because of Julia's prayers, we cried and repented. Instead of blaming each other, we all admitted our own faults. This was a truly amazing miracle. We embraced each other and cried loudly asking for forgiveness. We offered up our endless gratitude to the Lord and the Blessed Mother for the restored peace in our family.

In fact, my mother was always sad about the different religions and tension among her children and offered rosary prayers for each of us from 3:30 a.m. every day. God allowed this grace of conversion and restoration of peace in the family because of my mother's and Julia's prayers.

Through Julia's prayers for each of us that night, my 83 year-old father-in-law was cured of an intestinal inflammation, which everyone said was incurable. Four others were cured of various sicknesses like ulcers, arthritis, and pleurisy. My whole family converted because of these amazing miracles. We all came back to the Blessed Mother in Naju and began a life of prayers.

Praise to the Lord and the Blessed Mother in all eternity for curing and sanctifying our family. Amen.

*   *   *

2. Mary Lee, Busan, Korea (May 1992)

My name is Mary Lee living in Busan, Korea. When I was born, there was a hole in my heart. Doctors said I could not live more than a few months. But I did not die. I left the hospital when I was three years old.

Since then, I grew up without God in my life. It was a sinful life. But my condition deteriorated and I had to go to the hospital again. The doctor said the hole reappeared in my heart and was growing. He said I needed surgery. This was very painful to me, both psychologically and physically. I was not able to pay for the surgery, but my parents and the rest of my family helped. I was hospitalized on September 2, 1989 and went through many tests. The surgery was on September 11 and took eight and a half hours.

One month later, I left the hospital. I was weeping for joy in the taxi coming home. Then, I was visiting the hospital periodically for checkup and treatment. But, disappointingly, the chest pain got worse and there was also a lump growing on my chest. At night, I was unable to sleep because of the pain. So, I had to go through another surgery. One month later, there still was no improvement and, so, there was another surgery. By that time, there even was inflammation in my bones and bone marrow. Parts of my ribs had to be cut off. These operations were so painful. I had to take so much medicine and injections every day. I even wanted to die.

But, one day, I somehow began praying to the Blessed Mother. There was a statue of hers at the entrance of the hospital. I prayed before the statue every evening, *"Forgive me and rescue me. Let me get out of this hospital, please."* About two months after I started the prayer, I asked the doctor so persistently to let me go home that he finally did. But my condition did not improve and my bones continued to decay.

One day, I went to a prayer meeting at a church in Choryang, a northern suburb of Busan. There, I met a lady who told me about the weeping statue of the Blessed Mother in Naju. Again, that night, I was not able to sleep because of the pain.

The next morning, I went to the lady who told me about Naju. She lent me some video tapes from Naju. As I was watching them at home that night, I felt as if my heart were breaking up. I realized that God truly exists and also that the Blessed Mother truly lives. I cried and cried watching the tapes all night.

The next day, I asked the same lady if I could visit Naju. She introduced me to another lady who had experienced many blessings in Naju. She told me much about Naju and also said that I could be cured, both spiritually and physically, if I went there.

Later, I was able to visit Naju. There, I watched another video showing Julia's sufferings. I cried so much, repenting my sins. I was able to firmly believe that Jesus and the Blessed Mother were alive. In the past, I hated many people around me—my parents, brothers, sisters, husband and neighbors. Sometimes, I was angry with God, too. But, now, I realized that all the problems were because of my own fault. I cried continuously, beating my chest and thinking that Julia was suffering because of my sins.

I felt so grateful to the Blessed Mother, because I was led to the Lord and received so much grace from Him through the Blessed Mother's tears and Julia's sufferings. I came home filled with grace and joy.

A few days later, I wanted to go to Naju again. So, I did with a few friends. Since then, I went to Naju several times every month and found my health steadily improving. Soon, my bones became completely cured. I stopped taking pills and shots altogether. My stomach, liver and kidneys became healthy, too. My heart problem disappeared totally. Before, my body was a total mess with so many sicknesses and seven surgeries. When I converted and repented before the Lord, He completely cured my physical sicknesses as well. Our Lord also took care of our dire poverty. Now we even run our own store.

Blessed Mother! You called this wretched and unworthy

sinner with your tears and led me to the Lord. You are truly our Mediatrix!

Truly living Jesus! All the glory to You in all eternity! Amen.

*   *   *

3. Angela Lim, Busan, Korea (June 1992)

My name is Angela Lim living in Busan, South Korea. I divorced my husband 18 years ago and have been raising two children. No one will understand how many times I have cried or how much pain I have endured. Tears of blood have been flowing inside me.

I was so resentful and decided to take revenge by earning as much money as possible and raising the children in the best way possible. I worked like an ox, even though I had some sickness. My heart was always sizzling with resentment and anger, unable to forgive. I was angry with the world and, sometimes, even with God.

On December 8, 1987, I had an opportunity to visit Naju. There was a prayer meeting for the consecration of the new Chapel, to which the Blessed Mother's statue was moved from Julia's apartment. At that meeting, Julia relayed the Blessed Mother's messages to us:

The just anger of God the Father is overflowing. Do not criticize or judge others, but convert yourself. . . . Families are sick. Sanctify your family by loving one another. Never blame others, but always blame yourself only. Those who accept my messages will experience a renewal of their souls through my messages of love. . . .

I was totally shaken up by these messages and Julia's testimonies. I was crying loudly. Until that time, I always thought that I was right. I never admitted any fault on my part. As I had always been blaming others and been full of anger, I felt so shameful before the Lord and the Blessed Mother. My heart was shaken up in an indescribable way and I was crying uncontrollably. I cried and cried, as I was deciding to forgive and accept my husband.

People around me in the Chapel asked me to control the noise. So, I crawled out and began cleaning the bathroom floor. I cleaned it thoroughly remembering Julia's words: *Let us be-*

come a mop to clean souls. I wanted to become a mop for cleaning my husband, who was sick both spiritually and physically. I continued cleaning other corners around the Chapel. I felt so grateful to Julia, who suffered pains for the conversion of others, including me.

I went to the place where my husband was staying. He was in bed alone and very sick. He also had many debts. Momentarily, I felt angry, but soon this was replaced with an overwhelming sense of pity. We came home together and the Blessed Mother gradually restored his health. I got my spouse back after 18 long years, thanks to the Blessed Mother and her love. *"My dear children! Love even your enemies. If you live according to the love of God, you will be saved."* These words of the Blessed Mother given to us through Julia were the medicine that gave our family a new life.

How can we say we love the Lord without loving our spouses, regardless of the situation? When I see his shortcomings, I realize they are truly my own shortcomings. My husband now looks like St. Joseph to me, as the Blessed Mother is filling my ignorant heart with her love.

The grace I received was so precious that I have been encouraging others to accept the Blessed Mother's love, too. Sometimes, we rent a bus, as there were quite a few people who wanted to visit Naju. Many around me, my relatives, friends and neighbors have been baptized. Sometimes, even Buddhist monks and Protestant clergymen joined the group and converted with tears in front of the Blessed Mother's statue in Naju. My husband is always anxious that I do not miss the trip to Naju. Often, he cannot come along because of the business. When I go to Naju without him, he waits for me at home in the evening, praying with a candlelight lit.

Now, whenever we have any difficulties or pains, I rush to the Blessed Mother in Naju. So far, she has taken care of all our problems. She knows all about our problems, whether they are spiritual or physical. Whenever we rush to her, trusting her, she helps us—not just me but my whole family. We have experienced this so many times. Our Lord also cures, through the Blessed Mother, physical sicknesses which were declared incurable by doctors.

Before visiting Naju, I had tried many other ways: charismatic prayer retreats, fasting, overnight prayers and so on.

But I could not find peace of mind from them. The Blessed Mother cured my hardened heart and liberated me with love in Naju.

I am writing this testimony in immense gratitude to the Lord for curing my spiritual and physical sicknesses. I hope that others who are in difficulties will also find the boundless love of the Blessed Mother in Naju. Our Blessed Mother frequently said that we could reach glory only through suffering.

I cannot write here about all of the numerous sufferings I went through before conversion. Now I realize that even those many sufferings were given to me, because the Lord loves me. I give the Lord and the Blessed Mother my endless gratitude. I pray that each and every family in the whole world experience this healing by the Lord and become a small church.

*   *   *

4. Eli Saison, Manila, The Philippines (1992)

I am Eli Saison, living in Paranaque, Metro Manila. I am 53 years of age and married and have seven children.

I have been a professional musician playing the guitar and the piano for the past 35 years and am presently employed as musical director and pianist/singer at Concourse Bar of the Nikko Hotel Manila Garden.

Life was good to me, and although there were ups and downs in my life, no major tragedy had happened to me, not until September 6, 1991, when I lost the use of my right arm and right leg while I was driving my car. I had to deliberately swerve my car with my left hand to an electric post to stop the vehicle, since my right foot could not step on the brakes.

A bystander helped me and brought me to the Makati Medical Center. Four doctors of Makati Medical Center initially suspected a heart problem. However, after further medical examinations and heart scannings, they found nothing wrong with my heart. Two doctors, Dr. Jamora and his associate, recommended a brain scan. Four brain scans on me were done, and it was then that they discovered a brain tumor. Doctors recommended an immediate operation to remove the tumor. After a 12-hour operation, a mass or tumor as big as an egg was removed from the left side of my brain. This tumor was found to be malignant. After a recuperation of three months, I was able to acquire the use of my right arm and to walk with a limp, as my right leg had not fully recovered.

Tragedy struck me again when sometime during Holy Week, particularly Good Friday, I lost my left eyesight. My left eye had gone completely blind and only my right eye was functioning. I underwent laser treatment four times on my left eye, but nothing happened. There was no improvement to my left eye no matter how slight. During this time, although I had recovered the use of my limbs, I was still limping due to the weakness on my right leg. According to my doctors, the damage to my left eye and right leg, was done by the malignant tumor, which had been removed.

I confided this problem to Attorney Nordy P. Diploma. I told him that I was afraid of a recurring malignant tumor, considering that we could not be sure that everything was removed. Atty. Diploma advised me to put my faith and trust in God. He invited me to attend a healing Mass at Greenbelt Chapel on May 12, 1992, as at that time there was a visiting visionary from Korea, whom I later found out to be Julia Kim. During Julia's prayers and meditation, I smelled the sweet fragrance of roses filling the entire Chapel. Such a sweet smell, I am sure, was experienced by the entire congregation in the Chapel.

The following day, there was another healing Mass celebrated in a church in Katipunan St., Quezon City. After the Mass, Julia prayed and meditated. While she was relaying the messages of the Virgin Mary to the congregation, she felt some pain in her head. She announced that somebody in the congregation who was in a brain illness was being cured. She repeated this announcement twice since she must have felt much pain in her head. After Mass, I felt considerably better and proceeded to the residence of Atty. Diploma. It was there that his aunt and sister noticed a sweet fragrance of roses from me, which my children also smelled when I reached home about two hours later.

The following day Atty. Diploma and I went to Mrs. Mercy Tuazon's residence, where Julia was staying. I was introduced to Julia when we arrived. Julia then felt pain in her left eye and in her head. She was also limping. She then went to her room to rest. When Julia came out, she prayed for other people and, then, came to me and touched my left eye and left temple. She prayed for me in her own Korean language. While she was praying for me, I felt a coldness in my body. After Julia prayed for me, Atty. Diploma motioned for us to leave. I indicated to Atty. Diploma to wait awhile. I then noticed that my vision becoming clearer. I covered my right eye to test whether my eyesight on the left eye had been restored. Praise God! My left eye could see now! I told my friends the astonishing news. I thank God for this cure bestowed on me.

Atty. Diploma and I went home after the session at Mrs. Mercy Tuazon's residence.

Later that week I contacted the eye doctors who had treated me and told them the good news and the healing of my eye. They could not believe me. They told me it must be a miracle. Yes, there is no doubt in my mind that a miracle happened to me. Deep in my heart, however, I know that it was more than just a miracle of healing my cancer, which was a miracle of having been given back by Almighty God my playing skills as a pianist and my voice as a singer to be of better service again to my fellow men.

I have tried to tell this personal account of my healing with only one purpose in mind, which is to tell what happened to me as accurately as possible, without adding to or subtracting from what actually happened. I give this testimony with no other intention than to glorify the infinite goodness and mercy of God Almighty.

*   *   *

5. Danny Guilas, Manila, the Philippines (October 1992)

Dear Julia,

I am Danny C. Guilas, a civil engineer working for Mr. Nordy P. Diploma, an attorney, in Manila, the Philippines.

I have had a kidney problem since I graduated from college. It has become serious since two years ago. Both kidneys were not functioning any more. I also had a hard time financially, but did not blame God. When Mr. Diploma commissioned me to an extension work at the Chapel (in Manila), I was glad that I could continue supporting my family and pay my medical bills. But the medicines just gave me a temporary relief from the pain. Both arms were numb, back pains were all over, and every joint in my body was swollen for the last two years.

When Mr. Diploma arrived from Korea, he told me that Julia Kim, the visionary of the Blessed Mother, was coming soon and informed me about her healing power. I was not that religious, but, one thing for sure, I wanted to be cured.

On October 10, 1992, Saturday, Mr. Diploma told me to finish the work in his house before the guests, including Julia, arrived. He also instructed me to attend the Sunday service (the next day) and be prayed for by Julia.

On Sunday morning, I felt very tired and had pain all over my body. I took medicine which gave me some relief and enabled me to go to Mass.

My wife and I attended Mass just like any ordinary Sunday Masses. Things began changing when Mr. Diploma introduced me to Julia. Though I did not understand a single word Julia was saying, I was listening intently, partially ignoring the interpreter. When Julia asked us to close our eyes during prayers, I did so without knowing what would happen next. Though my eyes were closed, I could distinguish Julia's voice, because she was speaking Korean, followed by the interpreter. While I was listening to the prayer, I noticed that there were three female voices praying. Knowing that there were only two, I opened my eyes to see if someone else joined the prayer. I looked around, but could not see the third woman.

Moments later, Mr. Diploma was passing by, saying, "Hi!" to me. A while later, he came back and tapped me on my shoulders with both hands. At that moment, I felt a cold wind on my back and I felt freezing. I held on to my wife, sensing that I might fall down.

After Mass, I decided not to go to Mr. Diploma's residence, because it was hard to sustain myself. I asked my wife to drive straight home so that I could rest. I was going to visit the doctor for a shot by 5 p.m. When I woke up at about 4 p.m., I still felt very tired. But I got up to go to the doctor and get the shot, because I had to work on Monday.

At that moment, blood was coming out of my nose and did not stop. We hurriedly ran to the car. But, when I tried to start the car, it wouldn't. So, I told my wife that I was not going to get the shot, remembering the strange things that were happening since the Mass.

After dinner, while my wife was doing the dishes in the kitchen, I suddenly smelled a fragrance of flowers. I told my wife about it, but she said she did not smell any. But she said she did smell the fragrance that morning when we were leaving home for Mass.

I went to bed earlier than usual that night. I was urinating more often than normal that night. When I finally woke up at around 3 a.m., I found the strangest but the greatest change that happened to me. The usual back pains, the sore and swollen joints and chest pains were all gone. I was a little bit hesitant moving my body because of the fear that the pain might come back. But it didn't.

For more than 2 years, I was limping. The people living and working in Mr. Diploma's house can testify to this. I haven't done any fast walking, but this morning I ran two kilometers, just like three to four years ago. The village manager of Bel-Air knows about my sickness. She can also testify. The son of Judge Caguiao also knows about my sickness and can be a witness. I was not very religious, but now believe that miracles do happen. I know I was cured. I know that, through Julia, Mr. Diploma was made an instrument, an extension of her healing power from the Almighty that Sunday morning.

Praise God! Thank you very much, Julia and Mr. Diploma!

*   *   *

6. Viviana Lee, Kyungnam Province, South Korea (January 1995)

+ Praise Jesus!

I had been a Catholic for many years, but did not pay much attention to the Blessed Mother's Love. I was just too busy struggling with my own illness and for my own survival. I went to Mass on Sundays and offered the morning and evening prayers daily, but that was about all I did as a Catholic.

I had surgery eight times for my vertebra caries (decay of the spinal column). I suffered so much pain and got goose bumps when I even thought of surgery. Because of this illness, I was not able to do anything: I could not sleep on a mattress, but only on the bare floor; I could not ride a car; I could not wash my own socks; I could not walk up stairs; I could not do anything. It was my husband who did everything for me.

I needed another surgery, but it would cost us 10 million won (about US$13,000). My younger sister, who was a Sister working in the Naju Parish at that time, told me about the Blessed Mother's statue weeping in Naju. I went to see her statue, but it was so crowded that I came back without seeing her. The statue was in the beauty salon owned by Julia. Actually, I did not believe that a statue could weep.

Later I went to Naju again and saw the Blessed Mother's weeping through her statue. I wept, too, and I wept a lot. I said, *"Mother, why are you weeping? Are you weeping because of this sinner?"* By that time, my health had deteriorated even further. I also had cholelithiasis (the presence of gallstones), bloody urine, and jaundice. I said to the Blessed Mother, *"Mother, please do not cry. If I am to die, I can accept it."* Moved by the Blessed Mother's weeping, I repented my sins and wept so much—for the first time in my life. *"Mother, you are asking us to pray, because you feel so much sorrow in your Heart."* I began praying the Rosary fervently.

I did not ask for the healing of my illness, but, while I was offering prayers of repentance, I realized that my pains were gone and I was completely healed.

Since that day, I have never been sick; I have never taken any medicine; and I have never gotten any injections. I came home and told those in my home and Parish, but they had a hard time believing my words. Later, they also visited Naju and believed when they saw the Blessed Mother's weeping.

My love for the Blessed Mother has been growing, and I have been visiting Naju again and again in response to her calls. Other people who have visited Naju with me for the past ten years have also experienced many spiritual and physical miracles. I will introduce just one of them.

There was a young woman called Mi Sook Yoo. She was so sick that she visited many hospitals and tried many medicines. She even needed help in the bathroom. None of the treatment or medicine worked. She even visited a fortune teller who told her that her illness had been caused by devils and she needed an exorcist ritual. When I invited her to go to Naju instead, she refused, saying, *"I even have trouble sitting up. How can I ride a car?"* I insisted, *"Let's leave everything to the Blessed Mother and go."* She came along. I let her remain sitting up in the Chapel throughout the overnight prayer service.

Mi Sook spent the night in the Chapel crying so much. She received abundant graces from the Blessed Mother.

When she came home, her husband was in good mood. *"The Blessed Mother gave us lots of fragrance at home last night. I feel so good. How were you?"* He asked his wife to join the Catholic Church. Mi Sook was completed liberated from illness. They were baptized and began a fervent devotional life in the Church. Mi Sook received the baptismal name of *"Mary"* and her husband *"Joseph."* I became their godmother.

Besides Mi Sook, many others who had been staying away from the Church came back to the bosom of the Lord. Many who had not experienced the Blessed Mother's love before began living a life of much prayer and love after their visit to Naju.

I believe that we should double our prayers after we receive a special grace. I had been facing death, but was cured. Now, I pray 80-100 decades of rosary per day and attend Mass every day. Some say, *"You have been cured already. Why are you still going to Naju?"* Maybe they needed to be scolded by the Lord. Too many people forget about giving thanks after receiving graces.

My brothers and sisters! Let's not think about worldly things but about heavenly matters. Let us all hold the Blessed Mother's hands, get on board the Mary's Ark of Salvation and sail to the Harbor of Heaven. Thank you.

*   *   *

7. Marcia M. Czarnecki, Mechanicsburg, Pennsylvania (January 14, 1995)

Dear Julia,

I want to thank you for coming to Toronto, Canada so that I could hear Our Blessed Mother's messages given to you. I received many graces that evening and continue to do so through reading the book, *The Miracle in Naju, Korea—Heaven Speaks to the World*, and watching the videos concerning the miracles in Naju.

The greatest miracle I have received is the grace to see what the Will of God is for my life and to desire it alone. Before hearing Our Blessed Mother's messages to you at Naju, I wasn't sure what she and her Son Jesus were asking of me, especially in my relationship with my husband. I was on the road of doing my own will and doing what made me happy instead of doing what made Jesus and Mary happy. The messages from Naju seem particularly made for me and all sinners who have lost their way and are feeling very discouraged by their weakness and sinfulness.

When I heard Mary's words on the video, *Tears of Love*, *"How can you say you love me and my Son when you don't love those in your own family,"* I was shown my sinfulness and failure. I heard Our Blessed Mother calling me to unity by loving, trusting, respecting and being faithful to my husband. It was as if a light went on penetrating my darkened mind and softening my hardened heart. I heard Our Lady calling me to be obedient to my spiritual director, to renounce myself and my selfish desire, to suffer gracefully, without complaining, uniting my sufferings with Jesus for the salvation of souls, to pray for priests, bishops and the Holy Father, and most especially to a profound love and a deeper belief in the Real Presence of Jesus in the Eucharist.

In trying to respond to Our Lady's messages to you at Naju, my marriage has been saved after twenty-two years of enormous struggles and pain. My husband has had a profound conversion. He is now the husband that Jesus calls all husbands to be. We pray together daily as a family and share our joys and sufferings.

On October 25, 1994, when you walked into the Convocation Hall at the University of Toronto, a beautiful perfume emanating from you filled the room. You smiled at us all with such love I felt the presence of Jesus and Mary in the room. The vision you shared with us that you had during the Eucharistic miracle on September 24, 1994 about the large ships which were sailing in the ocean showed me I was stepping out of the safe boat with the Eucharistic Jesus, Mary and the

Holy Father into the other boat where my desires for worldly happiness would be satisfied.

Later that evening I cried and I heard many others crying while you prayed out loud in our behalf for the healing and loving hands of Jesus and Mary to touch our hearts. I felt a great hope and renewed courage to follow only Jesus and Mary as you left the room.

To my great amazement, you gave me the awesome gift of inviting me to meet you after you spoke. Before going to Toronto, I told my spiritual director my great fear of being in your presence because I had heard you had been given the grace to read souls. Because of my sinfulness, I was sure you would ask me to leave the auditorium before speaking to us that evening. Father promised me not only would you not throw me out but I would get to meet you personally and that you would hug and kiss me! You did just that! You stood up as I came downstairs and walked towards me, took both my hands, smiled at me and hugged and kissed me! I truly felt Jesus and Mary telling me through you that they still loved me even though I was a terrible sinner and that they were helping me to stand up and begin again with their love and strength to support me.

Whenever I have sinned again since then, I have received the grace to make a sincere Confession and begin anew. I sincerely believe it is because of your suffering and prayers for the conversion of poor sinners that I have received these graces. I feel Our Blessed Mother's powerful intercession and her merciful love for her children. I feel her leading me ever nearer to the Eucharistic Heart of her Son.

I have always believed in the Real Presence of Jesus in the Eucharist, but after seeing the video on Naju and reading about the seven miracles that you have had, my love and devotion for Jesus in the Eucharist has increased hundredfold.

Thank you, Julia, for being Our Blessed Mother's most humble and obedient servant. In doing so, you are showing me and others the narrow way Jesus and Mary want us to follow so as to bring peace to our hearts and homes and to enter Heaven someday.

*   *   *

8. Reverend Tae Hyung Kang, Kwangmin Presbyterian Church, Kwangju, South Korea (1995)

I am a Protestant clergyman at Kwangmin Presbyterian Church in Kwangju. First of all, I would like to express my deepest gratitude to the Lord for allowing me an opportunity today to write a testimony on the numerous graces that I have received from the Blessed Mother and also on my beliefs.

Earlier I had worked in the Kyungki Province, but the Lord led me to the city of Kwangju in 1993. One of the most impor-tant events that have happened to me since I moved to Kwangju has been that I have been frequently visiting the Blessed Mother's House in Naju. In the course of these visits, I have clearly experienced the love and graces from the living Lord and have acquired an understanding that Jesus, in whom I had believed since a long time ago, sent the Blessed Mother to all of us, sinners. In other words, I have discovered the impor-tant lesson that the Marian devotion, as taught by the Catho-lic Church, is pleasing to Jesus. For this reason, I, a Protes-tant minister, am ready to face any disadvantages that may fall upon me because of the call by my loving Jesus and my devotion to the Blessed Mother. The fact that I, who am un-worthy, have acquired the Marian devotion, has not been as-sociated with anyone in this world. I only hope that the Lord will protect me to the end. Sometimes, I have also restrained my desire to visit the Blessed Mother's House to avoid incon-veniencing the workers of Our Lady by frequent visits by a Protestant clergyman, even though these visits have not been caused by mere curiosity.

The Bible says that faith is a gift of the Holy Spirit (I Cor. 12:9). Therefore, my Marian devotion is also a gift of the Holy Spirit, which may have some bearing for my vocation, which I don't know yet. On September 24, 1994, the Blessed Mother gave us a message of love especially for the Protestants:

The small, separated churches have not accepted me yet, but will gradually accept me as the Mother of the Church.... Spread my words of love not just to Catholics but to all my children.

How wonderful it would be if the churches which have been divided since the 16th Century discontinue all the en-mity and fighting and become one based on brotherly love through the grace from the Blessed Mother! St. John of the Cross said:

Most merciful God! Please give the Spirit of Thy Son to all the souls. Without Thee, we cannot do anything.

The Bible further says that not even a bird will fall from the sky, unless God allows it (Matthew 10:29). It can also be said that the Reformation would not have occurred without God's permission. The important lesson from this is that this unfortunate event in Church history was caused by human sins and represented a chastisement from God.

Anyhow, the Blessed Mother's messages give a new mission and hope to both Catholics and Protestants. All of us should walk toward the Blessed Mother, hold her warm hands, listen to her loving voice, be embraced in her bosom and become one as brothers and sisters and, thereby, accomplish the important historical event of becoming one in the Love of Jesus.

The Blessed Mother has appeared and given messages at many places around the world during the past several centuries. Particularly, in Naju, Korea, she has been giving us very special signs and messages. In Naju, she has been revealing to us numerous signs, such as tears and tears of blood, fragrant oil, fragrance, and Eucharistic miracles, and messages for the past 10 years since 1985. I understand that there is no other place in the world with such powerful and objective manifestations for such a long time at one same location. Until now, numerous people have personally seen, heard, touched, smelled, and received the miraculous Communion; drunk the water from the mountain; and experienced graces! Many people have also experienced cures of incurable illnesses. In addition, countless people who had lost faith and left the Church have repented and returned to the Lord!

In the Bible, we find two persons who are contrasting examples. One is Judas Iscariot, who had accompanied Jesus for three years and yet betrayed Him and fell into eternal perdition. The other is the thief on the right of Jesus on the Cross, who believed the Lord and was saved at the moment of his death. What made the difference was "faith." No matter how long one may have been a believer, how lofty a position one may be in, and how much recognition one may get from others, he will be deserted if he does not have the kind of faith that Jesus can accept (Matthew 7:21-27). The leaders of Israel at the time of Jesus believed in God, but refused to believe in Jesus. Even the great St. Paul had not only been an unbeliever in Jesus, but judged Him as the head of the heretics and persecuted His disciples before his conversion. We need to remember the following words of God which apply to our world as well as to the past:

But I know that you do not have the love for God in you (John 5:42).

This means that those who believed in God but lacked the love for God failed to recognize Jesus as the Son of God and the Messiah. *The Kingdom of God is not in speech but in power* (I Cor. 4:20). According to John 7:31 and 9:30, a person who had been blind from birth and was cured was wondering why the Jewish leaders and Pharisees were not believing Jesus. The same kind of things are happening in today's world. Again, it is a matter of "faith." At the time of Jesus' public life, humans were tested on their belief in God's work through their acceptance of Jesus. Now in this end time, we are being tested in our belief in the work of Jesus through our acceptance of the Blessed Mother. What is important is the ability to discern. This ability is a power from the Lord which He gives to those who truly love Him.

As stated in John 10, we should become God's people who recognize His Voice through Jesus. By the same token, we should become the Lord's sheep who recognize His Voice through the Blessed Mother.

As stated in John 17:20, God and Jesus are One and the Blessed Mother is with Jesus. The early Fathers of the Church had this faith and the Saints possessed it. We should become people who inherit this tradition of faith. True faith means that one should have a sincere desire for childlike innocence and truth and courage to deny oneself, and willingly carry the cross for the Lord.

If anyone refuses to believe, continues to doubt, and throws vicious accusations despite so many signs and anxious calls by the Blessed Mother in Naju, he would not only be persecuting the workers of the Blessed Mother, but foolishly poking at the eyes of Jesus. The Blessed Mother is the Mother to all people. She is the loving Mother to Catholics, Protestants and unbelievers. I sincerely hope that her messages be spread to many people. As the Blessed Mother says, the corruption of humans worsens day after day, and the world is standing at the edge of a cliff, inviting its own destruction. Even the Church has been affected by the secular spirit and is sick. All of us must hurriedly arm ourselves with the Immaculate Heart of Mary, wake up from sleep, and change our lives based on the Blessed Mother's messages, which, in turn, are based on the Gospels. I pray in the Name of Jesus that we become one in the Lord and the Blessed Mother. Amen.

*   *   *

9. Mrs. Mercedes Diploma, Manila, The Philippines (November 14, 1995)

While I was visiting a friend's house earlier this month, I became ill, experiencing much difficulty breathing and feeling extremely dizzy. I felt that I was dying and went to a hospital. Doctors diagnosed my condition as stenocardia (the narrowing of blood vessels in the heart). My blood pressure was 240/130. To make things worse, they also found out that my lungs were filled with fluid. They sent me to an intensive care unit.

For almost four days, I was in a coma and did not know what was happening to me. Because I was not getting any oxygen, doctors decided to insert a tube through a hole in my neck. At that moment, my son, Nordy Diploma, asked the doctors to wait for a few minutes and gave me a piece of cloth that had absorbed the fragrant oil from Our Lady's statue in Naju. Julia Kim had given that cloth to Nordy. When the cloth was placed on me, a miracle happened. My blood pressure came down to 140/80. I felt my condition improving. There was no need for surgery, as my health was improving.

Later this cloth was lost while I was still in the hospital room. So, Nordy gave me his handkerchief that Julia had prayed over during her visit to the Philippines. I touched various parts of myself with that handkerchief. My health continued improving and soon I was out of hospital. Now, I am healthier than before. Thank you so much.

*   *   *

10. Peter Ryoo, Joo-An Parish, Inchon, South Korea

My beloved little souls! The sun is light. The Lord Who came as Light is shedding light on you by opening Heaven. These signs from Heaven signify the mystery of salvation. They also mean that the Lord is with you and is blessing you and this land.
—The Blessed Mother's Message in Naju on December 5, 1991

It was February 4, 1995 when I first visited Naju. It was January 5 according to the Lunar Calendar, just a few days after New Year's Day, a big holiday in Korea. It was also my 55th birthday. In previous years, there were lively celebrations on my birthdays with lots of food prepared by my wife, Theresa, and with many visiting relatives. But, this year, we asked our relatives not to come, because I was going to visit Naju together with my wife and my sister-in-law (my wife's elder sister), who was in her 70s. Many expressed concern about the trip considering my poor health.

We arrived in Naju at about 8 p.m. The Chapel, which is about the size of a school classroom, was completely packed with 700-800 people. I managed to step in the back corner of the Chapel, but could not find enough space to sit. I finally sat down with my legs crouched. It was hard for me because of the continuing pain in my heart. I kept feeling like running out of the Chapel. I could not pay attention to the talk given by Julio, Julia's husband.

I thought, *"People should be sleeping at this hour. Why are these people spending the night in this crowded Chapel?"*

I came to Naju after three months of struggling with my illness: the hardening and expanding of the arteries in my heart. It was my last effort. Doctors had told me that my heart was functioning at less than 20 percent of its capacity and that I could live only about six more months at most, unless I receive a new heart. How could I describe the shock to my family! I learned this only when my wife told me about it. But the operation for a heart transplant would be a very difficult and risky one. Besides, it would be extremely difficult to find a heart to transplant. I gave up staying in the hospital and began a life of continuous prayer.

I have been staying away from the Church for ten years since marriage. It has been a time full of vicissitudes: neglecting the Church, wandering and failing in business. How can I repent all of my sinful life? Will the Lord really forgive me? Because of my heart drooping down below the left side of my chest, it was difficult for me to sit up, lie down or move around. I had trouble sleeping and also frequently had severe difficulty breathing while in bed, which was a life-threatening situation.

I also had trouble eating and lost more than 20 pounds. As I was approaching death, I received the Sacrament of the Sick from the Pastor. Relatives and friends kept visiting me.

The first night in Naju was a difficult one for me because of the pain in my heart. My wife was watching me and asked me to go outside for fresh air. But I couldn't. Besides, I was listening to the readings of the Blessed Mother's messages. Near dawn, Julia began praying for individuals. Because I was sitting in the back, I had my turn only at about 7 a.m. When I went to the front where the Blessed Mother's statue was, I smelled a strong fragrance of roses. I did not know where it was coming from. I bowed before the Blessed Mother's statue and saw Julia, who was greeting me with a big, kind smile. I felt like crying like a child in the mother's bosom. But I hesitated. There has been so much pain in my life. My physical pain has been too great. I held Julia's hands. At that moment, my wife, who was standing behind me, said to Julia with much impatience, *"Sister, my husband is seriously ill. He can live only by a heart transplant. We came from far away, from Inchon."* Julia touched me where my heart was and prayed.

The prayer service was over and we were on the way back home. Because we did not sleep at all at night, we fell asleep in the bus. When I woke up, I could see the sign outside the bus: Chonan (a city about 150 miles north of Naju and 50 miles south of Inchon). Almost unconsciously, I touched where my heart was with my hand. I felt it was strange. There was no pain! I got excited and woke up my wife and sister-in-law, who were sleeping. I stood up, twisted myself, and pressed down where the heart was with my fingers. Still no pain! Alleluia! Thank You, Lord! You gave me a birthday present by curing me during my first meeting with the Blessed Mother in Naju. I remembered the Blessed Mother's message that the sign that she was bestowing upon us from Heaven was a Mystery of Salvation.

Later (June 9), I was examined by the doctors. They found out that my heart was functioning at 47 percent of its capacity, up from less than 20 percent only five months ago. Doctors said that a surgery would not be necessary. They were totally amazed by this. I sincerely realize that the Lord's Power is above the most advanced medical technology. I thank the Lord and the Blessed Mother for calling me to a new life.

*   *   *

11. Juliana Sun Yang Kim, Inchon, South Korea (November 25, 1995)

It was the second anniversary of the beginning of the fragrant oil from the Blessed Mother's statue in Naju. It was also the day when the Apostolic Pro Nuncio in Korea (an Archbishop from the Vatican) visited the Blessed Mother's House *(the Chapel in Naju)*. I came to Naju from Inchon before the Apostolic Pro Nuncio's arrival. I was praying in the Blessed Mother's House.

A while later, the Apostolic Pro Nuncio, his secretary (a Monsignor), Fr. Raymond Spies, and Fr. Sang-Chul Oh of the Choonchun Diocese arrived. There also were pilgrims from Sokcho, Seoul, Inchon, Busan, Daegu, Jeonju, Kwangju and other cities in Korea. I was paying much attention to Julia. While we were praying quietly in the Blessed Mother's House, Julia was talking to Fr. Spies briefly. Then, Fr. Spies and Julia together approached the Apostolic Pro Nuncio, who was praying, and suggested to him that a queen's crown be placed on the Blessed Mother's statue. The Apostolic Pro Nuncio gladly agreed and asked that the crown be brought to him. He placed the crown on the Blessed Mother's head.

Then, Julia walked toward Fr. Spies who was in meditation and said to him, *"Father, there is light coming down from the Crucifix."* Fr. Spies indicated that he understood. A moment later, Julia talked to Fr. Spies again quietly. Fr. Spies and Julia together went to the Apostolic Pro Nuncio. Julia asked the Apostolic Pro Nuncio and Fr. Spies to bless her hands. Fr. Spies received from Julia a small bottle containing some of the fragrant oil that oozed out of the Blessed Mother's statue about two years ago and gave it to the Apostolic Pro

Nuncio. The Apostolic Pro Nuncio blessed Julia's hands with the oil. Fr. Spies also blessed Julia's hands.

Then, Julia knelt before the Blessed Mother's statue and began praying. Suddenly she collapsed on the floor. I was frightened and rushed to her. Julia was trembling with pain and had a half of the large Eucharist that priests use between the fingers of her right hand and the other half in her left hand. Julia gave one half of the Eucharist to the Apostolic Pro Nuncio and the other half to Fr. Spies. The Eucharist had an image of the cross in the middle and also the letters "A" and "Ω," exactly the same as in the photograph taken in Naju on June 27, 1993.

The Apostolic Pro Nuncio and Fr. Spies each consumed a small piece of the Eucharist and then gave Communion to Julia and other people who were present. Seven priests and about 70 lay people received Communion. After everyone received Communion, two pieces of the Eucharist were left. Fr. Spies put them in the small pyx that he brought from Anyang. I learned that this Eucharist was brought to Julia by St. Michael the Archangel. I was wondering if this Eucharist had been received by someone sacrilegiously. But is it not possible that I also sometimes received Communion sacrilegiously? This was a very humbling thought. I was trembling inside and was shedding tears. The Sacred Host melted in my mouth softly like snow. A man from Soonchun was unable to swallow the Eucharist, because he had anger in his heart and did not go to Confession before Communion. Everyone who witnessed this amazing Eucharistic Miracle that God bestowed upon us was in total awe and an overwhelming joy. Some were crying loudly.

Julia said she was feeling cold and wanted to go to her house next door and write down the message that she just received. She said to the Apostolic Pro Nuncio, *"The Blessed Mother called Your Excellency here today very specially. She is asking Your Excellency to help prepare a tabernacle here and help allow the celebration of Mass here."*

Julia was about to step out of the Blessed Mother's House when the Blessed Mother called her hurriedly. *"Julia! Hold the hands of the priests, Giovanni and your spiritual director, whom I can put in my eyes without feeling any pain and come to me."* Julia held the hands of the Apostolic Pro Nuncio and

Fr. Spies, who were praying, and they approached the Blessed Mother's statue together. Julia began praying with her eyes closed, still holding the hands of the Apostolic Pro Nuncio and Fr. Spies with both her hands.

Suddenly, she raised herself while still kneeling and turned her head upward. At that moment, a small Eucharist came down upon Julia's tongue. The Apostolic Pro Nuncio took the Eucharist from Julia's tongue and showed the Host to people gathered there. Then, he put the Eucharist in the small pyx that Fr. Spies had.

After some time, the Apostolic Pro Nuncio gave us the Papal blessing and left the Blessed Mother's House. Later, we learned that he came to Naju not as a private pilgrim but as the official representative of the Holy Father. Also, we remembered the Blessed Mother's promise (in her October 23, 1994 message) that she would call the Apostolic Pro Nuncio. We were all overjoyed and thanked God.

For the past several years, I have witnessed many amazing miracles in Naju: tears and tears of blood from Our Lady's statue, fragrant oil from the same statue, Eucharistic Miracles several times, the fragrance of roses, healings of cancers and other incurable illnesses, and so on. But the miracle I witnessed yesterday was most amazing. I am overjoyed when I think that, by this miracle, the Blessed Mother is trying to lead us to her Son in the Eucharist, the living Jesus. I am making a new resolution to repent my past sins more sincerely and to live a better life.

(Note: The Blessed Mother was calling the Apostolic Pro Nuncio *"Giovanni."* Julia asked one of the priests, *"Is the Apostolic Pro Nuncio's name Giovanni?"* The priest did not know, either. He looked it up in the Catholic Directory and found out that it was indeed the Apostolic Pro Nuncio's first name.)

*   *   *

12. Fr. Francis Su, Sarawak, Malaysia (August 1995)

I, Francis Su Haw Hoo, a Catholic priest from the Diocese of Sibu, Malaysia, wish to offer testimony to the recent miracles which occurred in Naju, Korea, during the 10th anniversary of the Blessed Mother's first tears (1985). I went to Naju with a group of Singaporeans and Malaysians. We arrived at Naju on June 29, 1995, and spent exactly four nights there, and we participated in the overnight vigils for three consecutive nights in the Chapel (The Blessed Mother's House). The Chapel was occupied with lots of pilgrims coming from different countries. The whole place was filled with the fragrance of roses from the statue of Mother Mary.

On the first night (Thursday, June 29, 1995) our group brought a lot of flowers for Mamma Mary. Our Faith Tour Managing Director, Mr. Thomas Lui, brought a crown for Mamma Mary. Julia Kim asked me to crown Mother Mary. I felt so privileged to be given the honor to crown Mother Mary. Thank you Mamma Mary!

On Friday, June 30, we went to the mountain to collect water from the miraculous spring. The water had the fragrance of roses, indicating the presence of Mother Mary, her friendship and love for us, her children. After we all had collected the miracle water, some came to me for Confession. After that we prayed the Rosary. While praying the Rosary, many looked up towards the sun, which moved up and down; it started spinning and formed the shape of a big Host. Later, we heard that a group of people outside the Chapel saw the sun coming down slowly in the form of a Host and resting on the roof of the Blessed Mother's House.

In the evening at 7:30, we participated in the 10th anniversary concelebrated Mass in the Parish Church, which was packed to full capacity with pilgrims coming from all over the world. The Mass was said and presided by the Parish Priest, Rev. Fr. Julio Kim, in Korean language. The response was very good. Four priests helped to distribute Holy Communion. Julia, who was sitting in the back of the Church due to the huge crowd, received Holy Communion last. She went back to her seat, and after a few minutes, the Host in her mouth started to bleed. She was then surrounded by large crowds of people who witnessed this occurrence. Immediately after the Mass, the concelebrants also went and witnessed this. I saw the Host in Julia's mouth look like flesh mingled with blood. This is a confirmation to me that a consecrated Host is truly the Body of Jesus Christ in the form of bread so that it can easily be consumed.

After this we all went back to the Chapel for another overnight vigil. This night, the place was completely jammed with people both inside and outside the Chapel. Many people gave testimonies. I was also given the opportunity to give testimony about my experiences during my first visit to Naju in May 1995, when I witnessed the pain that Julia had to suffer for people who had aborted their unborn babies. While I was still giving the testimony, Julia, who was sitting behind me, was in pain again. Her stomach became big, just like a pregnant woman. This was witnessed by over a thousand people. I asked the people to pray and implore God's mercy and forgiveness on those people who are responsible for killing so many unborn babies. Many cried and begged mercy and pardon from God. After a while, Julia's stomach returned to normal size. Today the greatest evil is abortion—the killing of the innocents. At about 2:30 a.m. (Saturday morning), Julia asked me to anoint her forehead and hands with the holy oil which I brought along with me. I did the same to Julio, her husband. She held our hands in deep prayers and cried in front of the statue of the Blessed Mother. I felt very much like a child holding the hand of Mother Mary. After a while, I felt drowsy but very peaceful. I could then feel the very strong presence of Mamma Mary.

At 3:45 a.m., Julia, still holding my hand, suddenly jumped up and reached her hands towards the Crucifix above the statue of Our Lady. In that split of the moment as I jumped up with her, I felt she was asking me to catch something falling down. As she opened her hands, I saw, to my amazement, communion Hosts being placed in front of Our Lady's statue on the altar. I counted the Hosts, and there were seven. The Chapel was ecstatic as many present had witnessed this miracle, and their curiosity turned into worship and prayer, worthy of Our Lord Jesus in the Eucharist.

On Saturday (1st of July 1995), being the first Saturday of the month, we again had the overnight vigil. The night was crowded and filled with songs, prayers and testimonies from priests and lay people on how Our Lady had brought them closer to the Lord through healings and the Eucharistic Miracles. On Sunday (July 2) morning at about 5:30, I led the people to adore the Blessed Sacrament as taught by St. Michael the Archangel to the three children of Fatima, Lucia, Francisco and Jacinta, after which I took one piece out of the seven miraculous Hosts to bless the people present. Then, the people lined up in a long queue to see the miraculous Hosts and pay homage and adore the Eucharistic King. Julia and myself then prayed over the people one by one or family by family. It took us more than two hours to finish praying over them. I felt very sleepy and exhausted. I looked at my watch. It was 8 o'clock in the morning.

By Sunday night (July 2) most of the pilgrims had left Naju. That night, there were only about a hundred people in the Chapel: 45 of us from Singapore and Malaysia, 6 from Hong Kong, 2 Australians, and the rest were Koreans.

In obedience to the instruction by Archbishop Yoon in the Naju area, we decided to consume the seven Hosts. I was given the privilege to receive the first Host from Fr. Pete M. Marcial from Guam. Then, I gave the remaining Hosts to Fr. Marcial, Julio (Julia's husband), Rufino (administrator of the Chapel), Kap-Joo Choi (Chairman of Naju City Council), Andrew (a helper) and lastly to Julia. Before Julia received the Host, she felt very uneasy. But after she had received the last Host, she bowed her head in deep union with the Lord. I laid hands on her head and prayed over her. After a few minutes, she lifted up her head and opened her mouth. Her mouth was filled with Blood again. Those around us cried and worshipped the Lord. I put my finger on her tongue, and it was covered with Blood, and I showed it to the people. I wiped my finger with a linen cloth and the stain of Blood remained there. This linen with the stain of Blood is being kept in the Chapel as evidence and for further scientific laboratory tests.

I asked myself, why all these occurrences in such a short period of time? I began to understand that this is a gift from Mother Mary as a reassurance and reemphasis on the Eucharist. Many have lost the sense of the Real Presence of Our Lord in the Eucharist. As a priest, I have been given the power to make Jesus present in the lives of people through the Eucharist. The Eucharistic occurrences on these few days have increased my faith and strengthened my ministerial Priesthood. The celebration of the Mass and the Consecration of the Eucharist will be a different experience to me henceforth. I testify and reaffirm the presence of Jesus in the Eucharist and will give witness to these occurrences.

Monday, July 3 at 4:15 a.m., Yo Han (one of the volunteers

from the Blessed Mother's House) came to our hotel to fetch us to the Chapel to witness the big statue of Our Lady in the garden outside the Chapel. It also shed tears. Within a short stay in Naju, I witnessed at least eight miracles. Our trip to Naju is very meaningful and significant to me, especially the Eucharistic Miracles.

I believe wholeheartedly that Mamma Mary had led me to Naju to experience all these wonderful miracles in such a short time for a grave reason. She has undoubtedly put in my heart a strong desire and sense of urgency in responding to her pleas and repeated requests to pray for world peace and for the conversion of sinners. *"Pray, pray a great deal and make sacrifices, for many souls go to hell because they have no one to make sacrifices and to pray for them."* (Our Lady of Fatima on 19th August 1917)

"Come to me and spread my messages of love courageously so that people may be freed from the Red Dragon and that the Kingdom of the Lord may come. In union with the Pope and all the bishops, let the victory of the Resurrection reach the whole world. In this age, the devil is becoming more active to control humans by means of human powers. My numerous poor children are following the Red Dragon and walking toward the deep darkness, hell, in their extreme pride. They are working in many different cunning ways to confuse people about the messages that I give.

"Oh, my poor children. My priests, hold the hands of so many of my children who are recklessly walking into darkness.

"There are some priests who have broken away from me and do not follow the Will of Jesus. But, through my priests and on this soil made fertile by the blood of so many martyrs, many souls are growing under the light from my Son and me. On the other hand, the Red Dragon is becoming more violent. So, tell people to be awake and pray.

"Oh, my dear priests! I want even the most corrupt souls to receive the light from me. Therefore, be loyal to Jesus so that they may convert. Also, do not let my tears and blood flow in vain. I want my beloved priests to become sacrificial victims for the conversion of sinners.

"Oh, my beloved priests! My precious ones who perform the amazing miracle of the Sacrament! Do not turn your eyes away from my messages, but have complete trust in my Immaculate

Heart and entrust everything to my guidance. Rely totally on my Immaculate Heart through unending sacrifices and penances in order to crush the devils who are trying to afflict you by all kinds of cunning methods.

"My Immaculate Heart will surely triumph. You will certainly see the victory, if you accept my words." (To Julia Kim, Naju, July 5, 1989)

Woe to me if I do not put into practice these urgent messages and spread them quickly to everyone. I will inscribe them in my heart and have complete trust in the Immaculate Heart of Mary and entrust everything to her guidance.

"O Mary, my lovely Mother, I love you. I place myself under your maternal care. Carry me in your loving arms. Feed me with your spiritual milk and teach me to understand the Word of God. Cover me with your Immaculate mantle and protect me. I consecrate my entire life to your Immaculate Heart. I have trust in you, Mommy. I allow myself to be led and formed by you. Just tell me what I must do. Teach me to discover joy in prayer and to pray with my heart. Hold my hands, Mommy, and bring me to Jesus your Son. I love you, Mamma Mary. Amen."

Chronology of Events in Naju, Korea

1980 Julia Kim and her family convert to Catholicism. (They were formerly Presbyterians.) Julia is miraculously healed of terminal illnesses.

1981 (Easter Sunday) Julia and her family are baptized in the Naju Parish Church.

1982 Julia sees a vision of Jesus with His Sacred Heart torn and bleeding. She asks for sufferings for the conversion of sinners. A life of suffering begins for her

1985 (June 30) Our Lady's statue in Julia's home begins weeping. Intermittently, Our Lady weeps through her statue for a total of 700 days until January 14, 1992.

1985 (July 18) Julia receives messages from Our Lady for the first time.

1986 (October 19) Our Lady weeps tears of blood through her statue for the first time.

1987 (January 14) Fr. Raymond Spies, a Salesian missionary priest from Belgium, becomes Julia's spiritual director.

1987 (April 21) Julia suffers the pains of the Crucifixion.

1987 (May 12) Julia suffers the pains of the unborn babies being aborted.

1987 (December 8) Fr. René Laurentin visits Naju. Also, Our Lady's statue is moved from Julia's apartment to the newly-built Chapel.

1988 (January 1) Our Lady sheds blood from her nose.

1988 (February 4) Julia suffers the pains of the Crucifixion. She receives the Stigmata.

1988 (June 5) The First Eucharistic miracle to Julia occurs in Naju Parish Church.

1988 (July 29) Julia suffers the pains of delivery and abortion.

1989 (January 29) Julia suffers the pains of the Crucifixion and martyrdom of St. Andrew Kim. She receives the Stigmata.

1989 (March 25) Julia speaks at the Marian Conference in Pittsburgh, Pennsylvania.

1990 (January 13) Bishop Daniel Chi of the Wonju Diocese in Korea visits Naju. He stays in Naju for ten days and witnesses tears of blood flowing on Our Lady's statue.

1990 (September 26) Monsignor Matthias Perez Merino, a theologian at the Vatican, visits Naju. He states that Naju is the synthesis of all of the Marian messages.

1991 (May 16) The second Eucharistic miracle to Julia occurs in the Naju Parish Church. Thirty-three pilgrims from the Philippines witness the miracle.

1992 (January 14) Our Lady's shedding tears and tears of blood through her statue in Naju ends.

1992 (May) Julia, Julio (Julia's husband) and other pilgrims from the Philippines and Korea visit the Holy Land, the Chapel of the Miraculous Medal in Paris and the Shrine in Lourdes, France.

1992 (June 2) The third Eucharistic miracle to Julia occurs in St. Francis Church in Lanciano, Italy. The fourth Eucharistic miracle occurs in Rome.

1992 (June 3) Julia visits the Holy Father.

1992 (November 24) Fragrant oil begins flowing from Our Lady's statue in Naju. It continues for the next 700 consecutive days until October 23, 1994.

1994 (September 24) The fifth Eucharistic miracle to Julia occurs in the Naju Parish Church during a Mass celebrated by Fr. Jerry Orbos from the Philippines.

1994 (October 23) Fragrant oil ceases to flow from Our Lady's statue in Naju.

1994 (November 2) The sixth Eucharistic miracle to Julia occurs at St. Anthony's Church in Kailua, Hawaii.

1994 (November 24) The seventh Eucharistic miracle occurs during the Apostolic Pro Nuncio's visit to the Chapel in Naju. A large Eucharist is brought by St. Michael the Archangel. A few minutes later, a small Eucharist lands almost vertically on Julia's tongue. The smaller Eucharist and a piece of the larger Eucharist are being preserved at Fr. Spies' chapel

1994 (December) Archbishop Victorinus Yoon of the Kwangju Archdiocese, which covers the Naju Parish, organizes a committee to investigate Naju.

1995 (June 30) The eighth Eucharistic miracle occurs in Naju Parish Church. The church was packed with pilgrims who came for the 10th anniversary of the first tears from Our Lady's statue in Naju.

1995 (July 1) Seven Sacred Hosts miraculously come down from the Crucifix in the Chapel and land on the altar in front of Our Lady's statue.

1995 (July 2) The seven Sacred Hosts are consumed by two priests and five lay people in obedience to the local Archbishop's instruction. The Host received by Julia turns into visible flesh and blood in her mouth.

1995 (September 22) Another Eucharistic miracle occurs to Julia during a Mass celebrated by Bishop Roman Danylak from Toronto, Canada, and two other priests on the mountain near Naju.

For a list of other publications on Naju, contact:

Mary's Touch By Mail
P.O. Box 1668
Gresham, OR 97030
Phone: (503) 669-8443
Fax: (503) 669-7923